CAPSTONE:
INQUIRY & ACTION
AT SCHOOL

NINA LEACOCK & JON CALOS

W0010514

First Published 2021

by John Catt Educational Ltd

15 Riduna Park, Station Road,
Melton, Woodbridge IP12 1QT
UK
Tel: +44 (0) 1394 389850

4500 140th Ave North,
Suite 101, Clearwater,
FL 33762-3848
US
Tel: +1 561 448 1987

Email: enquiries@johncatt.com
Website: www.johncatt.com

ISBN: 978 1 913622 66 4

Set and designed by John Catt Educational Limited

Dedicated to capstone teachers and their on-the-ground expertise. We trust you to take this book as a starting point—or even a provocation—and to improve on everything we think we know about capstone.

ANONYMIZATION

We learn from stories. This book includes many examples gleaned from our own schools and from the schools of the National Capstone Consortium. All stories of student projects have been anonymized. Names and project details have been changed. In many cases, project stories represent composites of several projects known to us, but possibly carried out at different schools. Stories involving schools have been similarly anonymized. When stories involve capstone teachers we know, we use first names with the permission of the teacher concerned.

ACKNOWLEDGEMENTS

Teaching is a collaborative profession, and evey education book owes its existence to countless mentors and colleagues. In particular, we acknowledge the educators of the National Capstone Consortium, without whose expertise this book would not have been written. We also express particular appreciation for the students, families, teachers, and administrators of the Emma Willard School in Troy, New York and Bosque School in Albuquerque, New Mexico.

For various contributions, we thank: Chris Alvarez, Carly Andrews, Jess Barrie, Dagan Bernstein, Kurt Bratten, Josh Breault, Caroline Buinicky, Zach Cannon, Sheryl Chard, Steve Chinosi, Mark Coombes, Jim Daly, Jinni Durham, Kendall Evans, Tim Finnegan, Juan Flores, Judi Freeman, Nicole Furlonge, Gary Gruber, Gemma Halfi, Billy Handmaker, Geetha Holdsworth, Jeff Hooper, Doug Key, Arthur Knox, Meredith Legg, Eden Maisel, Sally Martell, Bridget McGivern, Kevin McGrath, TJ Middleton, Andrew Minnigan, Marisa Muoio, Seth O'Bryan, Heather O'Shea, Tom Penzel, Molly Perry, Ann Petit, Liz Radday, Jenny Rao, Anna Rutins, Kelena Reid, RJ Sakai, Louis Scuderi, Dan Shaw, Lindsay Slaughter, Matt Spearing, Adam Valenstein, Tamisha Williams, Jonathan Woolgar, Erin Zavitz, and Kristen Zosche.

Though work with these valued colleagues informs our understanding and enriches our teaching, we want to make clear that discussions, recommendations, and conclusions presented in this book represent our own opinion.

CONTENTS

A YEAR IN CAPSTONE

Each capstone program is unique to its hosting school. However, programs tend to share a rhythm created by the school calendar and the pace of senior-year activity. Nearly all capstone programs include both inquiry and action elements. For the convenience of the reader, we include below two typical schedules, one for a program centered on inquiry (research), and one for a program centered on action (off-campus placement), along with relevant chapter sections. Though both schedules cover a full year, we have found that shorter programs follow similar, though more compact, trajectories.

Milestones like those listed below structure the program and mark student progress. As in a traditional course, milestones can be set by the program in a handbook or on a program website. Even more effective for learning if time allows, students can create their own individual calendars.

Sample schedule

A year in an inquiry capstone

September
- All students engage in project design, *Chapters 3.4, 4.1, 4.2*
  - Brainstorm questions and write proposal or prospectus, *Chapter 4.2*
  - Gather working knowledge and develop research question, *Chapters 4.1, 4.2*
  - Panel review of project, *Chapter 4.2*
- All students conduct beginning-of-year reflection, *Chapter 4.7*

October
- Conduct in-depth text-based research, *Chapter 4.3*
  - Develop extensive annotated bibliography or literature review, *Chapter 4.3*

November
- Synthesize initial text-based research, *Chapter 4.3*
- Write preliminary analysis, *Chapter 4.10*

December *Structure program time to accomodate any long school vacation*
- Detailed and final written plan for any fieldwork or service elements, *Chapters 4.4, 4.5, 4.6*
  - Ethics review panel meets if needed, *Chapter 4.4*

January
- Heart of the inquiry project (usually an action component), *Chapter 4.3*
  - Primary source analysis, *Chapter 4.3*
  - Fieldwork or scientific experiment, *Chapter 4.4*
  - Community engagement, *Chapter 4.5*
  - Design-build, *Chapter 4.6*
  - Narrative or other creative reflection, *Chapter 4.7*

February
- Draft final essay, including any field data analysis, *Chapter 4.10*
  - Submit draft essay for defense, *Chapter 3.4*
- All students conduct mid-year reflection, *Chapter 4.7*

March *Structure program time to accomodate any long school vacation*
- Promotion slide, *Chapter 3.6*
- Write final essay, incorporating input from defense, *Chapter 4.10*

April
- All students practicing presentations *Chapters 3.4, 3.6, 4.11*
  - Multiple rehearsals; consider recording, *Chapter 4.11*

May
- For all students, final presentations and/or exhibition, *Chapters 3.4, 3.6, 4.11*
- End-of-year reflection on the individual capstone journey, *Chapter 4.7*
- Program evaluation by students, *Chapter 3.3*
- Program evaluation by all adult stakeholders, *Chapter 3.3*

Sample schedule

A year in an action capstone

September
- All students engage in project design, *Chapters 3.4, 3.6, 4.1, 4.2*
  - ◻ Create digital portfolio, an external communication tool, *Chapter 3.6*
  - ◻ Create internal shared document for tracking student work, *Chapter 3.4*
  - ◻ Create project poster with essential question and key product, *Chapter 3.6*
- All students conduct beginning-of-year reflection, *Chapter 4.7*

October
- Active on site, *Chapter 4.5*
- Conduct focused text-based research, *Chapter 4.3*
  - ◻ Develop short annotated bibliography or research notes, *Chapter 4.3*
- First monthly portfolio update, *Chapter 3.6*

November
- Active on site, *Chapter 4.5*
- Monthly portfolio update, *Chapter 3.6*

December *Structure program time to accomodate any long school vacation*
- Active on site, *Chapter 4.5*
- Monthly portfolio update, *Chapter 3.6*

January
- Active on site, *Chapter 4.5*
- Additional research, often a professional interview, *Chapter 4.4*
- Monthly portfolio update, *Chapter 3.6*

February
- Active on site, *Chapter 4.5*
- All students conduct mid-year reflection (part of portfolio), *Chapter 4.7*
  - ◻ Halfway done? Formal progress check to see if students are on pace to complete all that they planned. Also a time to modify projects as necessary, *Chapter 4.7*
- Monthly portfolio update, *Chapter 3.6*

March *Structure program time to accomodate any long school vacation*
- Active on site, *Chapter 4.5*
- Elevator pitch, *Chapter 3.6*
- Monthly portfolio update, *Chapter 3.6*

April
- Active on site, *Chapter 4.5*
- All students practicing presentations *Chapters 3.4, 3.6, 4.11*
  - ◻ Multiple rehearsals; consider recording, *Chapter 4.11*
- Final monthly portfolio update, *Chapter 3.6*

May
- For all students, final presentations and/or exhibition, *Chapters 3.4, 3.6, 4.11*
- End-of-year reflection on the individual capstone journey (part of portfolio), *Chapter 4.7*
- Program evaluation by students, *Chapter 3.3*
- Program evaluation by all adult stakeholders, *Chapter 3.3*

FOREWORD
BY JEFF HOOPER

Welcome—you must be one of us. If this book has made it into your hands, it's likely because you have found capstone education or, perhaps more likely, capstone education has found you. When the Capstone Consortium formed and hosted its first summer summit at the Thacher School in 2013, I had no way of knowing that it would attract so many kindred spirits. Over the years since, as the organization has grown, I've noticed that in schools of all sizes and kinds, the faculty members who become leaders of capstone programs have certain common traits. While the group photo from the end of each Summit represents a broadly diverse group (by measures visible and invisible), it also depicts educators united by a conviction that the work of their capstone programs produces the most powerful, durable, and rewarding experiences of their students' academic careers. There are more of us than we could have possibly guessed in 2013, and we're so glad to have you join our numbers by picking up this important book.

What else did those teachers have in common? On the surface, not much. There were teachers new to the profession and grizzled veterans. They came from all regions of the country. They worked at public, charter, independent day and independent boarding schools. They taught in a wide range of disciplines. We had teachers from institutions with tremendous privilege and teachers whose schools and students faced significant resource deficiencies. Most of them worked with twelfth graders, but some directed programs for students in eighth and even fourth grade. While we all had different problems to solve and different populations to serve, we found capstone education to be endlessly adaptable. Lessons from a large public school system in Vermont strengthened the program of a tiny independent school in Hawaii. A small rural high school learned from the experiences of a large suburban PK–12 school. What we discovered, in short, is that if your school has students and teachers, it can and should implement a capstone program, and both those constituencies will be better for it.

Beyond our superficial differences, though, I came to recognize a number of key traits commonly found in the scores of capstone educators that I've come to know through the Consortium. Here's an incomplete list:

- **An entrepreneurial spirit.** Many Consortium members are tasked with building a program from scratch. They must invent systems, recruit allies, bargain for time and resources, and make a compelling case for their programs.

- **Comfort with uncertainty.** Rather than guiding a classroom full of students along a pre-planned path, capstone education requires launching each student onto her own adventure. There will be unforeseen obstacles to overcome, and the eventual outcomes are unknowable at the outset.

- **A tinkerer's mindset.** Healthy capstone programs reinvent themselves each year. There are few absolute truths in this field, and educators drawn to this work relish the opportunity to iterate with each new group of students.

- **A "driver's ed" approach.** We may retain the emergency brake and be able to offer advice from the passenger seat, but capstone educators know that the student has to be the one to drive the car, and they won't be perfect at it. If you aren't comfortable handing over the keys, capstone education isn't for you.

- **Curiosity.** Seldom does one's expertise in an academic discipline come in particularly handy in capstone education. Rather, much of the joy comes from learning alongside the students, helping them formulate the next question and design the next avenue of inquiry.

While capstone education might not be a good fit for all teachers, we believe that it is a good fit for all students. Some students come to their capstone project having had great success and enjoyed great comfort "doing school." They appreciate clear expectations and knowing what will be on the test. They've mastered flashcards, formulas, lab procedures, and analytical essays. For these students, the capstone experience can be discomfiting. And it should be! These students need to grapple with uncertainty, with messy outcomes, and with ambiguity. We do them a disservice if we fail to present novel challenges before their high school careers conclude.

For other students, the capstone project becomes a welcome, if belated, breath of fresh air. They may have struggled with the strictures of the traditional curriculum at their schools and found it hard not to color outside the lines. They need this too! For these students, the agency to design their own learning and channel their native curiosity has been the missing piece on their educational journey. For these students, the capstone often becomes the one time when they feel truly confident and accomplished at school. There are of course many shades of gray between these two archetypes, but it seems intuitively obvious that all students benefit from a learning experience that *by design* differs from their previous experiences at school.

When I became director of my school's capstone program in 2006, I inherited a program that had evolved over a 20-year period, strengthened by the wisdom and experience of dozens of my colleagues and hundreds of students. However, while resources and professional development opportunities applicable to my work as a classroom teacher, a football coach, and a school administrator were abundant, there was precious little external support available to help improve our capstone program. We knew that we had much to learn and perhaps something to offer as well to a conversation about this transformative educational structure. This led us to pursue an E.E. Ford Educational Leadership Grant which allowed us to establish the Capstone Consortium and host a series of summer summits. At each of our gatherings, I was inspired and nourished by the passion and talent of the participants. The life and growth of that organization since then has surpassed our most optimistic hopes, thanks entirely to the extraordinary educators who have contributed to its development. Among that august group are the authors of the book you now hold, Nina Leacock and Jon Calos, two of the most creative, inspirational, and insightful teachers I've had the pleasure to know. You are in good hands.

Jeff Hooper
Thacher School

INTRODUCTION

Capstone: Inquiry and Action at School comes out of the diverse experiences of many teachers over many years. We, the co-authors of this book, have each taught at schools that hold capstone at the heart of their educational cultures. As teachers, we've experienced first hand the transformative power of capstone in the lives of our own students. As program leaders, we've likewise experienced the collaborative and organic nature of capstone programs in the ecosystems of their hosting schools. Jon participated in the launch and early development of a capstone that grew to become the signature program of his school in upstate New York. He piloted the creation of the course that has become a school tradition—the title, Signature, is part of the school brand. Nina joined a school in New Mexico where the capstone was already an established and thriving tradition. She participated in the collaborative evolution of that program to support a significantly wider range of students and projects. Our individual capstone teaching experiences at these two very different schools have cemented for us the value of inclusiveness, working with as many people and ideas as possible from the outset, and remaining flexible and open to change over time.

Growing only partly out of our individual experiences as capstone teachers, the story of this book is also intertwined with the story of the National Capstone Consortium. The two of us met at an early summit of the Consortium, held at the Thacher School in beautiful Ojai, California. Supported by a grant from the E.E. Ford Foundation, Thacher hosted the first summits of the then embryonic Consortium. As the summit's inaugural facilitator in 2013, Thacher's Jeff Hooper created a climate of humor, wit, and open exchange of ideas. Excursions into Thacher's beautiful natural setting were also part of the summit experience. As enthusiastic capstone teachers and avid outdoor fans, we found this combination irresistible. At those early summits, and especially on walks in the Ojai hills, we began the dialogue that resulted in this book.

The capstone community experienced strong growth during the Thacher years, connecting teachers from Massachusetts to Hawaii and many points in between.

Along with a core group of dedicated capstone leaders, we participated in the evolution of the Consortium into an independent national organization hosting summits on the East Coast as well as the West, while supporting regional meetings and growing an online network. Meanwhile, summit conversations fed our respective teaching practices in our home schools in New York and New Mexico, creating a feedback loop between our teaching experience during the school year and our teacher conversations over the summer. With independence from E.E. Ford and Thacher came more frequent meetings of the Consortium leadership team. Along with our individual experiences, the rich ongoing conversation with our colleagues in the Consortium informs the understanding of capstone expressed in this book.

The idea for the book itself hatched at a chance meeting at a conference in Atlanta, Georgia in 2018. The expansion of the Consortium had helped us to realize how powerful capstone is in an educational curriculum, how common it is in American high schools, and how lacking were resource materials. At the meeting, an interesting question arose. What do we do when we want to learn about something new? We read a book. But as far as we could tell, there was no book on capstone education at the high school level. At that moment of realization, this book was conceived in its current form: as a book by teachers, for teachers who are working with capstone students, so they can become citizens and professionals of the future.

> This is a book by teachers,
> for teachers who are working with capstone students,
> so they can become citizens and professionals of the future.

Though this book draws on long experience, direct and through the Consortium, we do not think of ourselves as "the experts" in capstone. Rather, we understand this book as one of many conduits of teaching expertise in the capstone network. It needs to be made explicit that when we say "we," we are not speaking for the Consortium as a whole, nor for the various schools where we have taught. We each bring an individual experience of capstone, while a dialogue carried on now over many years enables the two of us to speak together on the topics discussed in the book. One of the arguments we make in this book is that capstone expertise is emergent. It is context-specific and ever-evolving. The people who have expertise in a particular program are the people teaching in that program at that time. Though we hope this book will ease the process of launching and developing a new capstone program, or evolving an established one, we don't imagine for a moment that any capstone teachers will take this book as a fixed recipe, or be limited by the bounds of our experiences.

This book was conceived as a handbook for capstone teachers like ourselves. We were well into the writing of it before we began to realize how capstone belongs to and participates in a much broader movement of school reform in American education. We found ourselves writing about the many points of contact between capstone and a range of rapidly evolving alternatives to traditional classroom practice: experiential learning, service learning, internships, project-based learning, deeper learning, socio-emotional learning, 21st-century skills development, and performance or mastery assessment, among so many others.

As we considered these areas of overlap, it seemed to us that one distinguishing feature of capstone is the way that it radically shifts agency to students more effectively than any of these other movements. We recognize that this feature derives in part from the fact that capstone seniors are already developing beyond the bounds of their high schools. The approaches we recommend in this book might not work with younger students, but seniors are ready to do more than most teachers are currently asking of them. A second feature that seems to set capstone apart is that programs generally start with teachers rather than with school or district administrators, and then evolve out of organizational processes in which students play a crucial role, as do partners in the broader community that surround the school. As we discuss in Chapter 2.2, capstone is *networked* to a degree that is unique in our experience of schools.

Widening inequities in American society point to the need to educate students for a more active understanding of citizenship. Fast and radical changes to employment likewise point to the need to equip students with different skills than were needed a generation ago. In a study of employment trends since the dawning of the digital era, Frank Levy and Richard Murnane conclude that future workers will be doing *only* work that *cannot* be done by computers—that is, that which cannot be reduced to routine procedures.[1] Human work will consist of finding solutions to problems that resist categorization into cleanly demarcated factors—reducing events into the binary language of 1s and 0s. Teaching courses like capstone will always remain in the domain of humans. Our students today need to be developing flexibility and adaptiveness that go along with curricula like capstone. Capstone emphasizes the three skill categories identified by Levy and Murnane: "solving unstructured problems, working with new information, and carrying out non-routine mechanical tasks."[2] Project design, always left in the student's hands in capstone, is an essentially unstructured—or messy—problem. Capstone research never rests with reporting what others know, but always demands that students process and make use of new information. Design-build and off-campus experiential components ask students to interact with the world as whole embodied humans, and not only with books or screens.

The many points of contact between capstone and more familiar movements in alternative education also suggest another feature of capstone, which we might term its "universality." While capstone is always adjusted to local connection and conditions (capstone never transcends its school), in other respects, it lets go of tethers. In a single program, one student might be spending 90% of her capstone time in her garage, building an ion propulsion demo out of junkyard parts. Meanwhile, her friend might be interning on a local farm. Still in the same program, another student might have chosen a project that keeps him in the library, or interacting with research subjects online. We find inspiration in the idea of **universal design** in architecture. Universal design recognizes that ability and the term "differently abled" are defined in relation to an environment that is built and not natural. By building the living environment differently, architects can offer equal access—for example an attractive, broad ramp used by all—to those who previously had been divided by a staircase for the use of most at one entrance and an obtrusive lift for the few at another. Schools clearly are a built space in which not all students find equal access. We love the way that insightful design can solve many problems at once, and can do so unobtrusively, so that no one is spotlighted. Capstone program designs that offer students a menu of options, or take a portfolio approach to deliverables, or shift emphasis away from products and back to process, can be understood as taking a universal approach to their curricula.

A related feature of capstone is that it embodies what we call **forward design**. We say that while also acknowledging that the concept of backward design has been of great value to teachers and students in recent years—see project-based learning for a good example. When we say "forward design," we don't mean a return to the old topic-driven system of lesson planning that backward design was meant to replace. Rather, we want to let go of the idea that capstone teachers are in a position to set the learning objectives from which students would work back. Instead, we want to see no limit set on what any one student might accomplish. A starting point is established; planning happens in parallel with project development and in collaboration with students; adaptability and flexibility are essential. Our concept of forward design seeks to make explicit that capstone is a form of teaching in which it is assumed that by the end of the project the student will have become the master.

Through the writing process itself our understanding of capstone has grown, and with it our belief in its potential to change students, teachers, and schools. Part 1 of the book offers our definition of **what** capstone is, including the broad range of programs, while distinguishing it from other alternatives to traditional curricula. In Part 2 of the book we write about **why** we think this capstone explosion is occuring. Part 3 describes **how** capstone programs typically launch and evolve into organizational units in their home schools. Part 4 offers suggestions for **how** a curriculum and pedagogy of capstone can be created, simultaneously articulating some of the points of contact between capstone and other educational reform movements. Our conclusion offers a few thoughts about where capstone may be headed in the future—a future we hope that you, our readers, will take part in creating.

Author contribution statement
Nina and Jon contributed equally to the creation of this book from start to finish.

Notes to Introduction

Note 1, page 19: **future workers will be doing only work that cannot be done by computers**—See the report written by Levy and Murnane for the think tank Third Way. Frank Levy and Richard Murnane, *Dancing with Robots: Human Skills for Computerized Work* (Third Way), July 17, 2013.

Note 2, page 19: **"solving unstructured problems, working with new information, and carrying out non-routine mechanical tasks"**—See Frank Levy and Richard Murnane, *Dancing with Robots: Human Skills for Computerized Work* (Third Way), July 17, 2013.

PART 1: WHAT IS CAPSTONE?

CHAPTER 1.1
WHAT IS CAPSTONE?

Capstone defined[1]

Capstone...

- Thrives on the intrinsic motivation and choice of students.
- Shifts power and control from schools and teachers to students.
- Typically includes action elements alongside academic inquiry.
- Often connects students with experts off campus.
- Engages students over a sustained period and incorporates reflection as well as documentation of learning.
- Is forward designed, not backward planned, with student outcomes exceeding teacher goal-setting.
- Usually marks the end of high school with a meaningful culmination.
- Adapts its form in accordance with the unique culture of each school.

What is learning? What is schooling? What matters in education today?

When you ask people to tell you about their best learning experiences, you almost never hear about anything that happened in school. "Schooling" is a word that surely deserves its bad connotations. Too much of what happens in American schools today has little to do with joyful learning, with creativity, with celebrating the unique humanity of each student. Schooling equals rigidity more often than not. It means conforming. It means power differences that can be abused, killing the spirit of education. And yet schooling, along with the learning that animates it, is a meaningful and necessary part of American culture. In research and scholarship, from engineering to humanities, academic disciplines provide the paradigms in which novel and individual contributions can emerge. In art, creativity and constraint are interdependent, not mutually exclusive. In politics and business, understanding history is a prerequisite for changing it. In other words, one has to learn how other people do things in order to do them in one's own way. As has been often pointed out, if students only learned what schools set out to teach, we would all be in serious trouble. Student creativity carries learning forward, not only for individuals but also for the culture.

Capstones are student-generated and independent and invite choice. They plunge students into the complexity and disorder that accompany all genuine inquiry. They provide space for action, through which students experience making change in their communities. Capstone projects are not, however, a form of "unschooling." They happen in schools through capstone programs that are integrated into the larger institutional curriculum. They happen under the supervision of teachers who are experts in the methodologies of their fields, embedded in their communities through long-term professional relationships, and alive to the push-and-pull that categorizes rigorous and transformative learning and schooling. Capstone restores meaning in schools today.

Anthropologists refer to the process by which young people encounter the cultures into which they have been born as "initiation." We call this process "school," but it remains as meaningful and human a journey as ever. In addition to supporting learning, capstone projects are transformative rituals that manifest the relation of student to school, as well as consolidating and broadcasting the unique organizational identity of the school itself. As powerful manifestations of the originary meeting of young people with their own cultures, capstones point the way forward into the future. Capstones typically culminate in a celebration, a public demonstration of learning, or other community event.

A Natalie Dee cartoon depicts two eggs talking to each other. The cartoon eggs have preposterous stick arms and legs and worried expressions on their simple egg faces. "What is going to happen to us when our chickens come out?" one asks. "I don't know, man," the first egg's equally worried friend replies. "I don't know." Anyone who has taught high school seniors recognizes the confusion. Yes, the egg is going away, and it is hard to explain to young people just how little they will care about that broken, discarded shell in just a few short months. Capstone teachers could occasionally feel that their entire work consists of repeating, emphatically, "You will be the chicken! You will BE the chicken!" But no one in the throes of a major life transition can hear that message. It is because, so to speak, our future chickens are essentially unknowable that we need these rituals. They provide paths to walk, or a "container"—to use a psychological term—for natural change that feels inchoate and frightening.

Capstone projects are independent student projects that culminate and celebrate a student's journey through a particular school. For American high schoolers, capstone offers an academic ritual that parallels the school and family rituals of homecoming, prom, and high school graduation. Meanwhile, American capstones often offer high schoolers the most challenging and developmentally appropriate work of their high school careers, preparing them for college and after. Some capstones are research-based, giving seniors an unfiltered experience of the messiness and uncertainty of learning. Most capstones incorporate an action element through which students can understand their impact on others. Whether based in inquiry or in action, capstones allow high school students to experience themselves as adults, albeit young adults, in their learning communities. Capstones facilitate the transition students are making both in their relationship to their high schools and as unique individuals situated in contexts that extend beyond the school walls.

Capstone programs are school programs that support the individual student projects. Typically multi-disciplinary, capstone programs provide the instruction and infrastructure required for young people to do meaningful work. Some last only a few weeks in the spring of senior year, while the longest engage students for as much as two full years; most are either one semester or one year in length. These programs fit into the organizational structure of a school in a variety of ways. A small program supporting a brief activity-oriented project might be staffed, for example, by the senior class advisory team. A more extensive program might exist as a course in its own right, with full-time teachers offering regular instruction and assessing work throughout the year.

Capstone programs likewise structure student time in a variety of ways. Some capstones are required of all students, while others are opt-in, or may require a competitive application process. Some capstones are assessed using traditional grades and appear on the student transcript, while others have the status of a school activity. Some capstones invite students to work in cohorts or collaborative teams, while others support purely individual work. Some capstones dictate an elaborate sequence of skill demonstrations, while others leave more up to the student. Capstone projects are driven by student interest, so all programs offer a wide range of student choice and are structured to make room for exploration and reflection.

Capstone programs emerge out of and evolve with the natural ecosystem of a particular school. They are as unique as the school and local communities in which they are embedded. A school committed to community engagement might center an action project with an impact study as its capstone. At an art school, the capstone might have a performance as its deliverable. A religious school might ask students to reflect on their projects in relation to their faith. A science-specific program might culminate in an exhibition of capstone posters with the same elements one would see in the poster hall at a scientific conference. Because they rest in a web of human relationships, capstones are responsive to school and community change. Indeed, they often drive such change, as well as expressing it.

Because each program fits and evolves with the unique school that houses it, true capstone programs are easily distinguished from externally set curricula like International Baccalaureate (IB) and Advanced Placement (AP). The IB diploma program dictates a culminating project, the 4000-word "extended essay," which is assessed by examiners external to the student's home school. In 2014, AP introduced a two-year course sequence which is trademarked as "AP Capstone" and similarly builds to a 5000-word research essay. As with the IB program, AP students are assessed according to standards set outside the home school. Both the national AP and the international IB figure into what has become a complex and problematic college application process for American students. Additionally, though both entities have tax-exempt status in the United States, they are organizations necessarily driven by motivations that go beyond the learning and growth of individual students or communities. Given these circumstances, neither AP nor IB can support individual students in the young-adult experience of *giving back* to their home schools and local communities through their work. Neither can serve the ritual function of knitting the community together.

A closer look at learning and schooling as locally embedded human processes exposes a further distinction between "cake mix" curricula like AP or IB and capstone. The issue is not, as one might think, that standardization is intrinsically wrong, nor even that we only see what we measure. Standardization has advantages. And that we only see what we measure is as true locally as nationally—and we have to measure something. Rather the issue has to do with the distance of AP or IB course designers and examiners from the emerging knowledge of the rising generation. Standardized curricula like AP have to presume to know what needs to be tested and to measure students against a predetermined idea about what counts as knowledge. External examiners at IB who read student essays outside the context of a relationship with the student author likewise must decide what counts as knowledge, independent of context. Their standards will evolve over time, but at a pace that is glacial compared with a school program that can remake itself from one year to the next. The responsiveness and fluidity of a local program is qualitatively different.

Capstone programs differ from other programs in a school—its English or mathematics programs, for instance—in that they explicitly support learning and schooling that is always perfectly up to date. In effect, the curriculum becomes a joint creation of teachers and students, fundamentally shifting the balance usually in place in schools.

A corollary principle of capstone teaching is that "expertise is emergent." AP and IB offer teacher training programs through which "experts"—experts in AP and IB, that is—tell teachers how to teach. In contrast, capstone educators can engage collaboratively on a peer-to-peer exchange model through the National Capstone Consortium, for example. In other words, expert capstone teachers are the ones who are working with real students in real time. Only they know what actually works. Like army officers who must get the job done in the field with the soldiers and equipment at hand, capstone teachers are responsive and adaptive. They draw on pre-developed structures and systems rather than depending on them. The capstone teacher's expertise depends in turn on centering students and their work. Being emergent, capstone programming is fundamentally forward-designed. Because the outcome depends on students, it cannot be foreseen.

Capstones are likewise easily distinguished from project-based learning (PBL). Though the Buck Institute's PBL curriculum, for example, offers insights for new capstone teachers, PBL is not capstone. PBL lacks the powerful ritual element that carries individuals and programs to a next level of achievement. The Buck Institute offers workshops that centralize or standardize PBL methods rather than centering emerging teacher expertise. More importantly, PBL projects typically are embedded in previously existing classes and taught by teachers working solo within previously existing disciplines. Despite the choice that they offer students, PBL projects are typically backward-planned at a higher level in the sense that the teacher has designed project parameters to meet learning goals specific to that course. PBL projects, however well designed, do not shift the infrastructure of the school itself. Within those constraints, PBL is unlikely to have the impact on individual students, much less on teachers or schools, that a capstone does.

As flexible but also institutionalized school programs, capstones not only support the transition of students leaving the school but also structure the relationship of individuals to community. At the ritual public showcase of a capstone program, students are sharing their own work, but they are also representing their school. Based on their performance, their teachers and administrators will also be judged. This fact puts a healthy pressure on both students and teachers, clarifying the increasing responsibilities of those who are about to be independent young adults. The resulting outcomes are deep, meaningful, and impressive.

As schools seek programs that fully address modern educational goals, capstone offers a compelling option. In an era when uncertainty seems to be the only constant, capstone welcomes all comers, embraces their individuality, empowers school and regional communities, and provides a path for teenagers approaching adulthood. Capable of navigating the complexity and opportunity of teaching high school students, capstone is an educational philosophy and practice for our times.

Notes to Chapter 1.1

Note 1, page 25: **Capstone defined**—The definition we use in this book is our own, but draws on work done at successive summer summits of the National Capstone Consortium. Compare for example the report of the Consortium's inaugural summit in 2013. See Capstone Consortium, "Summer Summit 2013 Report." www.bit.ly/35xR11d

PART 2:
WHY CAPSTONE?

CHAPTER 2.1
CAPSTONE CHANGES LIVES

Capstone is a transformative educational program, influencing most aspects of schools and their inhabitants. The key to this developmental power is placing the student at the center of the experience. Success comes from supporting the student in clarifying her initial topic interest, ensuring she has the skills necessary to complete an involved project, and often helping her connect with members of the professional community off campus. This chapter also explores the value of career exploration and the revelatory aspects of final capstone presentations, including an example of how capstone changed the life of one student.

Passion is a result of, not a prerequisite for, a great capstone

It would seem that today's students live in a golden time, when everyone implores them to "follow their passion." Parents make great sacrifices to support their children as they explore cultural and athletic options from a very young age. Many of our communities harbor programs exactly tailored for this supposedly privileged youth, providing a remarkable number of resources and experiences for families and institutions with enough means. Most of these are all about nurturing "passion" in the next generation—or so parents would have you believe.

Consider travel athletics. After only a few years of participation, families often find themselves on the local school district team for the traditional season, as well as on a "travel team," for which they are really active most of the year, transporting themselves long distances to engage with similarly motivated young athletes and their families. Not only are the seasons extended, but the hours are long, involving early and/or late practices, as well as driving to widespread events. "Passion" must be alive and well given how large this population is, one would think.

Or college test-prep, starting at any number of ages depending on the time of entry into the standardized testing system. Examples include the SSAT (Secondary School Admissions Test) for independent school admissions and the PSAT (Preliminary SAT) for SAT (Scholastic Assessment Test) practice, which itself plays a large role in college entrance. Ignoring the corporate aspect of this testing machine—which has a grip on our American education system that appears to have been loosening recently—this testing apparatus accelerates children into adulthood, in which "passion" purportedly plays an outsized role. It might be surmised that kids cannot find their "passion" fast enough to pick the best college, the best major, and ultimately the best career. Ask the typical eleventh grader how often they hear, "What colleges are you applying to?" and you will observe gigantic eye-rolls and noted stress responses associated with this obsession with progression and the future. Kids are simply flooded with questions related to "passion."[1]

Here's the thing about "passion": it's amazing when present, actually rare in the population, and misses the point about life experience entirely. We all need to slow down and change our vocabulary—and also stop talking about college so much. We really should stop using the "P word" incorrectly. If one discovers a true passion, which is unbridled interest in something, this is an obvious area to explore and leverage in life—and it is not necessary for education. Passion is not nearly as important as it appears to be.

What is required for a capstone is interest in an idea and protected time to develop it. These prerequisites are all that is needed for capstones to grow and develop into the wonderful projects that they truly are. As students move through their timeline, adjusting to challenges along the way, there often comes a time when they enter a flow state, in which the labor is actually enjoyable and they look forward to finally attaining their goals. Engagement on this level is actually "passion" and we can use the word when it is warranted. Of course, capstones may remain at the "interest" level upon completion. In fact, gaining knowledge that an idea is *not* something to center your life around is just as valuable as discovering a passion, in our opinion.

Capstone provides a fertile environment to explore ideas of all kinds. It is a safe program to engage with interests, try out some ideas, and work on personalized goals. The beneficial outcomes are numerous, surprisingly many of which really lead to life pursuits. This is why we think passion as a requirement in our lives is overblown.

Young adults exercising adult professional skills

Discussion of 21st-century skills once garnered outsized space in our educational news. Representing cutting-edge goals, these skills were truly inspirational and worthy of adoption, and many teachers agree with them on a general and philosophical level. As we approach the end of the first quarter of the actual 21st century, we realize how far beyond our grasp many of these skills still remain in most schools. While it feels antiquated to reference them, America has done little to integrate these critical skills into academic courses, on the whole. The vast majority of our students continue in a conservative educational model that has existed for many, many years.

It must be noted that there are many versions of the famed 21st-century skills and they invariably reference similar themes. Reduced to the essential elements, one often finds the "Four Cs" in most variations of the skills: creativity, curiosity, communication, collaboration.[2] The value of these skills is that they teach students lessons that actually prepare them for real life. Done well, pupils greatly enjoy learning these readily applicable skills. Capstone provides an excellent way to impart these contemporary skills to our students. It makes use of them in natural and effective ways. Not only is the formation of a novel project "creative," but capstone demands inventiveness at every turn, as new opportunities present themselves, and challenges appear in a student's path. The initial spark that sets a student on the route toward a project is the "curiosity" inherent in all projects—and so are all the "aha" moments that appear throughout a student's experience. "Communication" plays an essential role in capstone projects. A few examples: progress must be documented for teachers; experts require formal messages to participate in the program; final presentations draw upon all of the communication skills in a student's educational quiver. Finally, exceedingly few capstone projects are solo endeavors. Virtually all of them rely on effective "collaboration" on many levels. As discussed in Chapter 2.2, the very work of teaching capstone is quite different from the traditional model. Partnering with people to complete a project happens often, and usually extends to members of the local community off campus, who provide expertise and/or opportunities to attain student project goals.

All of this illustrates the "real world" foundation of capstone. In addition to learning and perfecting life-long skills, students gain experiences that easily translate into actual careers (like Tena at the end of this chapter). These range on a continuum, from simply understanding what it means for a person to hold a particular job, all the way to embedded experiences like internships in which students take on actual professional duties. One can appreciate the value of these authentic experiences to satisfy student interest and illustrate what it means to work in a field of employment. Equally important, students may discover that they should avoid some career options, thanks to their early, low-commitment exposure. Consider the cost-savings of this decision before one begins a college education!

Capstone thus provides students with realistic and safe chances to role-play the professionals that they aspire to be. Together with their teacher, students identify their interests, connect with experts in the field, and essentially try on a career for size, to see how much they resonate with it. The jump from capstone to the real world is surprisingly short, attainable, and effective.

Learning outside the school walls

Experiential learning overlaps a tremendous amount with the skills that we want our students to develop in this century. Laid out definitively by Alice and David Kolb in *The Experiential Educator*,[3] experiences are the spark that begins a learning cycle which includes four transformative phases. Briefly, the cycle begins with an experience, then leads to reflection, next to conceptualization, and finally experimentation. The "experience" in experiential learning is traditionally interpreted as "hands-on" and/or "outdoor" activities, but is actually much broader than these, also including conceptual experiences in the classroom that feed the learning cycle.

Being out in the world is a powerful and effective experience to trigger learning and skill development. Not only does this naturally include many learning modalities but it also convincingly connects to real facts and concepts, which are directly important to what happens in our lives. If students are learning about people and events in our communities outside of school, they are by definition preparing themselves to be employable and productive adults when they graduate. Learning outside the school walls is then clearly a worthy goal to support.

Capstone provides compelling opportunities to engage with the community outside of school campuses. Student projects naturally require subject experts and people in the field for information and advice. Ranging from interviews of professionals to internships, resources from the surrounding community are essential to robust capstone programs. They require information to complete the project goals and people who can provide the necessary data. Many pupils wish to get a feel for a particular career, or to serve the community in a way that is beneficial to everyone.

Professionals from the community reciprocate by equally valuing the relationships developed by capstone. Their institutions often have parallel goals, like nurturing outreach and mentoring future professionals. They are able to connect their organizations with capstone schools, establishing relationships with institutions in the community, and they may even get capable youngsters who can help them with their work. Because capstone students are usually as energetic as they are motivated, this partnership makes for valuable connections for both sides of the social bond.

A case in point is Alex. He was fascinated with computer science and entrepreneurship. He and his capstone teacher planned an interview process in which he contacted six local companies and arranged to meet with key people from each institution and ask them prepared questions while leaving room for off-the-cuff conversations. Each meeting was engaging and exceeded Alex's expectations—in fact a couple of events led to shadowing experiences that Alex greatly valued. While he actually exceeded his goals, the professionals commented that they were more than pleased to provide information about their companies to young people, as a very advanced form of recruitment. They also just enjoyed sharing about their journey, what they do, and how their institutions contributed to the wider world. This was a clear example of a win-win situation, for the student and the career adult.

Capstone projects often connect with community programs that are equipped to engage students in the fulfillment of their missions. Many students seem to come up with ideas and plans that align with the work of local nonprofits, who are often able to support student learning. Student volunteerism is greatly appreciated, and the lessons that the students learn are important and profound. Many students meet people from very different walks of life and learn things that they never could in the classroom, from direct, meaningful experience. This learning changes people and lasts a lifetime, making it a powerful form of education. Combined with the wonderful partnership, this is another win-win for everyone involved. Students gain the opportunity to learn from people whose experiences may be different from their own, and community organizations gain as well.

Done well, capstones that venture off campus are the best examples of experiential learning and community outreach, putting the school's best foot forward. The projects truly do good in the world, effect change, and transform lives. They are a terrific example of how the surrounding community can connect and contribute to student learning in their districts. While they may lead to future careers, they always open the eyes of students to the needs of the local populace, and they create real-life examples that will stay with these young people as they age and join a professional community.

Career exploration

Throughout this book we use a forest metaphor for capstone because of the useful representation of many aspects of the programming, and this chapter is one with a tight connection. As explained more fully in Chapter 3.2, the major themes of the forest metaphor are interconnection and pathways, the latter of which is especially relevant to career exploration. One can think about students finding their way in the world, towards an eventual career, as a pathway that forms over time. It starts as a faint line with exploratory branches, and develops with repeated use. It is unclear where it goes or what land it travels over at the beginning and may remain that way for some time. Only when the destination feels close does the path become a trail that eventually travels directly to the site, naturally taking in the contours of the environment, and completed with trail markers along the way.

Capstone follows the same empirical model. Students start with an idea and some experience, then develop these together with their teacher, leading to impressive projects. What looks like a linear process is instead a dynamic experience involving trial and error, adaptation, analysis, and evolution, in keeping with the experiential learning model. Just as rudimentary paths become marked trails, students explore and change their plans according to what they experience and how this compares with their personal goals. This process is by design and is what leads to the remarkable projects that capstone students create. The emergent property of their experience comes directly from this selective process, in which the best option of the moment is preferred, and many of these projects add up to a surprisingly grand final product.

Learning off campus not only provides connections to career options via capstone but also does so in a manner that is natural and efficient. Most professionals found their careers through some forethought and a little luck. They were usually not identified early and with great accuracy, as many young people seem to think. A very impressive job can give one the sense that it was the product of a massive planning campaign, but the opposite is usually true. Career paths are replete with false starts, happenstance, and being in the "right place at the right time." Only when one considers the final outcome does it seem like it was foreordained. Capstone provides all of these elements by design.

Returning to Alex and his capstone project involving interviews, this theme is made crystal clear. In every single case, he learned that his contacts got where they were via some combination of a string of unpredictable experiences, meeting the right person at the right time, and "failures" that proved to be really productive in the end—the adults usually told stories that included more than one item from this list. This overall idea was obvious to Alex after synthesizing his interview notes, and he proudly shared this in his final presentation. As is often the case, experiencing a lesson like this is far more effective than being taught it in a traditional way in school, like memorizing a definition of a term.

Together with a teacher as a guide, and a flexible mindset, students explore opportunities, keeping the valuable ones and discarding the least desirable experiences. This is normal and encouraged in the evolving environment of capstone, and approximates what it is like for most people to find a career. Combined with the extensive community networks that many programs possess, students may try on all kinds of roles for size, deciding what is of interest and useful, and what may be ignored. There is equal value, in the long term, in understanding what is meaningful and what is a dead end, because students can direct their energies towards fruitful ends and avoid years of struggling with a job that really is a bad fit for them.

Presentations as self-discovery

Returning to the forest metaphor, there comes a time when pathways become established and relatively fixed. The environment is stable for a long period of time, and the walkways remain the same between visits to the forested landscape, after years of formation and adjustment and acceptance by all those who use them. The trails to and from popular destinations become reliable ways to travel throughout the area, so much so that one could imagine making a map of the well-traveled space.

Capstone projects reach a similar, concrete status after about one-third of the duration of the program. In a typical year-long project, students and teachers are settled into the real work of a project by November. Such a timeline is normal and healthy for the dynamic nature of capstone. Before this date, projects can change quite a lot, and even morph into something that seems quite different. Beyond this milestone, students discover the true nature of their activities, as well as their final goals and personal voice. During the latter third of a project, say in March, these unique and identifiable traits are refined and crystalized as students begin to prepare for their final stand-and-deliver moment: the presentation.

Most capstones end with a presentation of some kind, with one common format being the narration of slides followed by a period of audience questions and answers. Along with the summation and illustration of their extended experience, students develop their voice as it relates to their project. Their initial idea was converted into an impressive narrative, reflecting their interest and values. The sequencing of text and images in their presentation provides a lens through which to view a particular part of their education, married to who they are as maturing people. The capstone presentation becomes a snapshot of who the student was when they completed their experience and shared it with the school community. This is why capstone presentations are as compelling as anything students do in school. The result of extended work with ample support, including only the highlights of all their efforts, aligned with their personal beliefs, these sharing moments are always impressive and excellent examples of what a school can accomplish.

Adults change and students do as well. What was important to us during the adolescent years is often a shadow of what we become and do, and sometimes not even that. The capstone presentation may or may not lead to a career and/or lifestyle. It will offer a clear window into a student's history, complete with many successes and fond memories, and plenty of pivots along the way that seem intriguing in hindsight. There are few moments in the education of a child that create this specific and rich representation of their experience. The value in this justifies capstone as a fantastic opportunity for students to find themselves within the context of their learning. Unlike all other aspects of their educational experience, capstone gives them the space to explore their interests, the resources that they need, and a venue to share their work. It truly caps off years of lessons, creating a culmination of everything they know, personalized just for them—hence the term "capstone."

How capstone changed one student

The power of capstone has to be seen to be believed. Our students and projects are the best thing for public relations. They inspire awe through what they do and how they do it. The best way to learn about capstone is to dive into the details of student experiences and survey their impressive accomplishments.

Tena was, and continues to be, a model capstone example. She is about to launch into an exciting career in audio engineering, and capstone was at the core of her experience. Tena maximized the resources available to her, pushing herself and everyone around her to consider new and exciting aspects to add to her project. While Tena was always ready to accept the perceived risk, many aspects of her path were challenging to her. Her success was never guaranteed, yet it sure seems that way in retrospect.

Tena thrived in academics and athletics. She enrolled in an independent school to make the most of her opportunities in life. When this learning environment proved to actually limit her potential, Tena switched to another school that was better prepared to support her big life goals and ambition—one that had a formal capstone program—and it was there that her trajectory took off.

Tena loved music as well as technology. A gifted saxophone player, she excelled in regional orchestras, rising in the ranks of the local talent. Tena was also fascinated with audio engineering, which is a field without many women. Her capstone was about engineering and producing studio recordings.

Tena completed two years in her program during her eleventh and twelfth grades. During this extended term she continued playing in her ensembles, completed studio internships, and arranged stunning final performances, in which she played her music and presented her mixing. Tena was the star of her program.

Tena used capstone to her advantage in her college search and landed a spot in an institution with a terrific conservatory and an audio engineering program. Tena had a blog during high school, and she kept it up during college, so it is now six years old and going strong. Now a recent college graduate, she continues on her artistic and technical musical path, reveling in the wonders of audio engineering. Tena keeps in touch with her capstone teacher and is still writing about her experience. Her story is truly in its infancy.

Tena is amazing, and very typical of capstone. She began with an interest and some experience; she said "yes" to every opportunity that she met; she accepted challenges and risk; she traveled ups and downs over the years at different schools; and she successfully navigated a transformative pathway between high school, college, and a career. That is what students can do when given the right tools, and capstone is a powerful one among them. Tena ended with a passion that carried her through college, and stokes her engines to this day, but it started in a way that was less formed and obvious. Her program allowed her to realize her future, through collaboration, opportunities, and structure. This is how capstone changes lives.

Notes to Chapter 2.1

Note 1, page 34: **questions related to "passion"**—For an excellent take on the hyper-scheduling of teenagers and the feelings it produces, see Denise Pope, *Overloaded and Underprepared: Strategies for Stronger Schools and Healthy, Successful Kids* (San Francisco: Jossey-Bass, 2015).

Note 2, page 35: **the "Four Cs"**—Though definitions of the "Four Cs" or "4Cs" vary, they are often traced to the Partnership for 21st-Century Learning (P21). In their version, the four skills are critical thinking, communication, collaboration, and creativity. See P21's "Framework for 21st-Century Learning" at www.bit.ly/3w8rGWu.

Note 3, page 36: *The Experiential Educator*—See page 29 and following in Alice Y. Kolb and David A. Kolb, *The Experiential Educator: Principles and Practices of Experiential Learning* (Kaunakakai, HI: Experience Based Learning Systems Inc, 2017).

CHAPTER 2.2
CAPSTONE CHANGES TEACHING

Many capstone teachers will testify that capstone has offered the most meaningful and satisfying experiences of their careers. But the potential in capstone goes beyond providing a few sustaining career highlights. We have known capstone teaching to lead to a renovation of a teacher's whole practice, in and out of the capstone program. We attribute the change that we've seen—and experienced—to the invigorating effects of doing transformative real-world work with students in partnership with teaching colleagues from varied disciplines. This chapter makes the argument that what motivates us to evolve as teachers also motivates our work in capstone.

Energy creates change, change creates energy

Being a great teacher is a bit like being a great chef. The 1000th time you sear swordfish, it has to be as perfect as it was when you were enthusiastically devoting yourself to your first night in the kitchen. Unlike many other professions which offer visible stages and create an appearance of progress, however illusory, the work of teaching seems for most of us to follow the same round from year to year. "The students keep getting younger," grey-haired teachers say. Eventually the new teachers seem to be getting younger too. The challenges of staying fresh are many. Subject knowledge that was current when teachers first studied it grows stale across the decades, and the trajectory of the typical teaching career offers little opportunity to update disciplinary knowledge. The sheer labor of teaching loads combined with non-teaching duties can exhaust even the most extroverted personality. The disrespect sometimes associated with the profession as a whole doesn't help. Furthermore, as Robert Evans notes in his classic *The Human Side of School Change*, teachers tend to stay in one position longer than other professionals.[1] The consequent burn-out can lead us long-haulers to resist the kinds of organizational changes that might help us most.

Teachers know that the most potent antidote to career exhaustion is the joy of seeing our students grow. The previous chapter recounted how students experience the transformative power of capstone. Being witness to and partner in such transformations is what teachers live for. At the National Capstone Consortium's summer summit, teachers who have come to exchange pedagogical expertise and share ideas about improving their programs cannot help but spend much of their time telling *stories* from the year that just ended. What they care about isn't their programs; it is individual students and how they were changed by their capstone work. But the same teachers also know that their whole load was lightened throughout the year by the spreading influence of the joyful learning encapsulated in those capstone stories. Students driven by intrinsic motivation work harder and learn more, and with less unpleasant labor on the part of the teachers. A student whose essay on Shakespeare was not only boring but also full of sentence errors will miraculously learn to write prose that is electrifying—as well as grammatically correct—for her thesis on urban wildlife corridors. Meanwhile, another student whose zoology exam scores were mediocre will memorize half the fauna native to England in order to ground his project on woodland descriptions in *A Midsummer Night's Dream*. Even mundane tasks—learning the rules for comma placement or identifying "thorny hedgehogs" and "spotted snakes" with modern nomenclature—are eagerly taken on by capstone students who have discovered passion in their projects.

Poised between past and future

Moving from a subject classroom into capstone teaching can be one of the best transitions of a teacher's career, and also one of the most fundamental. Because of its emphasis on emerging scholarship, employment of up-to-date research methods, multi-disciplinary nature, and engagement with off-campus resources, capstone offers opportunities for teachers as well as for students. These opportunities for teacher growth, inherent in capstone, can lead to a renovation of the teacher's practice back in their home classrooms.

First, capstone teaching builds in organic and continuous ways for teachers to stay up to date in their subject fields and its methods. Let's take an example. It might be hard for a world history teacher to get motivated to rewrite the lecture on post-colonialism that he gave successfully last year and the year before. But in supporting a student project on Derek Walcott, another on ocean plastics and the economy of the Pitcairn Islands, and a third on K-pop, he reads along—occasionally ahead—and encounters new perspectives and new theories that will inform his framing of that well-worn unit the following year.

Second, more than amplifying this teacher's content knowledge, capstone teaching keeps his understanding of knowledge construction and distribution itself up to date. The landscape evolves weekly now. The best way to find information changes with it. By working alongside many students in support of their many projects, he maintains a "floating" expertise that combines up-to-date skills with up-to-date content knowledge. What this teacher learned through helping his capstone student Enrique is useful to Julia too. Reading Julia's bibliography made him realize that Anna's was one-sided. And Anna's, though not yet complete, referenced a book on C.L.R. James that sounded so interesting, the teacher read it too. Multiply this process over years, and it is not only single lectures that are being rewritten or replaced, but whole frameworks for this teacher's classes back in his home department.

Third, the chance to work on a capstone team with colleagues from other departments can likewise invigorate our teaching. Capstone teaching programs are typically multi-disciplinary and their teaching teams correspondingly drawn from across campus. One of us, Nina, taught in a capstone program that for many years had been housed in her school's senior humanities classes. When a directive came from the head of school to make the program more welcoming of science projects, the changes improved the program for all students, but they also led to permanent changes to Nina's teaching of English. A colleague from the science department came to her class to teach about research methods in the sciences and peer review, and Nina heard the lesson with them. Not long after, there was an opportunity for more science teachers to be involved in reading student research essays. The science teachers saw flaws in the student work and in the program instruction that had been invisible to the eyes of the humanities teachers previously leading the program. Nina was impressed, for example, with the care her science colleagues took to help students make only thoughtfully qualified claims about their evidence. They asked students to always note what was not known, along with what could be argued. Back in her home classroom, Nina adopted this approach when teaching thesis statements in English papers. When students want to extrapolate beyond their textual evidence in English essays, now they are asked to clearly signal that they have moved beyond argument and into speculation or questioning. In many other ways, the opportunity to interact with colleagues outside the humanities enlivened Nina's English teaching, as well as improving the capstone program itself.

Fourth, supporting student work off campus connects teachers to the larger community in ways that never would have happened had they remained in their subject areas. On this writing team, Jon administers capstone programs that place students in off-campus internships and service roles and also teaches biology. After a successful year with one student working in a lab at RPI in Troy, NY, the principal investigator approached Jon with an offer. Her graduate students ran a biophysics program aimed at high school students, all about molecules that glow for scientific applications. Jon arranged for the seminar to happen on his school campus, creating a wonderful opportunity for his students to have hands-on experiences with advanced techniques, as well as interactions with professionals in the field. Jon went on to incorporate some of the biophysics elements in his own courses and shared these resources with his colleagues. Again, this teacher's learning in his capstone program also improved instruction back in his home classroom.

Facing a fear

Capstone projects transfer power traditionally held by the teacher to the student. Student choice and intrinsic motivation drive the project. The transfer of power and choice from teacher to student implies a similarly radical shift in the role and even identity of the teacher. We believe that far from being something to avoid, this shift has the potential to bring energy and joy to a teacher's whole practice. But that said, we want to acknowledge that we understand: the fear associated with changing roles is real, and we've felt it too.

Most obviously, the role of teacher as content expert will be undermined in capstone work. With young adults choosing a wide array of topics, each student is likely to have more topic-area knowledge than the teacher within a few weeks of starting. The teacher role of judge may be undermined if a student's work in a program is not traditionally assessed, or if students come to care more about the esteem of off-campus mentors, or about the appreciation of public audiences, than they do about teacher approval expressed in the form of grades. But even teachers who understand themselves as "designers" of student learning experiences, to take a fashionable recent example,[2] may find this role likewise undermined by the sheer messiness and variety of project trajectories in a senior-year capstone. Capstone projects are forward-designed, not backward-planned. Anticipating such shifts can leave teachers wondering what they will actually be *doing* once they start a capstone program.

To put this all more fundamentally: if I am not the content expert, the judge of value, or even a designer of experiences, **who am I?** Lurking under the fear of not knowing what to do with my students lies the deeper fear of not knowing who I am. For teachers whose long hours sometimes take them away from the families, sports, and hobbies that otherwise contribute to a sense of identity and a balanced life, contemplating this question can be terrifying.

Redefining teacher expertise

But it is clear to us that teachers do not disappear, nor do they become anything like peers who merely learn alongside their students. It is just that in their capstone roles, teachers operate more like coaches than like lecturers.

In gymnastics, an athlete attempting a risky move may have a "spotter," a coach who stands in position, tracking and anticipating the movement of the routine. Search online for spotter videos and you will see some amazing catches— amazing both for the skillful anticipation which places the coach just ahead of the fall, and for the trust of the athlete who may have just sent himself hurtling headfirst toward the floor, confident that his coach will protect him from harm. In reality, these are not truly catches. Rather than physically stopping the movement of a flying body, the coach redirects that energy safely. Usually both teacher and student land unhurt on the floor. In a competition, the coach would be providing a "rescue spot," stepping in only in the case of a dangerous failure. But spotting also has a place in teaching. A young gymnast who has not yet experienced a particular maneuver can be helped through it by hands that guide or even provide a momentary impetus. By experiencing the movement from inside, the gymnast may acquire the trick more quickly than through mere observation and imitation. This is learning by doing—with a lot of very expert help.

In this example, it is easy to see the extraordinary expertise of the coach. In fact, spotting a gymnast requires a much deeper understanding of the sport than merely standing at the front of a room explaining a move or routine. The spotter understands what *should* happen, and also all the things that *can* happen with an inexperienced athlete. In addition, the spotter knows the athlete himself. She knows his experience level, his strength, and even the particularities of the way he goes wrong when he goes wrong. Beyond knowledge of the sport and of the unique student athlete, the coach brings to the moment her total attention. Spotting requires spontaneous, immediate action. Such action is only possible for the expert who is both fully prepared and fully present.

Translating this metaphor back into the language of schoolwork, we want to stress that as adult experts, capstone teachers still need the knowledge and skills associated with research in the academic disciplines. Likewise, when supporting off-campus internships or service work, they need their adult professional community relationships and life experience. Though the role of a capstone teacher may differ from the role of a teacher who understands himself as *primarily* delivering content, it is still an adult role. Likewise, capstone teaching does not require us to take any particular position in the debate over the relative importance of content as compared to skills, nor in the older debate about traditional and progressive models of education. As John Dewey suggested more than a generation ago, once things get practical, such dichotomies turn out to be less sharp than they appeared in theory.[3] This is why we understand expertise in capstone teaching as emergent, responsive to the students in front of us, and not a matter of mastering an externally developed method or top-down philosophy.

Now more than ever

Finally, the type of teaching needed in a capstone program guarantees the continued employment of human teachers. We are already seeing that significant content delivery can be done at scale without a live teacher. Once created, a video can reach an unlimited number of students. The success of the free Khan Academy more than demonstrates that educational videos can be effective for certain types of learning. Drilling, meaning the repetition of low-level skills to acquire fluency, can likewise be supported without individualized instruction through web-based systems like those offered by the subscription company IXL Learning. The enormous experimentation with remote instruction that took place while schools were physically closed due to the COVID-19 pandemic revealed more domains where effective learning can happen without guidance through a personalized student-teacher relationship. But the types of learning that happen in capstone go far beyond acquisition of factual knowledge or skills. Capstone learning is a more essential learning, and it does require the guidance of teachers who know their students as individuals.

Moreover, we argue that as more and more work once done by humans is taken over by computers, teaching and learning will have to focus more on work that only humans can do; there is no point in preparing students to do tasks that computers can do better.[4] The creativity and sense for human values that characterize capstone work can never be replaced by software. Software can already gather information off the internet and, thanks to machine-learning, deliver that information up in the form of natural-language sentences. At the time of writing, the GPT-3 program just published its first article in a mainstream newspaper,[5] and web profiles have been produced by computers for some time. But determining the use or meaning of information and relating to audiences by presenting that information within a specific human context cannot be done by a computer. Only human teachers can teach human students how to do this human work, which is the heart of capstone.

Notes to Chapter 2.2

Note 1, page 43: **teachers tend to stay in one position longer**—See Chapter 6 and especially pages 93–94 in Robert Evans, *The Human Side of School Change: Reform, Resistance, and the Real-Life Problems of Innovation* (San Francisco: Jossey-Bass, 1996).

Note 2, page 46: **"designers" of student learning experiences**—The concept has been developed by Grant Wiggins and Jay McTighe in *Understanding by Design*. (Alexandria, VA: ASCD, 2005). But see also the design process as outlined in free resources offered by the Stanford "d School."

Note 3, page 48: **dichotomies turn out to be less sharp**—See Chapter 1, "Traditional vs. Progressive Education," in John Dewey, *Experience and Education* (New York: Free Press, 1938).

Note 4, page 48: **work that only humans can do**—An excellent data-based articulation of this widely recognized argument is made by Frank Levy and Richard Murnane. See Frank Levy and Richard Murnane, *Dancing with Robots: Human Skills for Computerized Work* (Third Way), July 17, 2013.

Note 5, page 48: **the GPT-3 program just published its first article**—"A Robot Wrote This Entire Article. Are You Scared Yet, Human? | GPT-3," *The Guardian* (Guardian News and Media), September 8, 2020.

CHAPTER 2.3
CAPSTONE CHANGES SCHOOLS

The change driven by capstone starts at the grassroots, with students, and proceeds up organizational structures, impacting all levels of schools. The potential to transform schools is great and should not be ignored or underestimated. A movement is forming in American education toward capstone programs—whether they use the word "capstone" or not in the title of their programs—as teachers and administrators find their way to adopting 21st-century educational skills. People are realizing the importance of growing organic programs that originate in classrooms, not as top-down mandates from school district leaders. Teachers are empowered to create curricula that work in partnership with students in this fashion. This chapter delves into these issues, making connections with capstone programs, and highlights the importance of working with partners who are off campus and have similar aspirations to educate the future adults of our society.

Catching the wave

Capstone is having a well-deserved moment in American education. Capstone programs are popping up all over the country, following an organic process that begins with small teams of teachers and extends through schools, leading to school-wide change. In some cases, district-wide or even state-wide mandates put capstones in place in schools, but even in these cases, the capstone curriculum is being developed on the ground, by teachers in active engagement with their students.[1] We believe that this "capstone wave" or movement is happening for good reasons. Furthermore, we believe that the organic and grounded nature of capstone implementation promises a long future for the programs launching in this moment. We argue in this book that teachers can trust this movement and "catch the wave," without fear of adopting a fad. Capstone is the real deal.

The types of change that can be ushered in by a capstone program are precisely those broadly desired in schools today. Capstones are an excellent venue for students exercising 21st-century skills (see Chapter 2.1). Standardized curricula (AP, IB, etc.) feel increasingly restrictive as schools develop more personalization and flexibility for their students. Teachers have tried out methodologies that invite student independence, like project-based learning, and find themselves wanting more, and the students feel the same way. Schools recognize that off-campus experiences energize today's teens. Attempts to connect schools with organizations off campus are challenging, but this outreach is made easier and more authentic through capstone. Meanwhile, historical shifts in the social fabric of the country demand response from schools, and capstone helps to address this demand because it gives students the space to express and explore their concerns with support from trusted teachers and in productive ways. We feel that this is part of a broad movement with similarities to "deeper learning" as developed in the excellent book by Mehta and Fine.[2]

Capstone changes schools by allowing emergent, organic processes to drive systemic shifts. These processes start with students, but—once it comes to school structures—are typically developed by small teams of teachers who recognize the potential in the urgent student needs they see in front of them. In our experience, these organic processes can lead to lasting change to the infrastructure or curriculum in the school as a whole.

To put it another way, capstone is grassroots. At our own schools and in the schools of the National Capstone Consortium, we have seen time and time again how a small program, cautiously piloted by a team of teachers, grew and led to change impacting the school as a whole. We understand this as the "pilot" method of school change. Pilots are inexpensive in terms of time and other school resources. They have a planned end in case they are unsuccessful. With iterations built into the model, a pilot program grows to match a school's existing infrastructure and curriculum. Its growth is responsive to its specific environment, meeting the needs of teachers and students, while limiting conflict with other school objectives. Teachers try out ideas, keep the ones that work, and continue this selective process until a mature program is formed, minutely adapted to the specific school culture. The iterative process of growth and development allows the piloted capstone to become an accepted official program. In our experience, the capstone often comes eventually to be held up as the main embodiment of what the school stands for—the school's signature program.

Adaptability is one of the core secrets of capstone's success. These inherently dynamic programs are structured in ways that allow them to respond to changing circumstances. Their flexibility allows students to start with what they know, make new connections as they learn, and develop their projects organically. Events beyond the scope of a student's initial plans, or even the control of the school, can factor into the final composition of a project. In a year, capstone bobs and weaves, following a natural path that is the creative student process. Capstone can also adjust to big events that impact school at a higher level, beyond the scope of the program. The intrinsic adaptability of capstone works for students in the short term, and for programs and schools in the long term.

Take the global pandemic that emerged in 2020. Not only did capstone survive the shift from in-person to online learning, but some schools actually saw it thrive in this new, extreme educational environment. This was possible because capstone is uniquely adaptable. It works in nearly every educational setting, regardless of the amount of school resources. When the great educational shift happened, forcing students out of classrooms and onto computer screens, capstone programs revisited their goals, made adjustments, and finished the academic year in good shape. Pivoting was always in the DNA of capstone and this was a stress test of this feature, which it passed with flying colors. Without external requirements and pressures to cover a standardized curriculum, starting where the student is at, and planning from the ground up, capstone is designed to thrive in any learning environment. The pandemic cemented this core characteristic of capstone.

Centering diverse student experiences

Capstone changes schools by positioning and supporting students so that they can have a lasting impact on school infrastructure and programming. Students bring diverse life experiences to their inquiry and action projects at school.[3] When those projects are integrated, via healthy capstone programs, into the life of the school as a whole, their potential to bring lasting change to the school community can be realized. While engaged in their capstone projects, seniors are also in classes, clubs, and sport. Just by our social nature, the capstone experience gets shared. At the culminating event, other students, along with adult members of the school community, get to hear the academic conclusions of a student group that is almost invariably more diverse than its teaching faculty.

In a healthy program, support for action work at school can go beyond this level of sharing from diverse perspectives to actually help the school infrastructure evolve in a lasting way. Because the capstone student is supported from the outset, she has time and resources to develop a proposal that the school can take seriously. Because that support includes her teachers who know her well, and also have an adult perspective on the school, the likelihood that the school gets a proposal for change that they can implement is further increased.

Let's take an example. Jorge's capstone was an action project aimed at creating a common space on campus for affinity groups, which include people with similar identities, interests, and/or experiences. Jorge saw the need for a physical space in which students could have sensitive discussions with members of that group only, and a schedule to make the location available to the different groups. This was an ambitious project on many levels. The affinity space required approval from the administration, permission from the facilities department to repurpose the physical space, a budget to buy furniture, and a plan to negotiate and schedule with the calendars of many students in the various affinity groups. But Jorge was a force to be reckoned with at his school. Proud of his heritage, Jorge was known on campus for the respect and maturity with which he brought his ideas about diversity to conversations in and out of the classroom. Along with his developed world view, he was eager to tackle any challenge that he felt was important, undaunted by whatever complexity might arise. Jorge was an inspiration to his community.

The occasion of Jorge's presentation to the school administration demonstrated how both he and the school were growing because of his project. He was nervous for the big day—but with the support of his capstone advisors, superbly prepared. He came with extensive notes. His slide presentation was professionally formatted. His facts were well researched and supported and his ideas fully explained. He had anticipated most of the questions brought by his audience of administrators. His school had recently recommitted itself to systemic work in the area of diversity, equity, and inclusion (DEI), but it was clear when Jorge's proposal was approved that his individual efforts had led to a concrete change that would not have happened without him. His project came out of an urgent student concern, so its authenticity allowed it to accomplish more than the top-down approach that adults were rolling out. Jorge changed his school in just one year.

Jorge's example is one of many that speak to the transformative power of capstone. Empowering students to pursue their interests, with the dedicated support of teachers for their endeavors, impacts far more than just the classroom. Students bring their lived experiences and perspectives to their projects, inevitably introducing issues of urgent social concern into the school conversation. Their ideas are guaranteed to be heard better by their peers, because they are explained in familiar terms and come from shared outlooks.

Relationships with supportive teachers help them produce work whose value can be recognized by other adults, including school administrators. It's important to hold in mind the interplay between the flexible institutional structure of the capstone program and the individual passion of the unique student—for it is the combination of these two together that leads to change.

Partnering in the community

Capstone also changes schools by engaging students in off-campus learning and action opportunities, simultaneously creating long-term relationships between the school and its community partners. Though schools have long recognized the value of off-campus programs including internships and service learning, obstacles like the school schedule make them hard to implement through traditional course structures. The intrinsic motivation factor in capstone projects, along with the greater time allowed for student preparation, likewise increases the likelihood that the interaction will be of value to both student learning and the hosting community organizations.

Why do schools want students off campus? Because students learn more in real-world environments—as long as they are properly supported. Internships and job shadowing give students a taste of what a career feels like, as well as often leading to opportunities for actual jobs later on. Being engaged at sites in unfamiliar parts of their communities can expose students to difficult realities of the world that they may not have encountered before. Working with community activists, students may gain skills that they can later use in jobs or in their equally important roles as citizens. Any embodied experiences inform and energize the types of learning—text-based or discussion-based—more familiar to students inside their classrooms.

Though we all acknowledge the value, schools often find it very difficult to connect students to the world beyond the campus. The pressure to cover content in a traditional curriculum is one obstacle. Another challenge is that the school schedule and location do not align with the times and places when work needs to happen at a community site. Significant off-campus learning remains on the "wish list" for most schools, because schooling occurs as if in its own universe, making relationships with other types of organizations hard to create and maintain. Many schools even find that their community service programs run into resistance from teachers whose classes are disrupted when students leave campus—especially sad, since the opportunity to invigorate the traditional curriculum is lost.

Traditional service learning faces additional obstacles, over and above career-exploration programs. Schools are increasingly aware that unless very carefully structured, programs may wind up reinforcing the very social inequities that they meant to expose and dismantle. If service is a school requirement, the extrinsically supplied motivation may corrupt the learning mindset. With limited time for advance study, students arrive at community sites unprepared to understand the histories and systems that produced the conditions their service is supposed to address. If their service is fit into the school schedule, they are likely to wind up doing types of work (serving food or tutoring younger children are two common examples) that may lead to gratifying feelings of satisfaction in the short term, but never to lasting change; the work of addressing systemic injustice does not produce results on a school time table.[4] Even if opportunities for reflection are built in, what is actually learned in these service programs may be nearly the opposite of what the school had intended.

Capstone offers ways to begin to work through these very challenging obstacles and make progress toward a widely desired school goal. Starting with the students and their choices guarantees the kind of intrinsic motivation likely to lead to authentic relationships in the community and to the opening up of life-long questions about *why* our social world is the way it is. If adults on the capstone teaching team are supported in maintaining long-term relationships with community partners, they can match students with sites in ways likely to benefit all concerned. Academic requirements at the research stage of the capstone will ensure that the student has at least an initial understanding of relevant social systems, rather than going in as a naive observer. Unlike an ordinary volunteer, the capstone student has training and support that includes reflection on the fact that the perspective of the community partner on what is needed takes precedence over her necessarily less informed perspective.

We will consider an example here as well. Laurie had already done volunteer hours on her own at a local community clinic the summer before her senior year. Her role was providing information about nutrition to clients at the clinic. The experience led to an interest in food deserts and urban farms. Working through previously established long-term relationships between her school and a local network of small farms, Laurie developed a capstone project on community farming. Not coincidentally, the project dovetailed with the school's long-standing senior service week, during which all seniors spend a few days providing labor to the network. When spring came, the service director tapped Laurie to give a presentation to her peers in advance of their service. Her presentation was attended by all the senior advisors and teachers, a few of whom asked Laurie afterwards to share her paper and sources with them. Those teachers then integrated Laurie's work into the senior-year academic curriculum for future students. In theory, all of Laurie's sources and community connections could have been available to the teachers even if her project had never happened. In practice, without her passion and the time she committed to drawing connections between her academic classwork and her service learning experiences, those same teachers never would have made the adjustments to their own curriculum in support of the annual senior service week.

Like Jorge, Laurie changed her school in just one year. Jorge made an infrastructure change by making both a problem and a practical solution visible to school administrators. Laurie made a curriculum change by revealing connections between her on- and off-campus experiences, and by supplying resources to teachers. As in Jorge's case, it was the combination of the flexible institutional structure of the capstone program and Laurie's individual passion that led to change.

A culture change

Now we can visualize the power of capstone in a school. By starting with students, transforming their relationship with teachers, and connecting them with the real world, we have all of the ingredients for effective and lasting change. This is what capstone does. Students create the ideas for projects derived from their diverse life experiences. Teachers collaborate, share resources, and connect students with professionals off campus. Project topics are contemporary, meaningful, and worthy of exploration. Once all parties understand how capstone benefits students in ways large and small, short and long term, that is when capstone changes school. It is a culture shift that is organic and adaptive. A successful pilot merges seamlessly with a school curriculum, then grows connections throughout the traditional academic departments. The effectiveness capstone has at implementing 21st-century skills becomes evident, and soon teachers are re-planning lessons and incorporating more aspects of the program into their own classrooms. This kind of evolution is exciting and creates more change than the average new program on campus.

Growing capstone from the ground up ensures that students will be engaged and programs will flourish. There are many mandates swirling in the edu-sphere, with the majority of them established at the highest levels—too far from actual student experience. Capstone accomplishes goals that we consider vital to the future of the next generation, so let's use a model that is designed to teach students what they need to know. Capstone repays investment. This has been supported at a remarkably diverse array of schools across the nation, at all levels and forms of schooling. Its organic nature and malleability, allowing seamless adaptation to each school's unique infrastructure and curriculum, are the key ingredients to this five-star recipe.

Capstone achieves the change we are looking for, and it changes all who are involved. It makes use of skills that are essential for our future graduates, boosting their entry into the job market, and it teaches these skills in ways that are natural and inspirational to students. Students bring their personalities and lived experiences into their learning. Teachers join forces with students to complete meaningful actions that are memorable to all who witness them. Administrators benefit from the resources that they invest in capstone as they observe students learn and perform. Once they realize how powerful capstone learning can be, they realize the value of investing in the program. The benefits always align with mission and objectives. Schools become more connected to the communities that they serve, creating a beautiful give-and-take that integrates learning throughout the population, as schooling really should.

Notes to Chapter 2.3

Note 1, page 51: **district-wide or even state-wide mandates**—In this book, written for teachers rather than school administrators, the focus is on the single school. It is worth noting that capstone lends itself to organic networks of schools working in partnership. Likewise, capstone, as a fundamentally local type of curriculum, can be seen to model the type of change in which a successful pilot at one school is then replicated with adaptations (or "taken to scale") across a district. For a fascinating and relevant exploration of school reform carried out on models other than top-down standardization, see Anthony Bryk, et al., *Learning to Improve* (Cambridge, MA: Harvard Education, 2017).

Note 2, page 52: **the excellent book by Mehta and Fine**—This book develops the idea of deeper learning with fascinating case studies at innovative schools across the country. We think it should be on the shelf on any serious educational reformer. Jal Mehta and Sarah Fine, *In Search of Deeper Learning: The Quest to Remake the American High School* (Harvard University Press, Cambridge, MA, 2019).

Note 3, page 53: **Students bring diverse life experiences**—Diversity exists across many different spectrums. In fact, we teachers don't even know how our students are different from us until we give them space to show us. All of that said, race remains one identity category of predominant importance in schools. Research shows that many students learn better from teachers who share their racial identities. Since the national teaching force remains overwhelmingly White, even as the student population nationally becomes increasingly racially diverse, this particular difference constitutes another systemic disadvantage for students of color. A single project at the end of a student's experience at a particular school cannot make up such a disadvantage. Nonetheless, we see particular value when the impact of a student like Jorge can be amplified through a capstone program. On the demographic data, see Bruce Douglas, et al., "The Impact of White Teachers on the Academic Achievement of Black Students: An Exploratory Qualitative Analysis," *Educational Foundations* 22, no. 1–2 (Winter–Spring 2008): 47–62.

Note 4, page 56: **Traditional service learning faces additional obstacles—** Tania D. Mitchell offers a review of the research on the pitfalls of traditional service learning and the risk that it may "have no impact beyond students' good feelings" (page 50). Chapter 3.5 and 4.5 explain in more detail how capstone programs can avoid these pitfalls. See Tania D. Mitchell "Traditional vs. Critical Service-Learning: Engaging the Literature to Differentiate Two Models." *Michigan Journal of Community Service Learning.* 14 (Spring 2008), pages 50–65.

PART 3:
HOW? ORGANIZING
THE PROGRAM

CHAPTER 3.1
START WITH THE STUDENT

The personalized nature of capstone taps into student energy to start and continue projects, creating a relationship of trust with teachers to navigate the ups and downs of the experience, in a way that is categorically different from average classroom activities. This chapter provides an overview of the evolution of a project and an explanation of a capstone teaching philosophy. Students begin with their own plans and maintain a steady pace by setting goals and scheduling regular program meetings. As is always the case with capstone, students are at the center of every facet of the program. Skillful teaching lifts students when their zeal lags, employing techniques that are all about a growth mindset. Students and teachers work together to navigate the complexity and challenges of capstone together, making use of a rebalanced classroom power structure.

Capstone taps into student interest as a core source of energy.

Student interest as an energy source

High school is a fertile time for the development of the human brain as students begin to enter the next stage in life: adulthood. Proceeding at their own pace, each student follows a trajectory that eventually leads to life beyond school, taking on varying degrees of responsibility. Some students jump right into the professional world, others may remain in an academic setting like graduate school, and the rest make the switch some time after they graduate. There is a natural transition during this process, away from the rarified school environment, in which textbooks and tests are at the center, toward the real world which demands a very different kind of knowledge and type of skills. Along this pathway, student interest becomes more and more important, as "What do you want to do in life?" steadily transforms into an actual career.

Students begin their learning lives with open minds and natural curiosity. Their brains brim with questions as they study the natural world and their position inside it. Students are innately questioning, analyzing, synthesizing, and experimenting, mirroring the Kolb experiential learning cycle.[1] This expansive investigatory mode tapers as students move through the traditional American educational system. By the time they are halfway through high school, many curricula introduce radically different factors, like standardized knowledge and testing. This conflicts with the parallel career seeking process, which is decidedly not standardized, or at least is very different for each field. Right when students should be making broad use of their inquisitive brains, considering job options that align with their individual goals and values, many are enrolled in school systems that are seemingly opposed to this outcome. Capstone is a notable exception from this kind of curriculum.

Capstone taps into student interest as a core source of energy, providing just the kind of motivation needed to complete this student-centered program. The primary benefit is the sustainable intellectual drive required to do a capstone project from start to finish, with all of the modifications along the way. A secondary benefit is developing a growth mindset that is well suited to career development. Capstone begins with the most natural of mental states: curiosity about a concept or item. Together with a capstone teacher, a student frames the idea in a manageable way, setting the stage for a series of activities that lead to the completion of the project and resolution of the initial idea. It is the cognitive engagement of the student that pushes this process from the beginning to the end.

We addressed the distinction between passion and interest in Chapter 2.1, and this nuance is important here as well. Focused interest is the spark that ignites capstone, creating a robust series of activities that sustains student engagement throughout the project. This approach is an essential part of a successful program, and is enough without summoning the loaded idea of true passion. While some students may run with their ideas well beyond their final presentation, converting their project into some aspect of their college experience and professional career, others may stop it upon completion, content with a deep dive into a subject area before moving on to something else. Student interest gets the capstone job done every time.

Capstone provides a rich environment for student ideas to thrive. After the start, a recursive loop continually returns to the student and their ideas, surmounting challenges and updating the map that leads toward the end of the project. Capstone empowers the human condition of mental processing, harnessing this energy to run the project activities. Young adults are full of questions, just like their childish selves, when placed in the proper environment. These ideas and queries are generated and captured by design, fed into the capstone engine to get the students where they would like to go. This is especially useful when confronted with real problems because motivation powers the student through to a successful outcome. Capstone is impressive largely because of what this source of energy produces. Compared to their performance in other courses, student motivation and productivity can take people by surprise when they realize their true potential. Capstone projects are what can be accomplished in school when teachers tap into authentic student interest.

Collaboration through trust

Capstone requires a different kind of educational relationship with students. Trust becomes a very important part of the way teachers and students interact due to the student-centered nature of the program. The central idea, the motivation, and the sustainability of a project originate with the student, illuminating how much responsibility resides on their side of the working relationship. Instead of the typical classroom dynamic, in which teachers shoulder much of the managerial duties, capstone demands a considerable rebalancing of the educational workload. In addition to a shifting of duties from teacher to student, the entire nature of "teaching" changes, becoming much more of a collaborative process. Teachers retain ultimate authority and power, of course—especially when student effort drops and direct intervention is required. Some aspects of the jobs of teachers are essentially the same, but the overall nature of the interaction changes in capstone programs, allowing for the special features of capstone to flourish.

Trust is the best word to describe the base of this new course dynamic. Faith is placed in the ideas and actions of students after an initial screening. Teachers can rely on students for more effort once a few ground rules are established when they enter the program. They provide the original idea which becomes the core of the project. Students generate their personalized goals that align with their specific plans. They establish a pace that allows them to complete all of these items by the end of the project. Students also become the source of ideas when challenges pop up during the duration of their project. The spotlight in the classroom dramatically points away from the teacher and toward the student during the entirety of the project. This is especially obvious during the final presentation when students are literally the focus of attention of the entire school community.

Students simply take on more responsibility as many class duties are delegated to them. Capstone begins and ends with a strong sense of ownership. Students bring their own hopes and dreams to the classroom and teachers guide them through the pathways and processes for the extent of the project. A clear list of duties is continually revisited and updated, allowing students to understand what they have accomplished and what comes next. In taking on these capstone assignments, teachers are freed to focus on the higher order interactions for everyone in the program.

This relatively new kind of relationship between students and teachers requires confidence on both sides. Instead of doling out assignments and incentivizing behavior with grades, students and teachers enter a different working agreement. Students take on more of the tasks in this understanding and teachers shift their attention toward higher-level educational techniques. Students are more committed to their work with greater risk when challenges are presented. Teachers operate in different ways to make student projects as safe as they can be because both have more skin in the game. Personalization is what makes this possible. Risk-taking is more likely when teachers really know students and understand their potential. The project originates with the interest and experience of the student. This grounding forms the base of the relationship that operates on trust.

Capstone teachers should have music teachers in mind when they think about this kind of relationship. As is the case for a choral conductor who will appear on stage together with their students for the final performance, trust is essential. The conductor rehearses with the students, teaching them parts and coordinating voices. The conductor physically stands in front of the singers as they all learn their roles. The conductor's role shifts from a heavy-handed approach at the beginning, as they learn the work together, to becoming just a reminder to the students should they need a cue after they know the piece. Singers and conductors take the stage together to perform the piece and to accept the final applause and any mistakes made along the way. The students are in the central focus of the spotlight and the conductor shares the edge of the illumination. The kind of trust developed by this music teacher with their students also characterizes the relationship between students and teachers in a capstone classroom.

Finding the beginning

Capstone students get excited when they begin a project and usually aim for the stars. Given a chance to work on something that is important to them, they tend to go big, pitching ambitious ideas at the outset of the school term. Capstone is often the first time students are given permission to explore an area of interest for a long-term activity. Given the time and resources that are made available for their investigation, it should not be surprising that students really go for it when they enter the program. It is crucial to dial back some of these projects to a level that is more reasonable to avoid the risk of insurmountable challenges. What may seem less interesting by comparison to the student will be much better in the end because the project is more likely to succeed. There will always be time to add to a project—most projects are presented with opportunities to expand and transform during the course of events—but beginning too ambitiously without a firm foundation is risky because it can catastrophically collapse early on.

Developed programs connect with students as early as possible, when ideas are just forming and it is appropriate to consider all aspects of their plans. Even before they complete an application, students should sit down with capstone teachers to express their interest and describe their initial approach. A small group of students will share ideas that are actually good to go. Their plans match their previous experience, their scope of work is reasonable, they have the resources to complete their tasks, they have time in their schedule to do the work, and they have all the skills necessary to begin. Most students will need to reconsider some aspect of their plans because their ideas are some combination of too broad, too vague, or too involved. The best way forward is to focus on the key elements of their proposal. A series of questions will elucidate the core concepts, and actions can be used to make the project more specific, more doable, and often more exciting—when pared down to size, a revised project makes the student's ideas more immediate, actually boosting their engagement in the program.

An effective model for this conversation is to invite students to meet with one or more capstone teachers—two teachers are always better than one because of the synergy that comes from collaborating on ideas. If the initial proposal requires revision, teachers ask questions to identify the central ideas and activities. Here are some examples:

- What led you to think about this project in the first place?
- What previous experiences have you had that relate to your ideas?
- What resources might you need to complete your tasks?
- What else are you doing in school this year that might connect to your project?
- What other capstone projects in the program seem related to your proposal?
- What are the most important parts of your project?

Questions like these help students understand the magnitude and clarity of their ideas, giving them anchors for improving their thinking. They can begin to improve their plans once they visualize the essential elements hidden among some extraneous components, reconnecting them into a more cohesive and compelling concept.

Most proposals can be distilled to one or two central elements. Students can make a new blueprint with some of the original concepts built upon these core components. The best plan for assembly is the one that retains the key ideas at the center. Retaining parts of the first process is secondary to achieving what the student is truly interested in. The most important aspect of starting a project is ensuring that the framework is composed of the right pieces with room for future additions. With the bones of a project in view and articulated, one can be confident of the health of the project and be assured of future growth.

Beyond innate energy

Inherent motivation will likely be insufficient at some point in the lifespan of a capstone project. The original excitement and eagerness to get started will encounter enough challenges, or one major complication, calling for intervention by the teacher. Experienced capstone teachers have several options to choose from in their quiver of educational techniques. Primary among them is harnessing the power of student mental potential.

Carol Dweck's work on growth mindset is pertinent here. In *Mindset*, Dweck explains that a "growth mindset is based on the belief that your basic qualities are things you can cultivate through your efforts."[2] Dweck details the types of communications that are likely to help students develop a growth mindset and consequently engagement in learning for its own sake. In general, praising effort ("You worked so hard"), Dweck suggests, is more productive than praising supposedly innate qualities ("You are so smart"). The spoken word therefore plays an enormous role in capstone teaching. Centering ownership and framing feedback is of utmost importance to guiding student projects. Students are more in control of their project than their teachers. Attention must be given to how they approach their work and respond to difficulties, rather than directly solving the immediate problem. Capstone teachers must instead address the motivation and focus of the student, and get them to a mental place where they can sort through the issues and solve the problem at hand. This demands authentic listening, thorough consideration, and carefully measured evaluation. Teaching is never black and white, and this is especially true in capstone programs. Dweck's language shift is an excellent place to start when making the change toward a more suggestive and ultimately more successful technique.

68

Sample contract

*This student contract clarifies expectations in an **optional** program. Students are required to read and sign it during the first week of the program.*

Capstone contract

Student, review these expectations, then indicate your understanding by signing below. Remember that your continued participation in this program depends on these items. Should expectations be unmet at marking periods (when grades are generated), you may need to drop the program.

"As a capstone student, I understand that:

- I will attend all meetings;
- I will create portfolio events twice a month;
- I will arrange transportation off campus in person;
- I will participate in the final presentation event;
- I will seek clarification for any issues that I do not understand."

Print, sign your name, and add today's date.

Setting goals is a more concrete strategy for maintaining student effort. Students should establish some broad targets for each major period of the project, for example a general one per month. They need not worry how accurate they truly are because the act of creating them is the most important aspect of the process. Student plans will change as projects develop and so will the regular goals. Some may even be changed completely. What a goal represents is largely outweighed by making and revisiting it at the agreed-upon time. This is a flexible system that is designed to ensure persistent forward motion. Capstone projects will grow and develop in unpredictable ways, and may even backtrack if necessary. A calendar with equally spaced goals keeps students on a path that leads toward the eventual conclusion of the project.

Capstone projects are on the long end of school project timelines—more like an ultramarathon if they were a running event—and thus demand even pacing throughout the year. Slogging is inevitable at some point even for the most inspired and driven students. Progress will slow to a crawl, the way ahead will be unclear, and motivation will fall through the floor. In addition to repeating goals, regular meetings prepare students for these very challenging experiences. Like a pacer who runs with an ultramarathoner for the final stretch, guiding and encouraging the exhausted runner, meeting with teachers becomes essential during this time of tension. A pre-scheduled time to review progress, identify issues, and discuss options can become a turning point for a student's project. Students and teachers lead busy lives, making last-minute crises hard to deal with. A repeating calendar event is a proactive technique for anticipating problems and keeps challenges more manageable. Combined with repeated goals, pacing improves the odds of success in capstone programs to a significant degree.

Navigating senior year

Senior year is a busy time in the life of a student, filled with life events that may interrupt capstone projects, especially if their existence is excluded in the monthly plan. College-bound students are occupied with applications—whose deadlines shift earlier and earlier each year—and all the thinking, writing and energy that go into them. It is important to many students to maintain rigorous academic programs to improve their odds of acceptance into colleges, keeping many activities on their academic plate. Acceptance time also pops up during the year, when students hear from colleges, injecting a large dose of drama into school life. As graduation draws nearer, and the distracting warmth of spring rises, motivation becomes a whole different problem for some students. This is when "senioritis" can raise its head, sapping the life out of even the most driven of people, luring students to coast to the end of the year. How does capstone fit into this remarkably variable year? Very well, actually.

The student-centered, flexible nature of capstone makes it ideal for accommodating the ups and downs of senior year. Wise teachers scaffold their course ahead of time to accommodate the busy months during the semesters. They know when they can get a lot of work done, as well as when they need to dial back activities at times students must direct their attention elsewhere. Once the college season is largely complete, when students sometimes show signs of slacking, teachers ramp the capstone machine back up, re-engaging their students to work on projects of their own design. Because these projects are all about what students are authentically interested in, and have personal milestones leading to their ultimate outcomes, students happily jump back into the work, driving senioritis into the recesses of their minds. This is the work that they want to do when they get the time to do it.

A note about parents/guardians and capstones

Is your child ready to manage a year-long independent capstone project? Ask a group of parents and guardians of senior students this question, and you are likely to see some bemused faces—probably more than a few will be looking outright worried. The more the program is built up, and the success of former students touted, the more worry there may be.

So a fundamental responsibility of capstone program leaders is to make this early communication: the capstone is independent in the sense that the student's choices will guide the project, but it is not unsupported. The program—teachers at the school and adult community partners—will be providing the support. Students will not fall through the cracks, and if any students fall seriously behind, their parents/guardians will be notified just as they would for any other school requirement—no sooner, and no later.

Specifically, parents/guardians will not be called upon to compensate for any gaps in maturity that might make it hard for their children to stay on track in the capstone. Both parents/guardians and students will benefit from having the pressure taken off that relationship. Families of seniors have enough to navigate as it is, without forcing the adults to become last-minute teachers of project management skills!

If parents/guardians want to provide support, and their students welcome that support, that could be terrific for the students' learning and the projects generally. But family support should not be an expectation of the program, for any student, no matter their maturity level or general readiness. Besides relieving stress in the family at a time of transition, this program principle serves equity, helping to give each student a fair chance at an interesting and successful project.

Where parents/guardians and families generally can shine in the capstone program is as participants in celebrating each student's accomplishment at the end. So another communication responsibility of the program is to provide families with information enabling them to appreciate and acknowledge what their almost-but-not-quite-adult children have achieved!

Capstone also fits well into a senior schedule because it materially supports the college application process. A personalized project that makes good use of school resources sets a student apart from other applicants that lack this kind of opportunity. There is impressive overlap among the tenets of capstone and the characteristics of a successful applicant in many situations. Put another way, capstone projects are often just what a college is looking for in the students that they accept. We have found that the best way to incorporate capstone into the college application process is for the student to fit it in wherever and whenever they can. Students should talk about it during interviews, work it into their essays, and generally fit it into every opportunity that is discovered. This is because students are their own best advocates—which of course is another tenet of capstone. They provide the most convincing explanation of their work and motivation because it all starts with them. On the school side, institutions can best support their students by clearly defining their capstone program in visible spaces. Featuring it on websites and on school profiles (the information sheets that many schools make available to colleges) are two effective ways to define and exhibit capstone programs.

Some students immediately enter the workplace after high school, and capstone suits them in this endeavor as well. Employers love the tenets of capstone just as much as colleges, giving job applicants a similar leg up in the hiring process. On a related note, we have been impressed with the number of businesses that offer capstone programs themselves. Organizations often offer employees project opportunities that loosely follow what we outline in this book, in a professional setting.[3]

Notes to Chapter 3.1

Note 1, page 64: **experiential learning cycle**—See Alice Y. Kolb and David A. Kolb, *The Experiential Educator: Principles and Practices of Experiential Learning* (Kaunakakai, HI: Experience Based Learning Systems Inc, 2017).

Note 2, page 68: **"growth mindset"**—See page iii in Carol Dweck, *Mindset: A New Psychology of Success* (New York: Ballantine, 2006).

Note 3, page 72: **Organizations often offer**—We run automatic internet searches for "capstone project" and love what we observe each week. One can follow the capstone news and observe the development of capstone over time. Equally fascinating is the appearance of capstone in all levels of education, from middle school through graduate programs and in professional settings.

CHAPTER 3.2
TEACHING AND LEARNING
THE CAPSTONE WAY

Capstone at a successful school is like a community of plants in an old-growth forest, working together to create a sustainable system—complete with direct and indirect effects—with student experiences emerging from the woods. Like an ecosystem with multiple levels of plants extending from the ground to the canopy, connected underground via roots in a mutualistic fashion, capstone programs allow students to explore their personal interests by making use of local and regional resources. Students chart their own path—this is the capstone mantra—by beginning with their initial plans, working together with teachers and other adults, and incorporating lessons learned along the way toward the end of the project, creating an impressive and rich journey that is like a mature trail system in an ancient wood. This chapter describes how to teach in the capstone way, partnering with students to create an inspirational educational journey.

The forest metaphor

Schools are like mature forests, and each capstone project is a new expedition into an unexplored corner of nature. We find this metaphor useful to illustrate how to teach capstone in understandable terms. The idea of emergence is particularly well suited by this construct, as is the long-term benefit of project modifications. As two outdoor enthusiasts who hatched plans to write this book while on long walks outside, and who have managed many capstone projects directly related to the natural world, the forest is a topic that we love visiting and discussing whenever and however we can.

Consider the plants in an old-growth forest, untouched for hundreds of years. Above ground, one observes giant trees, forming the canopy with deciduous and coniferous crowns. Smaller trees fill in the gaps between the massive trunks, catching what light makes it through the top layer of leaves and needles. Shrubs and ferns cover the ground, mixed in with detritus that fell from the standing plants. Mosses form the lowest layer, adding a bright green carpet atop the soil, with mushrooms scattered throughout the forest floor. All of the plants penetrate the soil, seeking water and nutrients in close proximity to each other. It is a dense tangle of threads and thick roots extending far below the surface of the ground. Upon close inspection, one notices something amazing about all of these fibers filling in every available crevice. Despite all of the competition for limited resources, the roots are connected in a way that suggests that they are working together to create the massively complex vegetative structure of this grand landscape.

All of the plants are in fact connected in a mutualistic fashion.[1] Upending decades of thought about how roots interact below ground, trees are actually connected in the subterranean world by fungi. Fungi—the organisms familiar to us as "mushrooms"—have their own "roots" underground called hyphae, which actually make up the bulk of the organism. Most of a fungus exists in dirt as an intricate web of hyphae, seeking water and nutrients, composting dead matter like leaves and twigs, for which they are known as ecological decomposers. Some of these hyphae connect to plants, forming bridges that have enormous significance for the activity and health of a forest. It turns out that fungi provide essential nutrients to plants, and in return get food that they normally cannot access. On the scale of an entire forest, they then serve as conduits, moving vital chemicals from plant to plant. This is the mind-boggling news about fungi and forests: trees actually share resources indirectly through a fungal network that is found in mature forests.

Connection is the first important point in our metaphor. Healthy forests are connected in direct and indirect ways. We now understand that fungi plug into trees for immediate gain, and they aid the plants by transporting water and nutrients to second and third order organisms. These connections take time to form and forests suffer when they are disturbed. Logging and invasive species upset connections, making forests sick and unsustainable. Trees are also connected in a traditional way that we are all familiar with. Tall trees provide shade for saplings to get their start, and cast off leaves, twigs and needles for decomposition, forming fertilizer for general use.

Successful schools and capstone programs are similarly connected. Groups of people populate the buildings, interacting at many levels. Students attend classes managed by teachers. Administrators support teachers as they educate their pupils. Interactions abound in successful schools across all of the hierarchical levels to the benefit of all, with students at the center, because of the many and varied connections. Students work directly with teachers, learning lessons, completing assignments, and ultimately passing major assessments. Administrators make this possible by providing professional development, adding to the skill set of teachers, indirectly improving a student's experience in the classroom. When students need help, there are other staff on hand to help out, like counselors or nurses for example, waiting to form a connection right when it is needed. Capstone students often additionally rely on connections off campus to support their projects, extending this network well beyond the walls of the school. Some are direct, others indirect, and all of them are essential to the operation of the school and its programs.

Emergence is the next significant concept. Ecosystems have emergent properties that are only possible at the systemwide level. This is a characteristic that is true of the entire ecosystem and not found in the assembled parts. Put together, the members of an ecosystem create something that is more than just the sum of its parts. A biological example of this would be the resiliency of an ecosystem. In response to a disturbance, an ecosystem will adjust and return to what it was before if left to its own devices. For example, if a minor fire burns through a mature forest that historically experiences fire, a series of events will result that maintain the long-term composition of the landscape. Grasses, shrubs and trees will be replaced in roughly the same way thanks to the interactions among these plants. Shrubs may not be able to recover on their own without grasses sprouting first, which provide a protective environment for the germinating shrubs to get a good start in the shelter of the blades. Forests possess the ability to maintain themselves as a whole in the face of fire; shrubs on their own do not. This system-level response to an environmental disaster that creates a steady state despite perturbations is an example of an emergent property.

Schools are full of emergent properties. One example is culture, which remains roughly the same over time even though people depart and new people join— the high school student body turns over completely every four years. What a school is "known for"—sports, arts, rigor, etc.—is emergence happening in an educational setting. Another such property is the education of a graduate. It takes many teachers to provide all the learning that happens for a high school student. Considered all together, each course contributed to the four years of experience that led to a student's diploma. The formation of that experience, reliably formed for each student by a collection of teachers and administrators, is an emergent property.

Capstone is an excellent example of an emergent property. **Making use of direct and indirect relationships on and off campus, students pursue their**

individualized project, attaining levels of achievement that are special in high school. The ability of a fully operational capstone program to produce such projects and experiences is more than the sum of its components, and is often wondrous to behold—just like the beautiful forests that we love to explore.

Components of a capstone program are well understood in the context of this forest metaphor because events that happen in forests have interesting parallels in capstone. The rest of this chapter addresses some of these topics.

Planning experiences

Getting ready for a trip is important. Some people are unfamiliar with ways to be safe during a forest excursion, including the terrain, daily surface conditions, and changeable weather. Planning for a few possibilities is therefore an essential part of having a successful outing. Touring a natural space can turn into a miserable experience during a cold, windy rainstorm for which people are unprepared—these conditions can easily lead to life-threatening situations. Gear and its proper use becomes vital to an outdoor trip: shoes to comfortably traverse the ground, clothing to suit the immediate conditions, sunscreen for skin protection, and so on. Memorable excursions are often the ones in which all the "just in case" equipment remains in the pack, and what people set out with is perfect for the activities of the day. The insurance of the contents of the pack offers safety to explore, enjoy, and perhaps even push the boundaries of the outing.

Capstone requires an analogous collection of items. Each project should begin with an assessment of expected events and a plan for what will be needed during the duration of the project. Each student's kit is unique due to the personalized nature of the projects. Students need the most appropriate resources for the extended duration of their capstone project. For those who begin prematurely, without a developed plan and/or full list of necessary resources, trouble is bound to arise. Their fate depends on the degree of their unpreparedness and the ability of their teacher to rescue their ideas and activities.

Good preparation for a project is best in a small team, including the student, a teacher, and whoever can appropriately support the effort. Collaboration is always best at the outset, with many eyes and minds on the program, limiting the number of oversights, and benefitting from the indirect effects of the group. Some students can prepare all that they need by just working with their teacher. Others may need an extended network, including teachers from other departments, or even professionals located off campus. Team members who are the most flexible will be the most valuable, as new opportunities and challenges emerge. This is like packing a multi-tool instead of just a knife for a hike. The multi-tool has a knife, as well as other tools hidden inside that might be beneficial in the future, and it takes up about the same space in a pack.

A well-prepared pack is incomplete without a good map and compass. A visual representation of the landscape can make the difference between a nice venture and an unpleasant venture, or even life and death. The map should show any marked trails that go through the area. The cardinal directions must be represented. Water sources are important for drinking on long trips. The rise and fall of the land is wonderful to see on a map, usually shown with concentric topographic lines. Finally, a scale for distance provides a sense for how far apart things are in the real world. The conversion chart is used to translate the flat map to the real world, converting scale units to physical distance.

Capstone maps come in a few forms, like a timeline or concept map. Planning out major events for the duration of the project makes for a visual representation of the project and a sense of pacing that will be needed to complete the journey. This is by far the most common kind of map for capstone projects. Arranging major components of a project in a document, showing areas of separation and overlap is another kind of map, conceptually showing the project in a two-dimensional visualization. Other forms exist as well, which students should be encouraged to explore as appropriate, to find the best way to navigate their capstone experience. This is like some special maps that exist for exploring the woods, like geological maps, or ones containing demographics and political boundaries. One needs the correct map for certain excursions.

A teacher is the best compass that a student can have for their project, pointing in the general direction that leads toward their academic destination and translating what needs to be done into language that students understand. The student creates the plan, turns it into a map, and is then ready to embark on their journey. A teacher aims a student toward the best coordinates, setting them up for success, even if there is challenging terrain and unpredictable weather ahead. Even a well-prepared student can get dangerously lost if they head out in the wrong direction. Capstone teachers are like an analog compass, with a needle that responds to a magnetic field. It gives a generally useful bearing needed by a student, who needs to fill in the orientation gaps with experience. Capstone teachers never hand answers to students directly. Instead they provide wise counsel, allowing students to make final decisions, ultimately choosing their final destination.

Establishing paths

Paths of all kinds traverse the floors of forests, from faint traces by secretive animals to hardened trails built and marked by people. Their natural formation is a fascinating process with connections to capstone projects. As in the saying attributed to Aristotle, "nature abhors a vacuum," a pristine section of ground will soon show signs of some animal's passing. Foot action forms an intermittent track that deepens and changes orientation with time, use and weathering. It could be used just once and quickly covered by forest debris. More interestingly, other animals will use the path, as they journey from home to feeding sites and other important destinations. The path is eventually connected to the local network, as animals share routes seeking essential resources to live their lives—water is a good example of something that all organisms need. Where these resources are found—stream, pond, or dripping moss—one will observe paths made by animals seeking out their sustaining power. Water is ephemeral, as the seasons and climate changes, forcing the paths to change over time, as animals sort out the quickest and safest way to drink. This is true for all paths, which grow larger and smaller throughout the year, changing direction as activities shift, produced by animals making their way in the woods. In an old-growth forest, these paths can become well defined and complicated, creating a very efficient network for overland travel for any animal.

After a capstone student has prepared for their project, the real work begins. They have a good sense of where they are heading and what they hope to experience on their capstone journey. Students and teachers need to realize that there will be plenty of route-finding along the way. Choices will present themselves when students reach a junction. If the student has a good project map, they will ultimately reach their general destination, but the exact route is actually unknown until the journey is over. Like natural path formation in the forest, explorations must be made to identify good and bad paths. Students must invest time finding the most appropriate sequence of trajectories for their project according to their goals and interests. Like a wonderful outing in nature, the capstone journey becomes just as meaningful as the final outcome.

Capstone programs must provide the flexibility for students to complete their projects in an organic and personal fashion. The final route is revealed at the end of the project; it is impossible to predict at the outset. It must be experienced to be defined because capstone projects always contain an amount of uncertainty in the process. Students and teachers must be confident that they will prevail in the end and that the route will reveal itself over time. They cannot become overly frustrated when they temporarily lose their way, for that is the very nature of capstone. All projects demand some confidence that important resources will be identified in time. A capstone student who is prepared and adopts a growth mindset can trust that they will locate useful people and items in time to complete their project.

For the same reason that people can repeat excursions in nature and continue to have new experiences, capstone students can consider related projects successfully without fear of duplicating a previous student's work. It is impossible to fully replicate a project without a very detailed list of events in hand and a desire to follow them exactly. Curiosity and happenstance will always lead students in new and interesting directions. Teachers can comfortably allow students to explore similar capstone ideas from year to year, trusting that they will put their own spin on their projects, creating truly unique experiences. They will take different paths on their way to a similar destination.

Capstone often builds paths that no students have ever taken. The personalized nature of capstone leads to projects that are as unique as the students who envision them. Originating with previous experiences and shaped with current goals, each capstone project is like a snowflake falling among the trees, in that each one is unique and it is impossible to exhaust all the possible combinations. They are all made out of the same material, frozen water, yet the diversity is astounding and beautiful. Even the projects that have similar origins end up tailored to the personality of the student. Together with teachers, students create and travel through the woods together, leaving a network of trails in their wake.

Getting lost

Losing one's way is among the top fears of people venturing into the depths of an extensive forest, especially if the trip is long and the group small. One can minimize the chances of getting lost by packing well, including a map, and having practiced navigational skills. Becoming truly lost is a thankfully rare event, especially with our modern communication and positioning devices. People more often deviate from their route, realize the mistake, then make corrections that lead them toward their final destination. During the part of the hike that was unplanned but necessary to get back on track, delightful surprises appear, like a small pond hidden in a copse of trees or a rocky outcrop providing a novel view of the land below. The happy accidents were not part of the plan but join the list of waypoints nonetheless, merging into the totality of the experience. Sometimes getting lost provides the novelty which boosts the memory of the trip to a new level, making it stand out from the rest. Evidence of the benefit of getting lost in this example would be repeating the trip and including the diversion, to see the pond and view one more time. Recounting the hike is certainly improved by the inclusion of the "getting lost" part, adding the drama that always improves a story. Under certain conditions, getting lost may be advantageous indeed.

Capstone students often feel like they are lost in their projects, usually during the first third of the course. Even those that planned well and assembled all the necessary resources will experience some sense of aimlessness and reduced progress. The indeterminate structure of capstone almost always leads to a period of ambiguity with alternate options to choose from, none of which provide clear resolution. The well-prepared student collaborates with their teacher to assess the alternatives, selects one to explore to see if it becomes a viable path, and repeats until a new way forward is identified. The option may be an exciting new opportunity that was unforeseen at the start. If it proves to be a dead end, one can return to the decision point and try the alternate option. This loose form of planning leaves space for the chance inclusion of items which neither student nor teacher considered at the outset. A robust capstone network is sure to provide such connections if flexibility is part of the curriculum.

A capstone project is like a multi-day trip in which a party selects a trailhead, summit, and exit, packs all the essential equipment, and determines the daily plan only during the evenings beforehand. They arrive in their cars, carrying packs full of hiking and camping gear. They enter the forest, knowing only the destination of their first campsite and how they will finally leave the forest. Much less is known about the days in between. As they gather around a campfire to warm themselves and make dinner each evening, they agree on the details for the following day, filling in the planned voids of the trip, which will complete another section leading them eventually back to their cars. Their trip is broadly planned and includes short-term flexibility. Should they learn of a notable destination along the way, they can visit it and add to their experience. This is categorically different from a completely planned trip, which is composed of a tick list for every day that the hikers finish by marching along with their heads down, entirely focused on checking off the required elements of the route. If they fall behind schedule, they stress to get back on track, paying even less attention to the natural wonders that they pass.

Capstone is a student-centered, infinitely adaptable program that always produces significant experiences. Students plan just enough to ensure the completion of their major goals, leaving gaps to be filled in when they are best prepared to do so. It is the trip that allows memorable events to transpire. Capstone is never the predetermined trip—or even one standardized by other people—that precludes happy accidents. The final outcome of capstone is in fact loose and planned in a clever fashion. When people allow for opportunities to present themselves, the final outcome always makes for better stories.

Trip reports

All great journeys generate fascinating stories and capstone is no exception. The experience is as valuable as the outcome. The program creates remarkable stories by employing an adaptive model, planning just enough to ensure success, and leaving space to accept opportunities that add to the core plan. Novel elements are included by design, guaranteeing that capstone narratives are compelling.

The same is true in expedition literature that documents travels through uncharted terrain, like the forest in our capstone metaphor. Tradition calls for a report at the end, recounting the events, highs and lows, surprises, and meaningful reflection on the entirety of the encounters. Professional outdoor athletes share slideshows about their exploits, combining stunning images of themselves in nature, practicing their chosen craft—these are popular enough to support the athlete's career. Tales that include successes alongside challenges are the most popular, often becoming books and other media products. Innumerable stories include the protagonists getting lost, regaining their bearings, and the resulting lessons and morals. Heading into the forest with plans that evolve in memorable ways but end safely makes for captivating reading, resonating with the audience at many levels. These are stories that are real and impactful, accessible to people from many walks of life.

Capstone projects end with significant trip reports of a sort, modeled after the nature of each program. Some end with a major report, summarizing findings and encounters. This could be presented to a panel of teachers who ask probing questions and assess the degree to which a student completed their goals and understands the significance of their work and experience. The most popular report takes the form of a presentation delivered to members of the school community, ranging from a select group to the entire school, and even families and professionals who supported the projects. Some schools feature these on a special day, dedicated just to capstone presentations, creating a special schedule for the celebratory event. Representing examples of the most impressive activities on campus, presentation day is a day to pause and reflect on what the school can accomplish, as students complete their projects on the way toward becoming professionals. They are snapshots of young adults in development, transforming into citizens of the wider world.

Much material may come from a well-planned capstone presentation day. The presentations themselves can be filmed and posted for everyone to see, especially if friends or family were unable to see one because they were attending another. An archive of presentations is useful to future students and teachers, interested in what has come before and what may be done in the future. Anyone curious about what capstone is need only review student work to understand the nature of the program and the power of the curriculum. One quickly appreciates what students can accomplish in capstone after following the journey of a few students and considering what they completed by making use of the school and surrounding community.

The final benefit of a culminating report is the summative reflection, in which students gain a special moment to harken back to all that came before the ending of their project. Expanded upon in Chapter 4.7, this particular opportunity is unlike any of the other reflective times during a capstone project because it comes at the finish when there is the most to draw upon. It is the end of the trip, in the sense that a student made it to their destination, completing some version of the original plan, if not every single personal milestone. Gone are the stresses of navigating the middle of the project when one is less sure that the project will go as planned. It's over and there are plenty of stories to tell.

Notes to Chapter 3.2

Note 1, page 74: **connected in a mutualistic fashion**—For a great introduction to the fungal relationship among trees, see "The Social Life of Forests," written by Ferris Jabr and illustrated with beautiful pictures by George Ko. *The New York Times*, December 2, 2020.

CHAPTER 3.3
PILOT AND ITERATE

This chapter, we can summarize in a few words: start now, start small.

Don't wait until you get it all worked out. You need real students doing real projects in order to make progress in developing your program, and you need a program to have students. So start your program now. But don't implement on a big scale. You need to get it worked out, with the students. There are going to be failures, and it is better for the students if they are small at first.

Later on, once you have capstone students to talk to, capstone student work to review, and capstone stories to unpack with your colleagues, you can evolve the program. Probably you will want to do that by tinkering, not overhauling, developing the program bit by bit and year by year.

In other words: rinse, repeat.

By this we of course mean "iterate." This trendy word used to be just a synonym for "say again" (as in "reiterate"). Now what this little word signals is actually a well-theorized multi-step process in which what you say is different each time, not the same thing over again. Iteration is a method of making change incrementally through cycles of action, reflection, and finely tuned adjustment, leading to renewed action, reflection, and adjustment.

Experience, both direct and as accessed through the National Capstone Consortium, tells us that this is just how capstone works. Programs start as pilots. Teachers learn from their students. Even well-established programs continue to adapt every year. We believe that the organic pilot-and-iterate process we see across the Consortium is intrinsic to capstone as a philosophy and as a practice. On every level—from the individual student project, to the capstone classroom, to the teacher's pedagogy, to the school as a system, to school networks like the Consortium—capstone attends to what is emergent. Our core metaphor in this book, the school as forest, seeks to capture the way paths of practice are opened in the living school environment, manifesting energy in the community in beautiful and natural ways. If you are planning to start or develop a capstone at your school, this chapter may help you think about the big picture—how your program will grow and interact with that larger school ecosystem.

Zero to sixty

We hope that this book will offer teachers starting a capstone many shortcuts and inspire great aspirations. We also hope that this book communicates that capstone programs are unique to the schools that support them—much of what you will need to know, you will not find in any book, including this one. As with any good design process, listening to the people who will become the program's "stakeholders" is a first step. For example, the team might interview juniors about what they would like to see in the initial program when they are seniors. Interviewing school administrators is also a prerequisite: even if you know you have administrative support, you will want a nuanced understanding of their hopes and expectations. Unquestioned assumptions can lead to unnecessary stumbles. An added benefit to the pre-launch inquiry is the opportunity to develop a vibrant running conversation within the capstone team as a new unit in the school infrastructure.

Even more important than listening is observing: what does your school already do well? If the capstone is to become a culmination of your school's whole curriculum, you will need to start with an understanding of what unique written and unwritten features characterize that curriculum. In the next chapter we will talk about "housing" the program. Knowing what the program replaces, in other words what place it takes in the ecosystem of the school, will guide your design process. Make time and space for the team not only to gather data but also to reflect on what it hears and observes.

Given that failures are inevitable—since crucial learning won't come until the program is underway—we suggest that the initial design be simple, even if a more complex program is intended from the start. The pilot should:

- Enroll a few special students—later you can require it of all
- Assign limited work—later you can make it a work-intensive project
- Need few school resources like time, space, and money—later you can ask for more
- Grade pass-fail, if at all—later you can grade and include in the GPA
- Be transcripted as an elective, if at all—later you can add it to the school's graduation requirements

- Keep the stakes low—later it can engage the energy of a high-stakes program
- Engage a select group of teachers—later you can involve the whole faculty
- Launch quietly—later you can go for higher visibility

For a pilot that may need to win support from students, families, and administrators in order to expand, a final point is that the consequences of any missteps should fall on adults, not students. Adults are far more capable of anticipating missteps than teens. Later, once a program is established, it can afford to offer students the opportunity to learn from the natural consequences of their own mistakes. Early on, it's better to let adults absorb consequences. For example, you would not want the program to get a terrifying reputation in its very first year by failing students and preventing them from graduating. Instead, pilot an optional elective, and if you are offering credits, make sure none of the students enrolled in the first year depend on them to graduate!

Iteration: reviewing student work

Iteration implies review and reflection. Iteration does not mean blind repetition, which is what we get when we don't reflect. One of the refreshing joys of teaching in capstone programs is that they are not burdened with decades, much less centuries, of accreted habit. Still, you will want to build in protected time and protocols for the team to do a truly deep review at the end of the first year. Surveying students who participated is a first step. One excellent survey approach is to ask participants what advice they would offer to students who will be enrolling next year; you can likewise ask what advice they have for teachers. In the weeks before graduation, seniors enjoy being the experts asked to share their wisdom with those who will follow in their footsteps.

Listening to what students say is great, but it is even more important that the team look at their work together. Reflecting on student work is a vital school practice as distinct from grade-norming as it is from grading and from providing formative or summative feedback. Rather, those practical functions must be set aside in order for the team to engage in a true reflection on what their students have produced. As described by Tina Blythe in *Looking Together at Student Work* and by others, this is a practice of delaying judgment in order to allow deeper observations to surface.[1] In one English department, for example, teachers collectively discovered a correlation in the writing of their students between perfect obedience to the five-paragraph essay structure and shallow reading and thinking. Simultaneously, they collectively discovered that they valued messy, interesting writing over tidy, boring writing. Individual members of the department team had thought they were maintaining alignment with colleagues by emphasizing form over thought. Because of the practice of looking with an open mind at student writing, they discovered a previously unarticulated but collective concern about the place of reading and thinking in the department. The place of the five-paragraph essay, meanwhile, had seemed beyond question. Unless space is made for looking at the work and conversing openly, the capstone team may similarly be quite unaware of what their colleagues are taking away from the program's first year. Though capstone programs may be unburdened by disciplinary histories, they are under the same time pressures as any other program in the school. Unless time is made and protected, the urgent will overwhelm the important in capstone, just as it does anywhere else.

In addition to time for discussion, protocols are essential. Especially with a cross-disciplinary team, little can be taken for granted. The team will want to start with impressions or observations from student surveys and student work. What did they do well? What went as expected, and what came as a pleasant surprise? Even teams in established programs discover new trends every year. Thoughtful sharing of capstone stories belongs to the review process as well. Only after making observations will the team move on to a discussion of implications for the program. What aspects of the program design proved conducive to student inquiry and action at the highest levels? From there, the path to redesign in anticipation of year two is likely to seem clear.

Iteration: the program in the school

Capstone is grassroots. Programs are often started by a few interested teachers who share a commitment to student-centered teaching and learning. Programs frequently engage students off campus in ways atypical of the school's other academic programs. But as we emphasized in Chapter 1.1, capstone belongs to schooling. A fully evolved capstone program draws power from the ritual function of connecting individuals to the school as a community. Seniors in the program step up because they want to represent the school well at the moment of their departure from it. Established capstone programs are often the signature program at a school, epitomizing its identity in the larger community beyond the school walls. In the early years, then, the capstone team will want to look outward to other adults at the school as well as inward to its students when it does its annual review. How is the program showing up to adults across campus, including to school administrators? Seen from their perspectives, what were the successes and failures?

If the program aspires to growth that will require increased resources—teacher time, for example—frank conversation with administration in particular is essential. Capstone teaching can be highly exciting and energizing. All that enthusiasm brings out the best in teachers as it does in students. Especially in the early years of a program, teachers may be willing to go above and beyond, providing extra hours of work to the program without compensation. If the program requires little in terms of resources other than teacher time, the generosity of those teachers may go unremarked. It is perhaps inevitable that enthusiastic teachers will get out ahead of the institutional support available for the program, but it is likewise inevitable that allowing individual enthusiasm to outstrip the school-wide conversation will lead to a need for readjustment later on. Some of the teacher energy being poured into the program might be better directed to advocating for it on a school-wide level. To put this more bluntly: stretching resources can serve the program; stressing people will not.

Theory and practice

This book is aimed at teachers. We hope that it includes much that is of interest for school administrators as well, but we do not assume that our readers have the power to issue top-down directives at their schools or to command large resource reassignments—in fact, we recognize that administrators often don't have such power any more than teachers! Rather, we assume that you will be growing your program in circumstances over which you may have limited control. Capstone, as we understand it, is an "art of the possible." Capstone programs are at their best when they fit and express the unique qualities of their home schools; correspondingly, by their very nature they don't need more than those schools have to give. Capstone evolution never means transcending the setting.

We simultaneously recognize that the educators who get involved in capstone tend to be people alive to change. To pick up another trendy word, they are "innovators," though they may simultaneously have deep commitments to their home disciplines. A math teacher who becomes a capstone teacher does not cease to love math, nor cease to advocate for long-standing pedagogical values like procedural fluency. (After all, "radicals" are people who are all the more connected to their roots. Etymologically, radicals are like radishes: of the ground!) Likewise, capstone teams are cross-disciplinary, not trans-disciplinary. In other words, they are bringing methods from different disciplines to bear, not transcending the whole idea of disciplines and discipline-specific methods. Capstone evolution participates in the evolution of a school as a whole system.

Consider a few of the phrases that we repeat in this book that have become watchwords at the National Capstone Consortium summits and online events. Online or in person, our meetings follow a "peer-to-peer" model, meaning teacher to teacher. Though we occasionally invite like-minded professionals from other fields to share, most of our planned and unconference sessions are led by practicing capstone teachers who speak from recent lived experience. In capstone, we believe that "expertise is emergent"; only the capstone teacher knows what is emerging in the ongoing dialogue between the upcoming generation of students and this generation of educators. Each year is a new year in capstone. "Capstone changes schools" reflects our observation that programs in the Consortium are influencing change in their home school environments as well as being influenced by them.

Capstone story
A signature program

Jon's capstone program is the classic example of a grassroots idea that had its moment right when a school needed it. Jon moved from scientific research in graduate school to teaching high school, and then on to teaching advanced biology courses. Passionate about educating young adults and the scientific method, Jon soon developed several research-based classes, which asked students to determine what and how they investigated natural events—power was transferred from the teacher to the students. After a conversation with a colleague who ran a practicum program on campus and who regularly interacted with professionals in the surrounding community, he established a science internship program in partnership with local universities and technology companies. Though it was called something else at the time, this was the capstone seed being planted at his school.

The internship was very successful among all of the people involved with the program. Students deeply valued the hands-on experience of working in an authentic science research laboratory. They "did the work of the lab," and sometimes got an independent project to complete. A select few even became published authors with their work and thanks to the extremely generous support of their supervisors. Teachers supported the program because they understood the importance of the activities, and it did not add to their teaching load because Jon had dedicated time to run the program. Administrators touted the program because of its alignment with the school's mission statement. Parents loved how the program allowed their children to explore their interests, especially when they made a difference in the college application process. Supervisors and graduate students at the universities set aside volunteer time to host Jon's students because they wished to mentor the scientists of the future, and sometimes were able to add this outreach activity to their grant applications. The program grew each year that it was offered thanks to all of this support, which started as a ground-up, student-centered effort.

Jon's school found itself revising its mission, values and strategic plan right after the turn of the century. Committees composed of teachers and administrators took on this ambitious endeavor. It was during one of these meetings that the idea of a "capstone program" was identified and connected with Jon's science internship program. It soon became apparent that Jon's school had significant opportunity with the idea, because of the students who attended the school, the teachers who ran it, and the composition of the surrounding community—universities, nonprofits, businesses, etc.

A pilot was launched to test the idea and its potential. The program expanded to support any student who had an engaging idea, some experience in the area of interest, and time to do the work. An optional course was created, open to eleventh and twelfth graders. Importantly, the course fit into the other strong programs at Jon's school, augmenting and not competing with the full curriculum. After four years of evolution, the program became one of the signature programs at the school, so much so that it became part of the brand. For example, the alumni magazine adopted the name of the program, and featured alumni add their hand-written signatures inside the cover following the end-of-year tradition in the program. This capstone became a success thanks to the organic process that created it, the trial-and-error process that shaped it, and the many people, on and off campus, that supported it—and continues to thrive as our educational landscape changes each year.

Systems thinking in schools

Our experience in capstone aligns naturally with a systems-thinking understanding of schools and school change. Though it is not necessary to adopt systems-thinking terminology in order to develop or advocate for a program, it may simply be of interest to readers of this book to consider capstone through this lens. Systems thinking has roots in multiple fields, including physics, biology, and economics. An early landmark is the 1972 publication of *The Limits to Growth* by Donella Meadows, which considered the impacts of our global failure to think of economic systems as interconnected with the biological systems of earth's environment. Our forest metaphor draws on systems thinking in environmental science as well. Across fields, systems thinking has had considerable success in offering explanations when actions taken with one intention in mind lead to unintended and unwished-for outcomes. Overly simplistic understandings of cause and effect are a poor foundation for action in complex real-world systems—including schools. Systems thinking was brought into the field of education most famously by Peter Senge with *Schools that Learn*, an offshoot from his business classic

The Fifth Discipline.[2] Whether or not they cite its lineage, systems thinking is employed by many educators and education researchers today.

Coming out of systems thinking but focused on the practicalities of change within the individual school is the "cycle of experiment and experience" explained by Justin Reich of MIT's Teaching Systems Lab.[3] In "Launching Innovation in Schools," an online course he co-taught with Senge, Reich points out that teachers learn how to teach better from other teachers, more than from educators whose expertise is not based on current lived experience of the classroom. (We believe that as well, and also emphasize that we learn the most through our engagement with our capstone students.) Reich outlines the cycle, in which small teams of teachers try something new—the experiment. They observe what happens with their students and share their reflections— articulating the experience. Based on their collective learning, a new plan is made for the next iteration of the experiment. Reich's explanation of the role of school administration in this cycle is likewise well worth understanding. Though Reich does not use the term "pilot," his model beautifully illustrates what capstone teachers call the "pilot-and-iterate approach" to implementation. A few teachers start an experiment with a few students, learn from their experience and share their learning amongst themselves. In the next cycle, they make changes so that each iteration improves based on the particular conditions of their unique school setting.

Capstone is an "art of the possible."

In brief lectures and dialogues recorded for the online class, Reich and Senge speak persuasively to the point that the power to make positive change in a school is *already held* by teachers—and in some sense, perhaps only by teachers. As Reich suggests in the course of an explanation of the cycle of experiment and experience, school change only counts as school change if it impacts students through action in the classroom:

> First, all of the actual change in an instructional improvement initiative is entirely dependent on teacher experimentation and teacher learning. You can't have new practices without teachers and librarians and other instructional folks putting those practices in action, and you can't spread those practices without teachers sharing and teaching one another. Teacher leadership is essential, absolutely essential, to starting, scaling, sustaining new practices in schools. Full stop.[4]

Full stop indeed. And yet, despite the widespread use of terms like "teacher leadership," teachers who don't also have formal administrative roles rarely speak about themselves as leaders in the sense of being people *already empowered* to make systemic change. Reich and Senge again are refreshingly direct on the topic of teachers and leadership. "Leadership isn't a role," Reich says in the course's introductory video. "It's not a particular person in the department or building. But rather, it's a set of functions distributed widely throughout an organization. It's a way of working together with other people." Reich continues, "Teacher leadership is essential to improving teaching and learning in schools. Only people who work day-to-day with students can truly change classrooms and learning spaces."[5] We appreciate the way that Reich and Senge honor teachers here, and also the call to action represented by their insight: if not teachers, then who?

We have not found an education systems-thinking resource closer to the ground than this one. So we would like to add the emphasis here that—as important as peer-to-peer (teacher-to-teacher) leadership is—the real live layer in capstone at least is between teachers and students. In a tree, the largest percentage of matter is dead wood. Only a narrow layer, the cambium, carries the life of the tree and enables it to grow. This fine band of tissue lies just below the bark of real trees, moving nutrient-rich sap up and down, from where it is produced to where it is consumed. In schools, this live layer is the interface between teachers and students. It is the meeting that happens every day between the generations as knowledge is passed on or made new. As the years pass, the layer stiffens and dies, forming one of the many rings inside the woody trunk, marking the passage of time and environmental changes over the years. When we say that expertise is emergent, we mean first that it emerges from our engagement as teachers with students.

The death and life of great capstone programs

This chapter would be incomplete without an acknowledgement that not all programs make it. Sometimes pilots do not lead to established programs. Sometimes established programs fall prey to budget cuts or other manifestations of changed school priorities. The very same qualities that make capstone programs awesome—all related to their freedom from ties to traditional school structures—likewise make them vulnerable. No school cuts its math department, but some schools do cut their capstones.

A school is like a forest, and forests experience change, whether internally driven through the process known as succession or imposed by external disturbances. Emergent processes lead to the disappearance of whole species and to other startlingly visible changes to the landscape. Where trees stood, now grass grows. Or maybe paradise gets paved and now we have a parking lot. Humans may feel sadness or outrage over changes that we were not able to prevent. One outstanding program we remember no longer exists at the school where it started. At one time, it represented the vanguard in capstone, pioneering frameworks and practices that inspired teachers around the country, including the authors of this book. Now that program is no more, but we can see the enduring value of its trailblazing example in those schools where its ideas continue to evolve. Some program change originates internally, but external factors also impact and sometimes end programs. In the case of the program we honor here, it was not an internal shift, but rather changes in the school and district that undermined program support. Capstone belongs to schooling; capstone programs are not independent of school resources. We acknowledge here that external organizational realities can overtake the very best programs. Perhaps the next stage of learning for capstone teachers will have less to do with pedagogy or internal program management and more to do with advocacy and navigating the external systems which shape every school program, including capstone. The lessons learned in capstone may need to move beyond capstone.

A note about school networks

Systems thinking asks us to look at leveling up as well as leveling down. Systems thinking is often called upon in the education sector to help us understand why broadly implemented top-down initiatives so often seem to fail in schools. As systems, schools are subject to feedback dynamics so complex that it is difficult to predict standardized outcomes from standardized inputs. To put it simply, what works in one school may not work in the next because conditions we cannot map do more to determine the outcomes than any new top-down inputs. In the aftermath of the failures of many top-down change initiatives, systems-thinkers recommend an approach that starts on the ground. All of this is consistent with what capstone teachers know from experience.

The new field of improvement science, like earlier systems-thinking approaches, has been brought to education from other sectors, most notably health care. Proponents of improvement science believe that it can suggest ways to scale solutions to widespread problems, despite the differences between the contexts—individual schools or districts—where the solutions will be applied. Anthony S. Bryk and his collaborators at the Carnegie Institute propose connecting schools through Networked Improvement

Communities or NICs. An NIC formalizes school-to-school collaboration. In an NIC, problems to be addressed collaboratively are formally defined and organizational learning is formally measured through scientific data collection; solutions are shared across the network in an intentional way. Without a network, a school will have what improvement science calls Level A learning, which is the individual teacher's learning from classroom practice. It will also have Level B learning, which comes out of teacher-to-teacher exchange within the school. What it will miss out on is Level C learning, which happens when teachers at one school learn from teachers at another.[6]

Capstone teachers can be prone to isolation within their home schools, since their capstone work is discussed neither in the traditional departments nor in any other previously established unit at the school. The drive for capstone teachers to connect with counterparts at other schools is powerful; the National Capstone Consortium is only one manifestation of that drive. The Capstone Consortium is not an NIC, since it does not formalize scientific problems, analyze data, or redistribute learning in the ways mapped by improvement science. Most of the networking happens informally through one-to-one relationships between teachers at different schools, though they may have first met through our network. However, the Consortium does participate in a central tension that NICs seek to address: how do we benefit from what is learned at other schools, when our home school contexts are so different? How do we adopt good ideas from other places, while remaining alive to what is happening with our students in the present school year?

Notes to Chapter 3.3

Note 1, page 85: **engage in a true reflection**—See Tina Blythe, David Allen, and Barbara Schieffelin Powell, *Looking Together At Student Work*. (New York: Teachers' College, 2015).

Note 2, page 90: **systems thinking**—Though not about schools, *The Fifth Discipline* remains fascinating reading. See Peter Senge, *The Fifth Discipline: The Art and Practice of the Learning Organization* (New York: Doubleday, 2006). See also Peter Senge, et al., *Schools That Learn (Updated and Revised): A Fifth Discipline Fieldbook for Educators, Parents, and Everyone Who Cares About Education.* Revised Edition (New York: Crown, 2012).

Note 3, page 90: **"cycle of experiment and experience"**—Justin Reich and Peter Senge, "Launching Innovation in Schools." Online Edx course, archived open-access (MIT Open Learning Library).

Note 4, page 90: **"teachers sharing and teaching one another"**—The block quotation is from Reich's lecture on the "Inner Loop" in Unit 3b. www.bit.ly/3w7BkIY

Note 5, page 91: **"Leadership isn't a role"**—The quotations are from the course welcome video, "This We Believe" in Unit 0. www.bit.ly/3w7BkIY

Note 6, page 93: **improvement science**—The book *Learning to Improve* by Bryk and his colleagues is excellent reading, though it will not offer practical advice for capstone teachers. See also the resources of the website for the Carnegie Foundation for the Advancement of Teaching, where Bryk is president. In *Learning to Improve*, see especially Chapter 6, "Accelerate Learning Through Networked Communities." Anthony Bryk, et al., *Learning to Improve: How America's Schools Can Get Better At Getting Better* (Cambridge, MA: Harvard Education Press, 2017).

CHAPTER 3.4
ORGANIZING ADULTS ON CAMPUS

Capstone programs are student-centered, but experienced educators will understand that this does not lessen the complexity of the work of capstone teachers. Rather, student activity requires an elaborate apparatus to start and maintain a program. At the inaugural meeting of the National Capstone Consortium at the Thacher School in 2013, a cohort facilitated by Jeff Hooper developed the term "The Machine" to talk about the structures of adults running the program and advising, and instructing the students in it. "The Machine" includes the **people** and **processes** that enable the program to run. It includes the teams, standing meetings, events, and the program's pedagogy and curriculum. Though we in general prefer our organic metaphors, the reality is that some clarity and just a bit of rigidity are necessary to make a program work efficiently.

The capstone "machine" sits within the usual organizational structures of a school in an interesting way, involving challenges and opportunities. First, the capstone program may be liberated from many of the constraints that limit traditional academic programs. The program is unlikely to experience the kind of parental scrutiny that math and English programs do. Vertical alignment may be an issue for a capstone program, but programs are rarely under external pressure to align. Above all, capstone teams are free from a "business as usual" mentality or the inertia that leads us to do again next year what we did last year. Nimble and adaptable, the capstone program can try new things and lead the way for change at the school; that was the argument in Chapter 2.3.

Meanwhile, "nimble" can also imply "precarious." Many school administration processes that are taken for granted across the school may not function for the capstone program. Staffing, scheduling, and budgeting routines that typically involve department chairs, for example, may pass over the capstone program. Teachers are often not in the program full time and have their main responsibilities elsewhere. The usual lines of vertical communication between teachers and administrators cannot be taken for granted, which has implications for staffing, budget, and other program advocacy moments. Even if the program has a director, that director may not sit on the same meetings as the department chairs, so care must be taken to make sure the capstone is not left out of crucial processes. This chapter provides suggestions for creating an adult infrastructure that will allow the work of supporting students to get done as efficiently and effectively as possible.

Housing the program

Consider all the demands on the time of a high school senior. Even a partial list might include many or most of the following: academic classes, other classes, advisory programs, school-sponsored senior-year activities, college applications, service learning or volunteer work, sports or workouts, music or visual or performing arts, other school activities, non-school activities, afterschool jobs, faith groups, family. And that list leaves out friends and recreation, especially important in the teen years. **Which of those are your seniors going to give up in order to do the capstone?**

If you are preparing to start a capstone program, we strongly recommend facing that tough question up front and making sure that school administrators are on board with your answers. If you treat the capstone as an add-on, you virtually guarantee failure from the outset. Equally problematic is to launch a new program that outcompetes some existing school program or activity, provoking resentment or confrontation down the line. But there is also a positive incentive to understanding in advance what your capstone program will take the place of, because that will also tell you something about what continuing functions your program will be serving in the larger ecosystem of the school. Meanwhile, to the degree that the capstone hopes to introduce new functions to that ecosystem, it is only more urgent to understand precisely what you expect that system to lose and to gain.

A more practical way to approach that same tough question is to consider when in the school's daily schedule and annual calendar the program will show up, and where on the roster of classes and activities it will be "housed." Answers to the "when" and "where" questions will dictate the scope of the program, and also may force a decision on whether it will be optional or required of all students; they likewise will contribute to conversations about which of the adults on campus will be needed on the core capstone team, and who will be providing support.

Housing capstone programs

- Senior activity
- Extracurricular
- Extension of an existing program
- Element in an existing class
- Cohorts
- Independent class

Capstone as senior activity

One common strategy is to concentrate the program late in the spring of senior year, when schools often replace the usual curriculum and activities with senior-specific activities, or even just a lighter school day. In our experience, a well-designed capstone can keep students highly engaged at a time of year when they have lost interest in a routine that they have known since first grade. Advisory or grade-level time can likewise house a capstone program alongside and in symbiotic relation with the college application process, senior service, etc. The total time gained will be limited, tightly constraining the scope of the program. However, this approach works well with capstones required of all students and is relatively easy to introduce.

Capstone as extracurricular

Another strategy is to treat the capstone as a school activity, albeit a substantial one like mock trial, Model UN, or student government. This model asks students and their advisors to take on the responsibility of deciding what the individual students won't do in order to add the capstone to their varied schedules and fitting program requirements into their individual workloads. For obvious reasons, this model is appropriate for optional capstones, but not advisable if the capstone is required of all. Again, this method is relatively easy to introduce at a school new to capstone.

Capstone as extension of an existing program

Another strategy is to house the capstone in an existing program, within which it replaces a previously existing curriculum or activity. For example, a capstone centered on independent service learning might in effect replace (or become an option for replacing) a school's previous senior-year required service component. In that example, it could make sense to have the capstone run by the school's director of service learning. A new leadership team or standing meeting would provide support of the "thought partner" variety to the director, and a new adult teaching team, possibly consisting of the service learning faculty or of advisors, would be created or reassigned to enable the capstone to support a larger number of independent projects. Again, the total time gained will dictate the scope of the program. This model has the potential to work well with required or optional capstones, and is relatively easy to introduce.

Capstone as element in an existing class

Another strategy, securing a larger amount of time for capstone, is to house the program in an existing class or cluster of classes taken by seniors. English and science are disciplines sometimes called on to house a capstone. In this model, the hosting class gives up both class time and homework time to the program. Teachers and their departments will be more willing to give up time if they believe that their learning goals are being met through the program. For example, an English class might be willing to give up two months of instruction, two books, and two five-page essays, if during that same time each student will be reading and writing an equivalent number of pages. In other words, housing the program in English will likely mean having a program that requires a substantial amount of text-based learning and a substantial amount of writing. Correspondingly, a program housed in science classes would likely require some experiment or demonstration carried out according to the scientific method and shared out in a discipline-appropriate way, either in a scientific paper or poster. In either case, the capstone would be academic in nature. This model has the potential to gain substantial time for the program, allowing for deeper student work. The downside is that projects will be limited to include demonstrations of skill in the academic discipline providing the time. Depending on the classes involved, this model can work with optional or required capstones, as long as all students in capstone-designated class are indeed participating in capstone. Logistical challenges make this model difficult to introduce without considerable administrative commitment.

Capstone cohorts

The cohort strategy likewise houses the program in academic classes—newly dedicated capstone classes in this case—but provides more student choice. Students choose (or apply to) capstone classes or seminars that might be offered in any discipline. Each class includes a shared curriculum of texts, topics, and skills development. At some point, students branch out from the shared foundation to do individual projects. For example, a seminar in scientific methods could spend six weeks reading Thomas Kuhn and Karl Popper and engaging in assignments helping them to understand how to design effective scientific experiments.[1] Meanwhile, each student would be developing an independent project under the guidance of the teacher. The second part of the class would consist of time designated for individual student work along with ongoing project support from the same teacher. Meanwhile, across campus, other seniors at the same school might be taking a history seminar with a globalization theme. Students there would likewise have six weeks for shared reading and listening to invited speakers. Then they too would begin their projects, independent but clustered around the capstone seminar theme. The cohort model can work with optional or required capstones. Though it requires buy-in from many departments across campus, the cohort model can be easier to introduce because of its flexibility and incorporation of choice.

Capstone as independent class

Finally, the multi-disciplinary capstone class is a rare but highly effective model. By committing substantial academic time to the capstone, the school demonstrates that it values the independent work of its seniors. The question of teacher labor is simplified, since teacher time in the capstone is obviously equivalent to teaching in a traditional class. As we hope is demonstrated in Part 4 of this book, there is no shortage of material or instruction relevant to all capstone students—we think this use of time in the senior year of high school is of equivalent or higher value than any of the more usual demands on student time! If the capstone is required of all students, there will be multiple sections of the capstone class. In that case, a scheduling consideration would be to allow members of the multi-disciplinary capstone teaching team to visit other classes in the program and thereby share instruction across areas of expertise. Like the previous model, this one secures substantial time for student work and can function with optional or required capstones.

Adult capstone roles

Once you know where your program will be housed, you will be ready to think about the adults who will keep the program running. Ideally, a capstone program will involve many adults on campus at least peripherally. Given the way that senior-year capstones function as rituals, it can be very meaningful for teachers who taught those same seniors when they were much younger to play some role; meanwhile their current and recent teachers and advisors will feel invested and want to participate. At the same time, maintaining a coherent program with very large groups of adults involved can be challenging—or impossible. We therefore divide adult roles in a capstone into "**core**" or "**supporting**." The relative sizes of the core and supporting groups can vary, but you will probably want a very small core and a very large supporting crew.

Core capstone teachers devote considerable time, accept responsibility for collaborating with the core team and for maintaining shared program norms, and are compensated for their work with stipends or release time. In other words, their work in the capstone program is a significant fraction of their workload and would figure in any performance evaluation. If core team members do not do what's needed, the program will be in trouble.

Supporting roles, on the other hand, may be optional for teachers, or (if compulsory) rank alongside other low-level duties. They do not make up a significant part of the teacher's overall workload, nor do they figure in evaluations. Ideally, supporting roles are fun and low-stakes, so that if any expectations are not met, the consequences are small for students and for the program. We hope that the capstone program will be loved on campus, and part of that is to make sure as many people as possible have only wonderful experiences with it.

Unlike the core roles, the supporting roles are myriad and fluid. We make a distinction between roles for adults who work on campus and roles for members of the larger community, including community partners, outside experts, families, and alumni. (Younger students are a group not to be overlooked, but fall into none of the categories listed.) On-campus roles will be discussed in this chapter, while off-campus support will be discussed in Chapter 3.5.

The core capstone team

Diverse teams do better work. Most educators are aware of organizational research that has provided convincing support for this claim.[2] The core capstone teaching team in many programs is more diverse in terms of professional experience than most other teams at the school. Like capstone programs, capstone teams are often multi-disciplinary. More than multi-disciplinary, capstone programs are often multi-modal in the sense that students are connecting academic and off-campus learning; the capstone teaching team is correspondingly likely to invite collaboration between classroom teachers and educators who primarily work outside traditional classroom settings. In a typical high school, most teachers have never collaborated closely with a teacher from a different academic discipline, much less team-taught with a fellow educator who is not a classroom teacher. The diversity of experience on the core capstone team brings some challenges, but also enormous opportunities.

In building the core team, program designers will want to think about the capacities needed. As suggested above, these will be determined by when and where the program is housed—in other words, by what students are *doing*. If students will be participating in internships, the team will include someone with off-campus connections to local workplaces. If students will be involved in service, the team will include someone with an understanding of social justice and power dynamics. If students will be writing a lot, the team will include teachers familiar with strategies for responding efficiently and effectively to student writing. If students will be using design thinking or doing ethnographic research, the team will include someone with training or research experience in the social sciences.

The research that highlights the higher effectiveness of diverse teams also acknowledges that diverse teams experience more conflict and need more time for dialogue. Communication and documentation are key. A meeting of math teachers can start with many shared assumptions. When the capstone team meets, everything will need to be sorted out from the ground up. It is important that the team plan for this extra time and confirm its value—we do believe that conversations across disciplines and modes of education have enormous value beyond the capstone itself. It is also important that the team use processes or protocols to ensure that all voices are heard in meetings. Probably the team will bring meeting skills from their other roles on campus, but if not, the team could agree on a shared resource like the critical friends protocols in order to create common ground.[3]

Crucial to communication is documentation. Program deadlines and important dates need to be kept in one place that is visible to all. If the program has assignments, the prompts likewise need to be kept in a central location. In most programs, probably students and teachers can use the same materials. But whether or not students also access the team's core documents, the importance of these documents for the adults cannot be overstated. Either a website or a handbook can contain all program information and serve as an anchor for the team. If the capstone is graded, we encourage using rubrics. Whether or not rubrics are a preferred grading tool for individual teachers, they offer the team a way to get clear on assessment priorities. An added benefit is that they reassure students that grading will be fair across the program. (For more on rubrics, see Chapter 4.9.) Given how rapidly capstone programs evolve, meeting notes likewise take on heightened importance. A simple solution is to keep running notes in an online document that can be referenced by any member of the team at any time. Sorting in reverse chronological order means that the most current information will always be at the top.

Transparency takes care of accountability. Transparency means that the actions of each teacher on the team are visible to all. Transparency includes authentic conversation in meetings. A teacher might say, "I am grading using the rubric, but I am uncomfortable assigning so many Cs when the task was so difficult."

Whether the problem can be addressed that year, or whether the concerned teacher must live with his discomfort and wait for a solution in a future iteration of the program, it matters that the whole team know where each member stands. Transparency likewise includes any and all documents and records shared with students. The whole team should use a common online gradebook. When students sign up for meetings, the whole team should use a common sign-up system, with each teacher's schedule visible to others. When a teacher shares materials with students in the capstone, those materials must simultaneously be visible to the whole teaching team. Actions taken by an individual teacher without the knowledge of the team can lead to resentment, while the very same action taken publicly might lead to gratitude from the team—"What a great idea to meet with those students as a group rather than individually! You saved us so much time!" It is important to emphasize, however, that the goal is not uniformity. Once a basis of fairness is guaranteed, the program benefits from fully manifesting the diversity of its team. Not everyone does things the same way. One of the services a team-taught capstone can perform for its students is modeling respect for difference.

The directors of the core team

One common strategy is to designate one or more capstone program directors. Responsibilities include scheduling and facilitating meetings of the core capstone teaching team or advising team. If the capstone is graded, the directors would also supervise norming and provide a transparent grading system to keep teachers accountable to fairness across sections of the capstone (see Chapter 4.9). The directors would also take the lead on organizing ways for more adults across campus to engage the program in supporting roles. The directors would likewise take the lead in event planning.

Some less obvious responsibilities might fall to the directors of a new capstone program as well. The directors would want to be alert to the fact that the capstone program does not easily fit into previously existing organizational structures or processes at the school, increasing the chances of important work falling through the cracks. It is common for a capstone program not to have an independent budget, with incidental expenses associated with the culminating event, for example, being covered by a division budget, or other pool. The directors would want to know who is paying for what, and be ready to alert those paying colleagues early about anticipated changes, even if they themselves will never see a receipt. An even bigger issue is staffing in the program. The directors would want to understand the annual process for staffing sections, and to know when and how department leaders, division heads, and the registrar are involved. If the normal staffing process flows through meetings not attended by the capstone directors—for example, a standing meeting of department leaders—the directors would want to discuss in advance how the staffing needs of the program would be represented instead.

The capstone directors will also want to be alert to any ways in which aspects of the capstone program might introduce new conflicts at school. Capstone deadlines should not conflict with major deadlines set by the college advising department, for example. Likewise, the capstone culminating event in the spring needs to be carefully scheduled to avoid competing with other school events, whether prom or baccalaureate or an annual spring play or some other tradition. Capstone directors may even be working with the athletics director, since state tournaments for spring sports can produce seriously anxiety-producing conflicts for some students and families. Even if only a few seniors make it to the state track meet, for example, those individuals and their families should not have to choose between two events that, from their perspective, are both once-in-a-lifetime. Working with program directors and administrators across campus can in general help the capstone team understand complex contingencies and realities that students may fail to report. The student sprinting star may say that she does not mind changing out of her spikes and into her high heels in the car on her way back to school for her capstone presentation, but the athletic director can point out that the state 100 meters finals scheduled for midafternoon may not actually run until late evening. Events that are the highlights of a high school career deserve the care of many adult heads thinking together.

Every task listed here can be handled by a collaborative capstone team without a director role, as long as clarity and communication are in place.

> Events that are the highlights of a high school career
> deserve the care of many adult heads thinking together.

Key program partners on campus

Though they may have no formal designation in relation to the core capstone team, a few other parties on campus deserve special mention. An academic capstone will depend heavily on the school's librarian. In some schools, it may in fact be the librarian and not a classroom teacher who takes the lead, either for program administration or for instruction, or both. A capstone with an off-campus component is likely to call on the school's community engagement or service learning director, even if the word "service" is never mentioned to students. The reality is that the adult on campus with the most community connections will wind up involved. If the program has a public event, administrative staff who normally support events like graduation are likely to be called on. A parent association that supports school events may be involved as well. The person who handles alumni relations may be helpful in connecting capstone students with alumni resources. In addition to being thanked in any program publications, these special people on campus will be recognized and valued as allies of the program.

Volunteer advisors

Some supporting roles in a capstone demand commitment for the duration of a student's project, though the total amount of time invested may be very small. These roles can be figured in various ways: as members of the student's capstone committee, as readers, or as advisors, for example. If the students are aware that—unlike the core team—these adults are volunteering their time to help, that awareness can help them build important skills. In college and after, success will depend on getting help from people who are not obligated to provide it. Volunteer capstone advisors offer an opportunity for students to learn to write a courteous email, show respect for people's time, and write thank-you notes. As adults familiar with the developmental challenges of the teen years, volunteer capstone advisors can likewise provide feedback to students when they see gaps in their mastery of these important interpersonal skills. Though these supporting roles can be very substantial, they can be made joyful by keeping them clear of any "heavy lifting" for the program. For example, if the program is graded, that will be done by a member of the core team, not a volunteer advisor. Thus the volunteer role can be kept free of any conflict or unpleasantness that might belong to the institutional aspect of capstone as a school program.

In order to keep these roles more about joy than toil, it will also be helpful for the program to make sure that expectations for both capstone students and volunteer advisors are clear. When the students invite volunteer advisors onto their project, they might provide an "advisor commitment form" that details for the volunteer just what the commitment entails. The form should detail expectations and boundaries for both student and advisor—knowing of course that more might be taken on voluntarily.

Keeping expectations in check increases the likelihood of a positive experience for both students and volunteer advisors. But providing a bit of formality to the role helps students develop self-awareness and skills that may be useful to them as soon as the following fall when they arrive at college and begin to work with college faculty whose primary work is research, not teaching, and who expect students to signal respect for their time.

Sample capstone advisor commitment form

Aimed at students and their volunteer capstone advisors, this form clarifies expectations at a school where the advisor role is not compensated as part of regular teaching duties.

Advisor commitment form

STUDENT NAME: _____

FACULTY/STAFF NAME: _____

I have agreed to be the capstone advisor for the student named above.

_____

Faculty/staff signature (and name, if the signature is not readable!)

Capstone student expectations

Students are responsible for treating capstone advisors with the same level of respect they would give to an off-campus mentor.

- Students communicate courteously and professionally, whether in person or electronically.
- Students schedule meetings at times convenient to the capstone advisor, and show up on time and prepared.
- Students take notes in meetings and follow through on suggestions.
- Students provide copies of the project proposal and full-length draft to advisors on the day they are due.
- Students courteously keep their advisors in the loop as the project develops.

Capstone advisor expectations

Advisors are responsible for meeting with capstone students a few times each semester to share expertise and provide support in the form of dialogue.

- Advisors share expertise and support students with dialogue, possibly suggesting sources or off-campus opportunities, and helping the students problem-solve and strategize.
- Advisors ask challenging questions and help students recognize possible objections to their arguments.

- In addition to informal meetings, advisors participate in the student's capstone defense.
- Advisors read the student's prospectus and full-length draft, offering comments on the overall state of the project. (Advisors are *not* expected to provide written feedback on these assignments, nor to evaluate the quality of the writing!)

***

*This form should be returned **by the student to the capstone teaching team**.*

Committee members, panelists, moderators, etc.

While some supporting roles involve commitment over time, others allow adults on campus to be involved in the capstone and have an impact while demanding nothing more than an hour or two of their time. Sugata Mitra's "granny cloud" project rests on the idea that sympathetic listening, far from being incidental, is often the thing that students need most.[4] A lack of familiarity with the projects may even be an advantage, since a naive audience forces students to articulate clearly what they are thinking and doing. A beautiful consequence is that low-investment, high-joy roles for teachers across campus abound—and that these roles can also be high-impact. At so many stages of a capstone project, any adult on campus can provide sympathy and help getting thoughts sorted. There are a host of roles then that require no commitment beyond an hour or two, and also no continuity. An interested teacher can donate a few hours early in the year, then never show up again, and there is no problem at all. Let's look at some of the places where roles that are barely removed from "drop-in" can make a difference:

Review panelists

Each student gets 15 minutes with a panel consisting of two teachers who have volunteered for an hour or two. The student brings three copies of a succinct written project proposal to the review event. The student hands over the written version and speaks an elevator pitch. Conversation ensues; the students take notes. The written proposal stays with the teacher-panelists, in case they later want to offer further ideas to the student or to the program leaders.

Defense committee members

For sustained projects, defenses can be an excellent late-stage ritual. If the capstone includes a written component, core teachers will need to do the heavy lifting of reading and commenting. However, a defense that starts with a brief student presentation can easily include a teacher who shows up as a non-reading committee member. At the defense stage, students are still formulating ideas, and the naive audience member, new to the project, can be of enormous help.

Presentation moderators

At the culminating event, students presenting will need very little from adults. Nonetheless, an adult presence at each presentation serves many functions. Adult moderators can intervene with difficult audience members if asked to do so by the presenting student. They can keep track of time and signal to the presenter how many minutes remain. They can also offer moral support just by being present.

The program provides a sign-up opportunity so that teachers too can exercise choice, and a clear but succinct account of expectations. Properly managed with an emphasis on joy, these roles help students, generate good will toward the program, and provide meaningful experiences for participating teachers. They also augment the ritual function of the program by connecting students with the whole community as they make the transit toward departure.

For all supporting roles in a capstone, we strongly encourage programs to open the invitation to all adults who work regularly on campus—and not only to teachers. A school's administrative staff, its facilities crew, its development and communications departments—all of these employ adults with areas of expertise that are often unknown to the teaching faculty, and that may be of significant use to students whose project ideas are diverse and not necessarily "academic" in any narrow sense. Program directors should just be sure they clear the invitation with supervisors. It could be difficult for an administrative assistant to navigate a student request if the supervisor of her team is unaware of the program and its expectations. Again, to keep the program loved on campus, it behooves the capstone directors to foresee and forestall conflicts that might be introduced along with new practices and structures.

Student-centered organization of the adult team

In a program offering a wide range of student choice, the structure of core and supporting adult roles might be complex, with multiple adults involved in any one student project. In addition to the shared program documents that make requirements and deadlines visible to all, there will be a need for a system for student-centered documentation of each unique project. One solution is a collaborative online document holding key information and notes for each student. This organizational document can include important links to other online resources, like the student's portfolio or other digital elements. A list of adults who work with the student in core or supporting roles is also useful information to add to the document. Most importantly, this document may include regular notes following the progress of the student's work, ideas for development, and assignments with their future deadlines. The beauty of this shared document is that the student and all the adults involved can see the latest information in one spot, updated continuously—note that students often have full access to this document as well. This document is usually for internal use only. Only the student and the teachers in the program have access for reading and writing—it may contain private information for this reason. One practical use of this kind of document is for writing progress reports. When it comes time for a core member of the teaching team to grade a project, they only need to review this document to get the pertinent facts for their consideration, even if they do not work directly with the student.

Sample organizational document for the capstone team

Here is a sample of a document that one school uses to centralize all the information about one project for all the adults involved in the program. This school assigns a core advisor to be "in charge" of the student and their project. Additionally, a second teacher communicates with the student a couple times per quarter and has some professional or personal connection to the project and/or student. This works best as a shared online document.

Organizational document for teachers

Student information (The key information for each student.)

Student name:

Project title:

Portfolio link:

Primary teacher:

Secondary teacher:

Milestones (Simple, general goals for each month—one sentence. This school encourages students to be halfway done with their project in February, or to modify their plans.)

September:

October:

November:

December:

January:

February (50% done!):

March:

April:

May:

Primary teacher notes (Notes taken during each individual meeting with the student.)

Date:

Notes:

Portfolio notes (Notes about the student's portfolio.)

Date:

Notes:

Secondary teacher notes (Notes from the secondary teacher.)

Date:

Notes:

Resources (Special resources that the student might find useful. References, people, etc.)

Date:

Information:

A note about scheduling

The capstone sits in the school organizational structure in a special way, reaching across divides created by that structure. It draws participation from across departments and divisions. The challenges created for scheduling can hardly be underestimated. Imagine that you schedule all the review panel slots in parts of the school day when, unbeknownst to you, 90% of the teachers on campus have classes. Everyone is disappointed, and it is too late to make new plans. Or imagine that you invite teachers of lower grades to attend an after-school capstone event, but fail to register that all the teachers of younger students have sidewalk duty at that time. Now people may even be hurt or mad. Involving the registrar as an ally can be a game changer. The argument of this chapter is that it is the invisible work behind the scenes that makes centering students possible. The smooth functioning of many people in structures outside the usual school routine is not achieved without some behind-the-scenes work!

Notes to Chapter 3.4

Note 1, page 98: **Thomas Kuhn and Karl Popper**—We mean of course Thomas Kuhn, *The Structure of Scientific Revolutions* (Chicago: University of Chicago Press, 2012) and Karl Popper, *The Logic of Scientific Discovery* (New York: Routledge Classics, 2002).

Note 2, page 100: **Diverse teams do better work**—See Scott E. Page, *The Diversity Bonus* (Princeton: Princeton University Press, 2019). Or, for a very brief introduction, see Sian Beilock, "How Diverse Teams Produce Better Outcomes." *Forbes*, April 4, 2019.

Note 3, page 101: **protocols**—*The Art of Coaching Teams* is one source of meeting protocols. Elena Aguilar, *The Art of Coaching Teams* (San Francisco: John Wiley, 2016). The National School Reform Faculty website offers numerous free protocols on their website. www.nsrfharmony.org

Note 4, page 106: **"granny cloud"**—Mitra's project provides internet access and connects students with adult volunteers who are not trained teachers. See www.thegrannycloud.org

CHAPTER 3.5
COMMUNITY ENGAGEMENT AND INTERNSHIPS

Capstone students often venture off campus, seeking partners in the surrounding community to complete key aspects of their projects. Community engagement and internships are common forms of these interactions. These interactions with organizations off campus are often the most impressive offered by a school, and serve as shining examples of what the students can achieve. Schools would do well to support these teachers and students as they work to gain experiences beyond the school walls, and they will realize how remarkable these projects can become. A fully supported capstone program off campus is also a good opportunity for schools to advertise because they provide concrete examples of their mission statements in action.

Along with these special projects come extra requirements to ensure that students have meaningful experiences that are productive and safe, including aligning student interest with placement off campus, establishing contacts off campus, scheduling, transportation, and safety. Great care is needed to structure these aspects of the programs. Assigning dedicated teachers to them is the best policy—schools should formally assign and compensate the work of cultivating the off-campus network. Communication is especially important in these projects, with students serving as the hub of their information network. This chapter will review all of these topics, supporting capstone teachers as they set up this relatively complex part of their programs.

Do no harm

"First, do no harm." Doctors have their Hippocratic Oath, but we teachers often think we can manage without this reminder, at least while inside our own classrooms. Once we contemplate sending our students out into the community, however, we would do well to consider the many ways in which helpful intentions can produce unhelpful impacts. We need to consider the ways in which our well-meant programs may cause problems. It is better to keep students in class than to send them off campus in thoughtless ways, even if the perceived benefits seem great. Students can do a bad job in the library without necessarily harming any living persons. When students are out of school and in the surrounding community, the possibility for harm is immediate because the work is happening in the real world, and the minimum bar must therefore be set much higher. This should be of particular importance to teachers and administrators responsible for these kinds of interactions. They must understand the risk involved and make sure that all participating parties have the same level of understanding.

Capstone projects out in the real world tend to fall into two broad categories—service learning and internships—each of which has its own subcategories of activities. Both involve students working with professionals on site, engaged in meaningful work related to supporting the host institutions and gaining life experience that may amount to career exploration. The degree of personalization is less than most capstone projects because students are often doing the work of the organization as laid out by their supervisors. These are roles defined by the supporting professionals which can be done by anyone assigned to those particular jobs. Students have less flexibility customizing their projects in the traditional sense. The tailoring comes in including these action events into their project—they choose to be off campus, working with adults who are practicing their specific jobs, incorporating these mentorships into their larger plan.

Educators designing a capstone program that will be centered on service learning—or incorporate service learning as an element—will quickly become aware that resources on service learning are aimed at *service learning* programs, not *capstone* programs. Service learning in the context of a capstone program presents overlapping but not identical challenges and opportunities. That said, if the capstone is to incorporate service, it would be best for the capstone teaching team to work in collaboration with the school's service learning director, or someone with expertise in critical service learning (see Chapter 4.5) and relationships in the community. This is the best way to engage in this important and nuanced work. Entering a service learning relationship without the right framework and mindset can lead to poor outcomes. This is a good reason to expand the capstone team, building upon the inherent benefits of collaboration in groups—capstone works best in diverse teams.

All of that said, service learning elements are of enormous benefit to capstones. Outcomes for students make them more than worth the effort of preparation on the front end. Furthermore, educators designing the service element of a capstone will likewise become aware that many of the challenges faced by typical service learning programs are removed or mitigated in the capstone context. Capstones support individual or small-group projects generated by student interest. Capstone advisors do not have to worry about placing large numbers of students appropriately, nor about lack of intrinsic motivation. The fact that seniors are old enough to take public transportation (or drive themselves) obviates some of the challenges of scheduling. Commitment, communication, and compatibility, named by Dadit Hidayat and his colleagues as the "three Cs" of a successful service learning placement, are much more easily cultivated in a capstone context.[1] Meanwhile other challenges of service learning appear in capstone as they do in service learning programs; we discuss the need to prepare and support capstone students doing service projects in Chapter 4.5.

Internships are superior opportunities to learn what it is like to work in a field of interest. We have extensive experience placing students in research institutions with an emphasis on STEAM (science, technology, engineering, arts, math) topics. The truly interdisciplinary internships that draw upon more than one of the STEAM fields are wonderful student experiences as they give them direct involvement in modern research that draws upon the expertise of diverse researchers. We have found these professionals to deeply value the importance of mentorship, creating an avenue into STEAM careers, carving time out of their very busy jobs to include students in their workplace. We have placed students into entirely different organizations, ranging from small to large businesses to local government departments, and have observed them gaining the same level of life-changing moments. There is a lot to be said for investing the time and energy into developing these programs and relationships. They have the potential to deeply impact the lives of our students.

Aligning interest and placing students

Capstone students naturally gravitate toward community and internship projects as they consider their personal interests, their places in the world, and how they can make a difference or engage with the local communities. Students may know of people who they would like to work with, they may have interests that align with institutions in the surrounding area, they could be involved in current events and looking for an outlet, or they may have another significant reason why they are keen on these activities. Protocols are therefore needed to keep up with this regular demand. Capstone teachers should be prepared for the kinds of questions and proposals that will likely emerge because of the complexity involved with getting students off campus and working with appropriate people. One cannot really create these experiences in the moment.

Requests by students for community involvement are as common as they are diverse, sharing some elements and also bringing with them many pleasant surprises. Students love to incorporate people from outside the school community in their project plans, hoping to connect with them as they create goals to complete during their work. Preparing for these proposals presents a real challenge because capstone teachers never quite know what resources they may need to find to support a student's meaningful idea. A network of people and places is essential to managing this aspect of capstone programs. A teacher team sorts queries and helps students clarify their core interests and motivations. Members of the school community may serve as resources required for one project, and others will direct attention off campus in search of project partners. The network expands in circles, with the first one centered on the capstone classroom, then concentric rings expand outward, existing in wait for future project ideas. In concrete terms, a network is a group of people who could serve as off-campus supervisors for capstone students. Each has a skill set or is affiliated with an organization that is commonly connected with a capstone project. They are professionals in the surrounding community who, in addition to their professional talents, understand how to work with adolescents and have personalities that suit this unique task.

Assuming that teachers can secure resources for students located in or out of school, aligning interest and need is an essential part of starting a capstone project to avoid doing harm to any involved party. In addition to the importance of positionality discussed in Chapter 4.2, capstone teachers need to help students assess what they really hope to accomplish and identify the key underpinnings of their projects. Initial project proposals are usually too broad and inherently risky, stemming from student enthusiasm and grandiose ideas about what they can accomplish in the program. This ambitiousness is created by the interaction between the embedded complexity of these topics and the aspirational motivation of the students. They wish to tackle important topics that contain many threads woven into a multivariable structure. A teacher's first job is to ask a student to narrow their interests to the fundamentals, then consider how they could be dealt with by employing the simplest solutions. This grounding process will increase specificity and reduce risk, and can always be expanded in the future, but only in ways that are logical and safe.

Compatibility is most significant in service learning projects where the boundaries are less clear than in internships. Students take on projects that relate to deeply human issues, making any misjudgment potentially more significant. Projects that aim to improve the lives of the most at risk in our communities are intended to be helpful, and ensuring that efforts truly go directly toward documented need is of utmost importance. This is especially challenging for privileged students who have little personal experience in this realm to build their projects upon. They must do even more work to understand where they come from and what their impact will be, compared to what they are hoping to accomplish. Again, we point to the importance of addressing positionality and collaborating with teachers who specialize in these topics.

Internships are usually many steps removed from the delicate topics involved in service learning—unless one interns at a service learning organization. They are more often slotted in the "profession shadowing" category of academic experiences, giving students a sample of what life could be like in a particular career setting. Alignment is nonetheless very important for a different set of reasons. One example is that students are operating on their own at a physical distance from their teachers, often with adults who are unfamiliar with the nuances of interacting with teenagers. Another is that students represent their schools due to the simple fact that they are the only ones on location, regardless of how well they embody the mission of their educational institution. Much can happen before the capstone teacher figures out that something is amiss in the internship, creating fertile conditions for potential harm.

In all cases, it is vital to distill a student's project proposal down to its essence and investigate whether the ideas in their concentrated form match up with the opportunities provided by the program. Hopefully they do, and plans may be approved and enacted. Any misalignment is more easily spotted in this reduction step and can be addressed before any harm is done to the student or the people that they work with. Efforts to align interest and need early on will be amply rewarded later in the program when these two factors will combine to produce important and lasting outcomes.

Complicated situations are best handled with a phone call, not by email!

The paradox of the database

We noted above that a network of people is a terrific resource for capstone programs. Near the top of the list of capstone teacher wishes is an extensive, diverse contact list of people who can be connected to students right when they are needed—this is the address book for the people network. In this database would be adults who have skills that are particularly suited to the topics that capstone students are interested in. This theoretically should be a manageable resource to develop because many adults support the idea of sharing expertise and introducing others to their professional world. They are willing to dedicate some time even if they are busy and the interaction is essentially voluntary. Generating this matrix of who can do what faces a surprising challenge.

Capstone projects on average need expert support from professionals. Predicting the exact resources that will be required from year to year is very difficult, unfortunately—and this is the paradox of the database. If a capstone teaching team could amass a collection of people qualified and willing to work with high school students, there is no guarantee of when or if they will be called to duty. The personalized nature of capstone drives a unique collection of projects each year, following the interest of each graduating class. The exact nature of each project is hard to predict despite the fact that there are trends every year related to popular areas of engagement—service learning and internships are common proposals, for example. An actual database would gather some dust as people waited to be contacted by a student who would like to request their services, demanding patience of the people contained within it. It is the rare professional who has this discipline, assuming they even stay in their job long enough to be present when their number is called up.

Teachers who wish to create a database need to have these issues in mind to keep their partners engaged and content. It would be wise to pair a project like this with other school needs to make it more likely that people will be asked to follow through with their initial agreement. Capstone teachers could partner with other groups on campus who are also looking for adult support, who are more likely to call on them in the short term. An active database could be made in this fashion, which makes people feel like they are needed and acknowledged and will be more sustainable in the long term. Publicizing these interactions becomes an important activity, demonstrating the needs and outcomes, which is good for the database and school communications in general.

Whether teachers develop a database or not, a truly useful goal is gathering a team of networkers to provide the contacts with other professionals. Setting up relationships with people who themselves know lots of different people is a profitable capstone activity. Every school has a few of these people, who seem to know just the right person one is looking for, either due to their disposition or position or both. A short list of people who can find the professional that a capstone teacher is looking for is priceless and worth every effort to assemble it. When a student pitches a project that requires adult support outside of the capstone program, a networker can quickly lead to some options for the student to approach. As always, the networkers will operate the best in a team, sharing ideas and listening to each other, identifying people collaboratively.

Systems for matching capstone students and experts are largely similar for community engagement and internships, with internships presenting fewer challenges because of more consistent demand. A focused internship program has a relatively predictable need that regularly draws from a contact list, making a database a viable option, well worth the time invested. A key difference with internships is that the students actually have less say in the goals of the experience as they are dictated by the professional environment. Students often engage in activities that contribute to the work of an organization, rather than deriving their own essential questions and key products.

Working with partners off campus

Along with the remarkable potential that comes from students working off campus are several unique challenges. The most significant of these issues is the disconnect from the classroom and the teacher. There is fundamentally less predictability with respect to what a student can expect from day to day and fewer opportunities to control the outcomes. It can take some time to realize that things have gone sideways when students are located in a place of business or university, for example, due to less frequent communication as well as the physical distance between the site and school. Establishing clear ground rules is imperative in these situations for these reasons. Here are some essential points for any capstone project that will spend time outside of school boundaries:

- Prepare the students
- Educate the adults
- Establish regular communication
- Invite adults on campus
- Thank everyone afterwards

Capstone students represent their schools as soon as they step across their school's border, regardless of their awareness of this important fact. Their actions will be recognized as emblematic of their school, for their successes and missteps and everything in between. Students must be aware of their representation and comport themselves accordingly. They simply need to follow some guidelines taught to them by their capstone teachers. They will have stellar experiences if they are punctual, proactive, and honest. They must be on time for transportation and for any meetings scheduled by their adult sponsor.

Students should be one step ahead of daily activities, anticipating what they may need to take care of before events become problems. Should their candor be required, students need to share all that they know in the moment, to ensure that adults have all the information necessary for decision making. These are fundamental characteristics that take on new importance when students are working with adults who are different from their teachers.

The professionals supporting our students off campus face an unusual challenge because school is very different from the operations of most institutions, especially because capstone is unique among all other school curricula. Capstone teachers must provide an overview of their program for their adult partners in an easy-to-find format like a website, using terms that outsiders will understand. They should also share a list of duties that they expect professionals to perform, again using very direct language. The adults should be aware of how the student will travel from school and back, particularly if the location has any safety issues or if transportation will happen when it is dark out. Special capstone projects may require further education if unusual activities are required. Finally, it should be made clear which members of the school to contact for any pressing needs and how to do so.

Communication with adult supervisors is an important part of supporting capstone students while they are off campus. After explaining how the professionals can get in touch with the appropriate people at school during the initial meeting, it is wise to plan a few points of contact throughout the duration of the project, ensuring that most communication will be about productive topics and not just when there are problems. These reinforcing messages will improve the retention of professionals in a capstone program. The initial invitation to join is the first opportunity to reach out, followed by a program update in the middle, and another invitation to attend the final presentations at the end of the year on campus—or some equivalent culminating event. This three-part plan keeps the channel of communication open and the messages light and easy to compose. Of course, it should be made very clear that the adults off campus can contact the capstone teacher at any time for any reason so that it is obvious that the adult has all the support that they will need to sponsor the student at their location. In fact, the regular updates are really an excuse or prompt to reach out to the capstone teacher should they feel the need. Modes of communication are important to consider and should follow this simple rule: complicated situations are for phone calls. Capstone teachers should be aware of the power of the phone call and when to use it, avoiding long and/or intricate emails that run the risk of being misunderstood. When in doubt, make the call.

School is a mysterious place for many adults who work with our students, even more so due to the open-ended and ever-changing world of capstone. Inviting adults on campus is a very effective way for them to learn more of the goals of the capstone program and the lives of the students enrolled in it. A tour of campus followed by a meeting with capstone teachers and students will make the adult feel even more engaged in the program than they already are. They agreed to participate in the first place, after all, indicating their inherent interest in school. Hosting them on campus always leads to improved understanding and appreciation for the program and its participants.

A formal thank-you to everyone who supported the program is warranted at the end of a capstone experience. Traditional cards and envelopes from students are a nice touch and have the added benefit of teaching students how to address and mail them—many students will need assistance with this basic and apparently vanishing life skill. The thank-you expresses gratitude for the adults' contributions, crystallizes the special nature of relationship for the student, and illustrates how students should behave once they are in the professional world.

This is a good point to note that developing good relationships with adults affiliated with capstone projects off campus is vital because students come and go over the long term and capstone teachers need to maintain a healthy network if they are to have a sustainable program. It is apparent that teachers need adults for the current year when there are immediate needs as demanded by the students. It is also true that ongoing work must be done to keep professionals engaged for subsequent years as student interest ebbs and flows. Maintaining a robust network like this is challenging work and giving this focused task to a teacher is a great way to make sure this assignment happens. Committing a teacher demonstrates the school's investment in the program.

Planning the first meeting

Here is a sample agenda for the first meeting with professionals off campus. The purpose is to align everyone's expectations about a capstone project, on and off campus. Students and teachers at school and adults off campus need to be on the same page about some crucial project elements. This example includes these items as well as a simple framework for arranging them.

Sample agenda for first meeting with professionals off campus
Aimed at students and their off-campus supervisors, this agenda ensures that the initial meeting covers all practical topics, as well as clarifying behavioral expectations for adult-student interaction.

Off-campus project
First meeting agenda

Supervisor:	Student:

Our first meeting will be on site, together with the supervisor, student and a capstone program representative. The goals for this time are general introductions, scheduling and behavioral expectations.

Agenda

- Introductions of supervisor, student and capstone representative.
- Review of school program:
  - Weekly visits, for a three-hour session (including travel time), for academic year.
  - Student participates in a project on site. Activity up to supervisor.
  - Student enrolled in course at school—integrated with project—student maintains digital portfolio.
    - Privacy notes: clarify what can and cannot be shared publicly.
  - Protocol for missed weeks. Online work for student if possible.
  - Student presents project in May. Supervisor invited.
- Confirm weekly meeting times.
- Confirm location of research and transportation stop.
- Exchange supervisor and student contact information.
- Review standards of behavior (below).

Student meeting time:

Contact information:

- School phone number
- Capstone teacher phone number and email address

Standards of behavior

Examples of behavioral standards regarding interactions with students and colleagues include, but are not limited to, the following:

- Act as a role model to students and colleagues, being especially conscious of your actions and words at times and in places where students can observe you.
- Maintain only professional relationships with students, acting transparently and unambiguously.
- Act and communicate in a professional, respectful, and courteous manner with all school community members.
- Take responsibility to set and maintain clear and consistent boundaries with all school community members. Boundaries need to always be appropriate for the circumstances.
- Promote best outcomes for students by acting always in accordance with the mission, values, and expectations of the school and in ways that reflect well on the school.
- Understand the imbalance of power that exists as a result of authority, whether that be between adults or between adults and students. The imbalance of power between adults and students is of particular importance in a school environment. Use your influence to promote healthy student development. Also understand this imbalance can often continue after the student has left the school.
- Accept responsibility for the impact of your actions and words, regardless of your intent.
- Relay community concerns to appropriate people at school, including referring students in need of counseling or health services.

Scheduling, transportation and safety

Capstone teachers should create a thorough plan for students to travel safely to and from sites off campus. There are several important procedures to establish regardless of the actual mode of transportation because of the significant risks associated with these activities. These rules apply whether students drive themselves or the school provides transportation; they exist to keep track of trips and make the best use of the time invested by everyone participating in the program on and off campus.

A central calendar is an invaluable asset, containing scheduled times of actual departures and arrivals. Sharing this calendar clarifies who is travelling when and is very helpful when plans need to be changed because all linked parties are notified immediately. Each calendar event may contain critical travel and contact information, again providing essential information in one spot for anyone who might need it. Consider including the departure and arrival times, the street address, email and phone numbers of anyone directly interacting with the students, and who to contact at school if any questions arise. Quite a bit of information can be included in an event without distracting from the essential purpose—departure and arrival times—for "just in case" planning.

Students need to closely follow transportation guidelines and will likely require constant reinforcement. They need to check out with the correct person on campus using the designated system, and repeat the process when they return to campus. Include them in the formal calendar event as well, giving them access to all the critical information, and train them to be able to find what they need when they need it. Students who miss a day for any reason need to inform the correct people as early as possible. This will involve multiple modes of communication, and students cannot relent until the key people have confirmed the change of plans. This last point is of utmost importance! Students cannot assume that an email or text will suffice. They need to be sure that the recipient received and understands the message before they go on with their day. Nobody wants a volunteer off campus worrying about a no-show student. That is a stress that capstone teachers will be happy never to experience. Constant reminding is a necessary task, making sure that students will know exactly what to do when they get sick or something like it, even after prolonged periods of regular trips when there was no need to change the normal operating procedure.

Syncing school calendars with people off campus is of special importance because of how different a school schedule can be. Changes for vacations and holidays should be made well in advance, and reminders sent out as the dates draw near are quite helpful. Schools that have a rotating schedule will need a way to educate their off-campus partners about how it will influence transportation. Students working in institutions like universities that have their own unique schedules must take extra care to align calendars and watch out for changes on both sides due to extended vacations. One must always keep in mind that most organizations will be very unfamiliar with a school schedule, making extra information particularly useful even if it feels like overkill.

The first trip off campus is an opportunity to identify a couple of required elements. The physical address is needed to determine the actual location where students enter and exit a building. This spot should be easy to find, well lit at night, and regularly frequented by others. It should be determined if any extra security will be involved like a passcard to gain access to a locked door. Additional directions must be clarified so students know which stairs and hallways to take all by themselves, including who will greet them upon their arrival. More travel details should be added as required by sites that require them.

Parents should be part of this planning as well, especially if they are driving or their student is using a family vehicle. Each school will have their own culture to dictate what and how to share with parents. Schools that provide transportation should make parents aware of any extra fees and how often they will be billed, avoiding any surprises at the end of the program.

Capstone teachers should not assume that everyone is aware of the risk associated with transporting students off campus. It is good practice to have a conversation with an administrator who is responsible for this kind of risk about what is happening in the program and what might concern people who are in charge of this aspect of the school. This might be a financial officer or another person in the business department. Insurance issues may come into play for capstone activities and school officials need to be aware of any significant activity.

Communication

The key to good communication in capstone is to put the student in the center, in keeping with the ethos of the entire program. Maintaining all of the connections that can form in a project may become complex, demanding an efficient, reliable system of communication. Consider a sizable capstone program with 50 students, each with a teacher relationship, some with a connection to another school community member, some with student partners, and a few working with professionals off campus. What once seemed manageable really is not, even with adult helpers beyond the school walls. All of this is really more than one teacher can handle, so students must be the central conduit of communication to distribute the load.

Despite the fact that students seem to thrive in a digital communication world, they need specialized training for capstone communication—really any type of formal message composition. The good news is that they are familiar with the speed of communication and the ability to quickly get in touch with people who are important to them. There are several skills that they need to develop beyond this point:

- Be proactive
- Share first drafts
- Use proper grammar

Anticipating when to send a message is the most important part of student communication. Many requests to share information will come from the teacher, and students just need to meet the respective deadlines. This kind of communication is routine and easily managed. Communication becomes more complicated in the moment, when a task needs to be completed quickly, or a surprise pops up which requires strategizing and resolution. A typical example is transportation, which was addressed above. Students who get in touch with the requisite people immediately avoid the ugly mess that can form around a canceled trip off campus. They know who to write to, have the contact information, and are the first to understand that a drive needs to be halted. They are therefore the best person to handle the bulk of the communication. Another example is a project snag that changes a schedule, necessitating calendar changes for meetings that the student was going to attend with other people but then have to be modified. The student is again the best person to deal with the involved scheduling minutiae. In all cases, the capstone teacher is included in the communication loop continuously.

Students need to seek approval for formal messages that are sent on behalf of their program. A message to an adult, a mass email to the school community, or a survey for a large population should all be drafted by a student and edited by a capstone teacher before any of them are seen by the intended audience. There is nuance to any kind of formal communication that students must consider, which a teacher can easily identify and correct. Two simple rules are to use good grammar and capitalize. Nothing fancy, just a level of writing that will accurately convey what the student intends without confusing people or angering them with another form of spam in their inbox.

A final point about communication is that regular updates are crucial for keeping up with projects that are inherently out of sight of teachers. Student-centered projects are self-focused by design, placing much of the work in the students' purview. When married with any work off campus, one can appreciate how much work could be done beyond the notice of a teacher. It is important to ultimately get up to speed on student progress, and essential to know what is going on if problems arise. It is remarkable how problematic events can become in a short period of time without regular communication. Students keeping teachers in regular touch is the ounce of prevention that avoids a pound of cure (i.e. clarifying all of the resulting confusion).

When to intervene

The stakes are higher for capstone projects that include elements from off campus in many different ways. Finding a compatible and willing person is the first factor that adds to the extra variables involved in these kinds of experiences. Thankfully it is often hard to say no to an eager high school student who sends an earnest and well composed message, but professionals are busy and many of them are unable to meet the needs of the program. Keeping in touch with the student is a challenge that we have reviewed along with the risky aspects of problems arising at a distance from school over an extended period of time. In addition, supervisors may be willing, but few of them are real educators who have the actual skills to deal with students like their capstone teachers.

Teachers should be more hands-on with these kinds of projects (compared to typical capstone activities) for the reasons noted above. The value of failure takes on new meaning here because things can truly blow up (consider the story of Trevor shared at the end of this chapter) and the impact may be felt by more people, some of whom are not members of the school community. The probability of failure is the same as for all projects, but if there is a major problem, it will put out partners from the external community, which capstone teachers should avoid to maintain their sustainable network of supervisors. These professionals are busy and they volunteer their time, so there is a likelihood that relationships can sour more easily. There is still a balance between failure and intervention, but the scale is tipped further away from failure as a learning experience, closer to avoiding harmful failure.

Regular updates from students become extremely important when they are working with members of the surrounding community. Capstone teachers are justified in demanding that students update their digital portfolios weekly, even if they are unable to attend their site (see our section on digital portfolios in Chapter 4.6). We often ask our students to just post "Could not go today because it snowed" to maintain the habit and to keep the channel of communication always on.

Professionals work with all kinds of volunteers and may sometimes confuse the role of the capstone student. Even after a thorough introductory meeting in which duties were reviewed for all parties, actions can slip on site, and students may find themselves doing jobs that surprise them and making mistakes. Again, these adults supporting students are not teachers and may need reminding every once in a while. The capstone teachers must keep close tabs and always be ready to get involved if they get any signals of this sort from a student. In our experience, this is a rare event, but it does happen, and a quick intervention has solved most of the situations.

Take the case of Trevor, who was participating in an internship in a regional neuroscience lab at a university. He inadvertently posted some microscopic images in his online portfolio that were due to be published and were therefore private, very sensitive information. These were pictures of animal tissues that were part of the work of the lab. Trevor did not realize how important these images were—they were secret data that was to be used for publishing and fundraising. His portfolio was public and crawled by Google. Thankfully, the capstone teacher was in good communication with the scientist and got an email the same day asking for the images to be taken down, and they were. But Google has a long memory for uploaded images, as everyone learned the next day when the professor wrote a harrowing email to the capstone teacher, begging for help to remove the pictures that she needed for her research. She was quite upset because a grant application was on the line, all because of one high school senior who made a simple mistake. In the span of 48 hours, Trevor learned all about how Google keeps track of images and how to clean out every digital nook and cranny, eventually deleting all of the sensitive content online. Several years later, the scientist still hosts capstone students, and Trevor has an interesting story to tell!

Notes to Chapter 3.5

Note 1, page 113: **the "three Cs"**—See D. Hidayat, S. Pratsch, and R. Stoecker, "Principles for success in service learning—the three Cs" in *The unheard voices: Community organizations and service learning*, eds. R. Stoecker, E.S. Tryon, and A. Hilgendorf (Philadelphia, PA: Temple University Press, 2009), 146–161.

CHAPTER 3.6
MAKING CAPSTONE VISIBLE

Visible manifestations of capstone learning—presentations and events, individual artifacts and collective documentation—serve many functions for the students, the program, and the school. In Chapter 4.10 and 4.11, we discuss how to support students in producing "deliverables" like essays and presentations, and we also discuss their value for the learning of the students themselves. Deliverables are judged independent of the person or process used to produce them. Seeing something you have made judged on its own merits is a growing-up experience. Meanwhile, precisely because of this grown-up quality, capstone deliverables also serve functions that go beyond the learning of the individual student. They serve as boundary objects, bringing capstone students into new relationships in the adult world. They are used by students later for applications. As anticipated shifts in assessment take place, they will also serve as natural performance assessments. They are archived as individual and collective memory objects. They promote the program, making it visible to the larger intramural and extramural communities. Understood as performance assessments of the school's whole multi-year curriculum, rather than of individual work, they also serve the school as artifacts documenting organizational rather than individual learning.

Program communications

The program will want to communicate capstone activity to multiple audiences, including adults across campus, families, and younger students. A simple all-staff email blast from the capstone teachers can give adults across campus a heads-up at times when students are likely to be approaching them for support, or inform them about opportunities for volunteer roles in the program. (For more on engaging adults across campus in low-commitment ways, see Chapter 3.4.) Messaging out to families is best coordinated with the school's director of communications. Program leaders can provide content for the school's social media, or write blog posts for the school-wide newsletter celebrating major milestones for the capstone cohort. Depending on the number of students involved, the school newsletter might want to either spotlight a few stellar projects or even run a year-long series highlighting the work of each student in turn. If, for example, a year-long program has 60 students enrolled, two profiles a week from October to May will allow all students a turn. To make this possible, program teachers would have students fill out a survey that drops into a spreadsheet shared with communications. The survey would ask for a brief project description, along with a few questions designed to elicit engaging student quotations. The office of communications would then be able to use this ready material to draft profiles on their own timeline.

Promoting the program by promoting individual projects

Ways to promote individual projects include:

- Promotion slides, formatted into a slideshow shared around campus
- Project thumbnails, advertised on the school or program website
- Posters, displayed digitally or in print
- Elevator pitches, given to a panel or at a "speed date" event
- Short presentations given to internal audiences, often younger students
- Student profiles, written by the communications department for the school newsletter
- Digital portfolios, or individual project websites

To make the program visible to younger students (a recruitment consideration for optional programs), the best ambassadors are the seniors themselves. Outstanding projects can easily spin off short presentations to be delivered in classes taken by juniors. Capstone students can also present at school-wide meetings. Seniors approaching graduation appreciate appearing as experts and giving back to the community. Meanwhile a low-stakes presentation to younger students is a great opportunity to build confidence in public speaking. Another internal strategy aimed at recruiting or inspiring younger students is to run a slideshow on screens placed around campus. Each capstone student submits a promotion slide with an image and their name. If it is early in the year, the slide will also show the research question. Later, anticipating the capstone exhibition, the slide may instead advertise the project title or even thesis statement. Slideshows make it possible to showcase each and every senior's project, increasing the likelihood that younger students will see something in the mix that sparks personal interest. Similar to slides, but allowing for more complex content elements, individual project posters (whether digital or print) share the diversity of projects to the school community.

A very different strategy with similar impact is to engage younger students in documenting and publicizing the projects of their older peers. In a media studies class at one school, younger students created a podcast series that shared information about senior projects with students and families alike. Journalism classes that include younger students might likewise enter into a symbiotic partnership with the program.

Sample poster guidelines

Capstone students make project posters for several reasons. In this action capstone program, they help focus projects on the core ideas, and they are excellent advertising for the program. They are complete, accurate, and attractive once they are done.

Project posters

Format

Include these required elements:

- Title: a short description of your project. Two parts often work well, for example: "Plastic in the Great Lakes: an investigation into the presence and effects of microplastics in the Great Lakes ecosystems"
- Your full name and graduation year
- Headshot: a picture of you
- Essential question: a question that frames your project. The primary idea that your project is centered upon
- Key product: the ultimate idea, object, or goal of your project. Can be a physical or conceptual item
- Pictures: relevant pictures for your project
- QR code: a code that links to your portfolio

Completion

Posters need program director approval before they are complete. Add your completed poster to your portfolio.different font.

A flourishing capstone program may eventually become the school's signature event, serving to make the school more visible in its region. In this case, the program is promoting the school, rather than the other way around. If the school is prepared to support the capstone exhibition as a fully public event, a significant step—advertising it in the local newspaper or radio and on the school website—may be appropriate. A few schools even partner with already visible organizations in the larger community for joint events.

Digital portfolios

Most program communication strategies, including those that promote the program by promoting individual projects, distinguish between the public face of projects and the personal learning trajectory. The public gets a promotional snapshot, while documentation of the learning itself stays between student and teacher. One widely used strategy, however, makes the capstone journey itself fully public.

Digital portfolios, in the form of individual project websites with regularly updated blogs, offer an excellent option for action capstones like internships or design-build projects. In keeping with the idea that "transparency takes care of accountability," public sites make it apparent who keeps up with work and who falls behind. In ungraded capstones especially, this can be a helpful motivation.

Students post in response to assignments made by the program teachers, creating a timeline as the project evolves, complete with twists and turns. Visitors to the project website will appreciate how much has been accomplished, how plans shifted over time, and how the final product came into being. Teachers additionally find the documentation they need for any project assessment. For both public and school audiences, portfolios are inherently creative and should be visually engaging.

Reflection is an important part of the digital portfolio. The formation of the project, including comparison of expectations and reality, is an integral portfolio topic. By integrating reflection into the main vehicle of project documentation, the portfolio assignment conveys a program's value for student learning.

Sample portfolio guidelines for an action capstone

These guidelines explain to students how they will document their internships or community placements. In this program, the digital portfolio is a major deliverable as well as a vehicle for documentation and reflection. As a bonus, the portfolios make the program visible to the larger community.

Digital portfolios

Overview

Your capstone portfolio is the primary mode of communication for your project. You will use it to share your work, and it will be used to publicize the capstone program. Following guidelines is therefore very important.

Frequency of events

General capstone students create portfolio events twice a month. Deadlines will be posted for planning purposes.

Capstone students in the science internship program must create portfolio events each week. Should a week be missed for any reason, simply create an event that says "trip cancelled" and a very brief explanation, like "snow day." There are no extra guidelines for these students other than greater frequency.

Content

Privacy is very important in portfolios. Please carefully follow these rules:

- Only use first names in your portfolio. This applies to you and everyone that you write about.
- Science internships: publish data only after approval from your off-campus supervisor. Information like numbers, pictures, etc. may be sensitive and permission must be secured before posting. When in doubt, do not post right away.

Here are some things to consider including in an event:

- Include the assignment date, which is *not* necessarily the posting date. For example, if it is the second event for October, write "Second October event."
- Your regular activities.
- Interesting connections with other parts of your life.
- Reflections on past and current work.
- Changes that have been recently made.
- Long-term goals.
- Media to illustrate your work.
- References to all sources using a proper format. See our library for details.

These are some options for events:

- A written narrative. Two paragraphs. Use proper grammar.
- Written piece. Two paragraphs.
- Video of student discussing event. 2 - 4 minutes.
- Graphic (or series of graphics) of event. Significant information content.
- Digital.
- Sketch and take a picture.
- Audio entry discussing event. 2–4 minutes.
- Timelapse of work being done.
- Must include written reflection.
- BE CREATIVE!

Reflections play a big role in events. Consider these questions when deciding what to write about.

- What was the assignment and how?
- What are you sharing in this entry?
- Why is this entry submission valuable and what did you learn from it?
- How will this entry help determine what you do next in your process, whether that is positive or negative?
- How do you feel you are progressing towards your finished product with this entry?

Platforms

Students choose the best web platform for their portfolio. Some common choices are WordPress, Weebly, Google Sites, and Wix. Consider the topic of your project and what you hope to accomplish, then select a platform.

Review

Each student has a primary teacher who will review and provide feedback about the portfolio. Be sure to respond to their feedback, or any other comments that you receive.

First portfolio event: autobiography

Introduce yourself and your project to your readers. Compose a very brief autobiography which summarizes your life experiences and interests, as they relate to your project. Include the key events which led you to propose your capstone project. Only share information that you would like to be in the public domain.

Second portfolio event: timeline

Assemble a project timeline for your capstone. Write out a few goals for each month, spanning September through May. These will be used to make sure that progress is made, and all necessary adjustments completed. This will be like your own personal milestones, to be done in addition to the official program milestones. Start with the timeline that you created for your Signature application, then edit it to become this portfolio post.

The final exhibition

The majority of capstone programs culminate in an exhibition event at which each student offers some form of presentation. No event in the capstone year is so visible and so important for the students involved and for the program as this final exhibition, expo, demonstration, or celebration. Though a presentation is not the only form of capstone deliverable, it is the most common. Perhaps the power of a human speaking to other humans is craved even more in this digital era. Perhaps the flexibility of the presentation format, which allows diverse projects to shine, makes it popular. Whatever the reason, we know of few programs that dispense with this step. In Chapter 4.11, we discuss how to prepare individual students for their individual presentations; here we offer support for the capstone team as it designs the event itself.

As we've noted throughout this book, senior-year capstones are rituals which facilitate the rite of passage that is a student's graduation from high school. At the same time, capstone rituals strengthen the school by embodying and making visible relationships within the school, and between the school and its larger community. No aspect of the program benefits more from a thought experiment that we might call "thinking like an anthropologist." First, what is a ritual? A ritual is a repeated, formalized set of actions. Rituals organize space, time, and action in a way that carries meaning. Rituals contain wonderful and risky transformations. With their reliable protocols, rituals hold up the celebrant whose spirits are flagging, even as they amplify the joy of those ready to fly free. Rituals "work" even if some of the participants are not "feeling it" at that moment. They offer a safe outlet for exuberance. In considering a ritual, we watch what people do and how they move just as much as we listen to what they say.[1]

Seen through an action or academic lens, what matters in a student's project may be details that are too small to make it into a short presentation. For the teacher, those details are the project. But on the night of the exhibition, what matters more may be the way the student performs the role of expert to an audience that knew her once as a small child. Members of that audience may not even care about the details that were so important to the teacher. What they see is the student stepping up into a new relationship with adults. In designing the final exhibition, then, the capstone teaching team may want to engage in some "defamiliarization" in order to think on a broader scale about the different meanings different participants will attach to the final exhibition event. In a section of this chapter, we offer a defamiliarization thought experiment activity for the capstone team to try out together.

****

Thought experiment

Defamiliarize your capstone's culminating event by thinking of it as a ritual

(an activity for the capstone teaching team)

Physical performance

- How are objects used (if they are)? What meaning is carried in the objects?
- Do students receive a certificate? Are essays printed and bound in an attractive form? Will the exhibition have a printed flyer or program that can serve as a memento?
- How is space used? What values are embodied in the use of space?
- Is there any transformation or decoration of everyday space for the exhibition? Or is a space not normally used by students opened up for the presenters? Is the space conducive to social connection between presentations? To family gatherings?
- How is time structured? What meanings are carried in the use of time?
- Does the exhibition feel like part of the school day, or is it more celebratory? Does the schedule of the event allow for social connection before or between presentations?

Participants

- Who is visible? Who is invisible?
- How are students and adults positioned? Who is recognized and honored as supporting each student's long journey through high school? Are families acknowledged? If the capstone culminates the whole curriculum, are *all* teachers acknowledged, or is only the capstone team visible? Are staff members who may have been as important to students as teachers equally honored?
- Who is included? Who is excluded?

- If the program was optional, was it truly accessible to every student, or did systemic factors determine who participated? Do the timing and the framing of the exhibition event make it accessible to working parents and guardians? To younger siblings and younger students? To out-of-town relatives who may otherwise visit the school only for graduation? To alumni?
- Who is centered? Who is marginalized?
- Does the ritual truly center the student presenters, or are adults still most visible as the ringleaders of the show? Are all types of projects and all kinds of students equally celebrated? If not, what systemic rather than individual factors determined who was given center stage?

Meaning

- What's the meaning for the student?
- Do the student presenters get to feel like the experts? Do they have a sense of agency in the event? How are they oriented toward friends, family, and former teachers in the audience? What does the event experience contribute to their self-confidence or sense of self-efficacy? To whom do they feel connected through the event?
- What is the meaning for the community?
- Do families get to see their children positioned and acknowledged as young adults? Is this an opportunity for former teachers to say goodbye? How does the school as a whole see its work, perhaps over many years, reflected in the exhibition?

Mission alignment

- Is the meaning carried in the capstone ritual congruent with your school mission?
- If the capstone is optional, how does this subset of the senior class relate to that class as a whole? Even if the capstone program is on the vanguard in some respects, do you nonetheless see a healthy relationship with the school as a whole? Or are there signs that the program is an outlier?
- Does the meaning expressed align with your values as an educator?
- What do *you* see that you value? What leaves you uncomfortable or concerned?

****

Event planning

Just planning the event as an event is a major task, one that *cannot* be undertaken by program leaders without support from across the school. Depending on the size of the event, the planning process may need to start more than a full year in advance, when the school's major dates calendar is being set. The list of people to contact will be long. We suggest a few considerations below:

- The administrator who keeps track of the school's major dates will need to put it on the master calendar.
- The facilities manager will need to schedule and manage space needs.
- The head of school, division head, and any other administrators who may need to be present will want to put the event on their calendars.
- The director of communications will need to plan for promotion, and may have advice about flyers and signage.
- IT will need to provide tech support before and during the event.
- The business office may need to help a program without its own budget decide where to request funds to cover any incidental expenses.
- The administrative support staff usually responsible for catering and decorating will be invaluable if food is to be provided to guests, or academic spaces to be altered in any way for the celebration.
- The school's parent/guardian association may likewise be helpful with food or decoration; the administrative support staff will know whether this is an appropriate request.
- Student organizations like student government who often provide event support may be helpful for welcoming guests, handing out programs, etc., while the drama tech club may be able to assist with moving furniture and generally preparing spaces for showtime.

This is just an initial list. Just as capstone programs are unique to their home schools, so are their exhibitions. The capstone team will want to plan an event that is in alignment with the school's event culture. A capstone teaching team whose classroom roles have not previously involved them in this aspect of the life of the school will want to seek support early. For example, working parents and guardians will not be able to attend an event held during the work day, while events that run late in the evening are difficult for families with much younger children at home. An event held during the week of graduation puts two high-stress dates in proximity, but allows families who have come from out of town for graduation to see the capstone exhibition too. The timing will dictate who can or cannot attend, and thus shape the character of the whole ritual. Someone at the school will have experience navigating off-campus factors like these, which may not occur to the capstone team. As a final note, all of these supporting adults can be thanked in the program.

Promoting individual projects also promotes the program.

The schedule of presentations

The capstone team will need to do some math. If 60-odd students each give a 20-minute presentation, with five minutes for questions and a five-minute passing period, it will take 30 hours, or four school days, to run them sequentially. One person can see every student over the four days—but probably not even the capstone teaching team wants to experience that marathon! Also, on that schedule, audiences are likely to be tiny, giving the event a low-energy feeling. If the same students present for the same length of time, but 15 rooms run concurrently, the event now fits comfortably into an evening. The number of people on campus at one time for the event will be large, creating a high-energy feeling. The likelihood, however, that students and families will miss presentations of interest to them is high. Each program must find its own happy medium, carefully building a schedule that probably does run a number of presentations concurrently, but also allows friends to celebrate the capstone success of friends. Keep in mind that in a close-knit community, families may have forged very powerful connections with the friends of their children, or the children of their friends, and feel heartbroken if a student who "practically grew up in my kitchen" is presenting in the same time slot as their own flesh and blood. A good overall planning strategy is to think about the event experience from the audience perspective. Realistically, families may enjoy seeing perhaps three or four presentations in an evening, or a few more over the course of a weekend. If the presentations are longer or shorter, that of course changes the experience, and the math.

How the program celebration uses space is as meaningful as its use of time. An audience of 20 feels robust in a classroom, but disappointing in an auditorium. Another consideration is whether each student will have an identical amount of time in an identical space, or whether outstanding projects will be honored with more time and space. As always, such considerations depend on the school context. Which is more in line with the school culture: to foreground great accomplishment or to give each participant equal billing?

Show time

No matter how good the planning, something will go wrong on the day of the event. A video will have been taken down from the website where the student counted on accessing it. A strap will break off a presenter's shoe. Someone will have forgotten to override the automatic four o'clock shut-off on the building air conditioning. The administrator who gets stuck in traffic will have the only key to the supply closet where the podiums are stored.

The capstone team will want to be prepared to respond to small emergencies like these without disrupting the students' special day. Knowing that glitches are inevitable, presenters and some of the adult support will need to arrive early. One place to go for advice is the school's drama or music directors, who have experience getting people onto campus in advance of fixed start times. If musicians arrive on campus by five-thirty for a seven o'clock concert, your capstone students should allow a buffer for unexpected delays as well. If the event is at a time of day when the capstone group is not normally returning to school, they will be unfamiliar with traffic patterns, for example. Once on campus, students will want to check their technology and any props before guests arrive. Arranging the presentation spaces themselves can be empowering and lessen nervousness. Meanwhile, the capstone teaching team will want to equip themselves in advance with cell numbers for facilities and tech support. Even if these departments are providing in-person support at the event, it may be difficult to locate them in the moment without a cell number. Lastly, in our experience, having safety pins and duct tape on hand never hurts!

It is as troubleshooters that adult moderators shine. As we discuss in Chapter 3.5, the presentation moderator role allows adults from across campus to participate in a meaningful way without making a large time commitment to the program. And as we discuss in detail in Chapter 4.11, it can be better for students if the moderators remain in the background unless truly needed. But their mere presence can be a comfort to nervous young presenters, and they will be absolutely vital when something goes wrong. As at any school event, it is simply good practice to have a responsible adult in each and every room where students are gathered.

Publishing and archiving capstone work

The many deliverables—essays, presentation videos, posters, or other artifacts—produced by students in a capstone can have a life beyond the limits of the campus and beyond the end of the senior year. Capstone deliverables are boundary objects which carry different meanings in different contexts. Since many students will not do a project of this size again until graduate school, it is common for them to use their capstone essays or presentation videos in applications for jobs, internships, or research placements during their college years. If the college application process moves to include electronic portfolios, as some anticipate, capstone deliverables will of course be a natural fit. For such individual purposes, each student will keep digital copies of their own work.

Some programs publish capstone artifacts, most often presentation videos, on the school website. Programs that include blogging have an obvious platform for publishing final deliverables as well. Capstones that start in the junior year, though rare, do position students to seek publication independently. Outstanding capstone students have produced articles for newspapers or magazines, for instance. And each year, a few capstone students nationally self-publish a book.

Some programs archive capstone work for off-campus or future audiences. Archiving is different from publishing. Given the relatively ephemeral nature of many forms of publication, it is worth considering the goals of collective documentation taken on by the program, so that the appropriate medium may be chosen. Digital and print media bring different affordances. In his now-classic work on thoughtful technology use, *The Distraction Addiction*, Alex Soojung-Kim Pang explains why print media continue to survive and thrive in our digital era. Print has affordances—portability and stability are two he names—that make it preferred over phones and computers for some functions.[2] Consider a program that aspires to archive all its student capstone essays. What is gained by creating a searchable digital archive as the school's own internal student database? What is gained by displaying each essay in an attractive printed and bound form? Which archive, digital or physical, is likely to serve the school's goals more effectively? Answering such questions may require the expertise of the school librarian. Taking the long view of the archivist will also push capstone teachers to think carefully about the value of capstone deliverables beyond the program context.

Given the ritual function of capstone and the intensity of high school graduation as a ritual in American culture broadly, the future role of the capstone artifact as memento or memory object has to be considered as well. A copy of the attractively printed and bound capstone essay might rest in a box in the closet along with the high school diploma, sports trophies, and concert programs, not to be examined for many years. When the box is opened again, the value of the essay is not academic; rather it serves as a more elaborate documentation of an earlier version of the self. Here, the stability of print comes into play: there is no risk that the former student won't have the software needed to revisit their long-ago efforts. This sentimentality can also be valued in capstone.

Notes to Chapter 3.6

Note 1, page 133: **capstones are rituals**—We are indebted to Tamisha Williams and Sheryl Chard for our understanding of school events as rituals. Our material is adapted from their workshops at the Sofia Center for Professional Development, where Sheryl Chard is founding director. Readers interested in thinking about school through this lens might start with Peter McLaren's *Schooling as a Ritual Performance: Toward a Political Economy of Symbols and Gestures* (Lanham, Maryland: Rowman & Littlefield, 1999).

Note 2, page 139: **Print has affordances**—See pages 150 to 154 in Alex Soojung-Kim Pang, *The Distraction Addiction* (New York: Little, Brown, 2013).

PART 4:
HOW? SUPPORTING STUDENTS

CHAPTER 4.1
THE QUESTION

Nothing more powerful. Nothing more mysterious. Nothing more crucial than the question.

Every capstone starts with a question. More than a starting point, the capstone question remains open and alive, guiding the project right through to its conclusion. Teaching students first to ask questions, and then to evaluate and sort their questions, and then to focus the project through the lens of a single guiding question, and above all to sustain that question over time—that is core work of every capstone program. Good capstone students understand themselves first and foremost as people asking questions, and only secondarily as people answering them. In fact, in a year-long program, teachers might expect students to revisit and reopen their question every few weeks, right up to a month or so before the final deliverables are due. Many strong projects may even conclude with questions unanswered; adult audiences respect a high school senior with the wisdom to share what he knows he doesn't know after a year of good work.

Questioning is a skill, and this chapter will include practical resources for teaching that skill. But questioning is also a way of being in the world: open, ready to engage authentically with others, committed to the long game. Joseph Campbell once joked that some of us participate in organized religion as a kind of inoculation against religious experience[1]—in other words, so we don't have to think about it the rest of the time. Likewise, schooling at its worst might be a kind of inoculation against questioning, with teachers sadly standing in as the ones who say "Have no fear, the answers are right here"—no need to tolerate any uncertainty. In setting itself against quick and easy answers, capstone also sets itself against weak ideas of what a school should be.

Feeling interest

The question articulates the student's interest. Very understandably, high school students don't yet know what interests them and what does not—the project design phase of a research project is even more important with young researchers than it is with professionals. Interest can be understood psychologically. In an anecdote retold by Adam Phillips, a country clergyman asks D.W. Winnicott, at that time a rising figure in British psychoanalysis, how he can tell whether a parishioner needs professional medical care, or whether his own listening ear will suffice. Winnicott reportedly replies that the clergyman should ask himself if he is *interested* in the parishioner, or whether he is bored by their conversation. If there is interest, then all will be well. If, however, the clergyman is bored, that is a sign that something may be terribly wrong.[2]

Winnicott's insight could of course be reapplied as advice for teachers, rather than clergy. It comes to mind when a student tries to propose a pre-existing opinion as the basis for a capstone project. The opinion is sometimes not even the student's own, but rather belongs to a parent or other authority figure. (Often, though not always, the opinion is political.) The student may start "I want to write about how X is ruining Y." There is no question, and we are already bored! Such projects rarely go well. The passions that motivate any of us to reiterate long-held opinions may be strong, but they are not of a sort that lead to learning. A student with a genuine question, on the other hand, will salvage something from the project, no matter how awkwardly framed the question may be, no matter how imperfect the work that follows. A student who wants to know something she does not already know is in a healthy space for working and learning. In our experience, her curiosity is unfailingly infectious: if she is interested in her question, then so are we! Like Winnicott's country clergyman, teachers don't need a medical degree to tell if a budding project is likely to thrive.

In order to build up student stamina to tolerate uncertainty about themselves and the world—to sustain questioning—it is helpful to acknowledge that research and action projects have an emotional trajectory. The psychology of research has been well studied, and the work of Carol Kuhlthau, for example, may be of interest to capstone teachers.[3] For students, however, simply validating that the feelings they have about their projects are normal feelings—signs of health and growth—may be more than enough. High school seniors will rise to meet adult standards, but they also love a little psychological regression. Eric Carle's *Mixed-Up Chameleon* can be repurposed in a capstone class to show students how it feels to be trying on different ideas through a rigorous project design phase. If I don't know whether I am doing the flamingo thesis or the giraffe thesis or the fox thesis, I am just going to feel *weird*, and there is nothing wrong with that. In fact, some of the uncomfortable feelings often taken by students as a sign that something is wrong are actually indicators that something is very right. The capstone teacher's role includes providing the support that enables inexperienced researchers to stay present for the process.

Interest, as explained here, is the psychological term that names what happens when something *in me* encounters something *in the world*. Discovering an interest is a profound experience for a young person. In capstone, in order for a question to guide a project over time, it must genuinely be a question for that student. In other words, that unique student must truly not know, and truly want to know, the answer.

Learning questioning

Many resources exist to help students and teachers understand and work with questions. Though the ultimate goal is a single question that will guide the capstone project, learning to work with questions has great intrinsic value as well. We value what we schedule, and students who are accustomed to think of school as a place of answers may need a concrete demonstration of the value of questions to capstone. In a capstone course, an entire unit on questions would not be out of place, teaching the practice by example and not only through protocols. Rainer Maria Rilke's concept of living the question, from *Letters to a Young Poet*, validates the emotional experience of uncertainty that is the researcher's lot. *The Souls of Black Folk* by W.E.B. Du Bois shows how a framing question can reveal the social positions of those who question and those who are challenged to answer, to powerful effect. The essay "The Question Concerning Technology" by Martin Heidegger can be read successfully by motivated high school seniors and demonstrates how questioning can form the structure of the investigation itself, rather than being only a preliminary step.[4]

Whether or not there is time to study questioning more deeply, capstone students will need to be introduced to a few strategies and a few taxonomies in order to be able to work with their questions at a basic level.

First, **question storming** follows the rules of brainstorming to dislodge resistance and quickly generate a lot of material to work with. As in any other brainstorming activity, students will simply write down all the questions that occur to them, avoiding both judgment and censorship. The Question Formulation Technique (QFT) developed by Dan Rothstein and Luz Santana incorporates question storming as its first step and is a great way to help students working in groups to build up their questioning "muscles." Rothstein and Santana describe their QFT as "a shortcut, not a detour": in other words, it is a tool that helps students and programs further their own ends. The QFT does further the ends of capstone, and other question storming techniques are also helpful. Simply having students individually write down as many capstone questions as they can in a timed window gets things going. Prompting them further to ask questions not only about their topic but also about their process can help them stay focused on the all-important interest factor. Make sure to archive this early work generating questions, as returning to it later in the process can be very helpful.

As Rothstein and Santana emphasize, inviting students to ask the questions, instead of preserving questioning as a right of teachers, shifts the center of power. Such empowerment of learners is at the heart of capstone work. Because it may feel unfamiliar to students, it is important to explicitly teach the question-generation phase and to validate that it is difficult but valuable work, well worth the time invested. Materials related to the QFT can be accessed through the book *Make Just One Change: Teach Students to Ask Their Own Questions* or through the website of the Right Question Institute.[5]

> Confirmation bias is the nemesis of all researchers.

Types of questions

All research projects involve many types of questions. Understanding that different types of questions lead work in different ways further empowers students. Once students have generated a body of questions, teaching a few taxonomies can help them to gain facility as questioners, sort and evaluate their questions, and work toward the goal of developing the one question that will ultimately anchor the project. The QFT distinction between "**open-ended**" and "**close-ended**" questions is a good place to start. As the QFT illustrates, the goal is not to prioritize one type over the other, but rather to recognize their different values in different contexts. But a sustained high school capstone project will require other ways of thinking about questions as well.

Students are likely to be familiar with the concept of "**essential questions**." This term is used differently by different educators. In particular, essential questions may play a different role in a teacher-planned unit than they do in a student-generated capstone project. Among the many resources on essential questions, *Essential Questions* by Jay McTighe and Grant Wiggins stands out.[6] Meanwhile, the useful *Dive Into Inquiry* by Trevor MacKenzie offers question stems that can help students brainstorm.[7] Essential questions capture our deepest motivations in an inquiry. As important as they are, essential questions are so deep and so broad that they can never be answered definitively. In particular, answers to essential questions are personal: it will be difficult for a student to argue that her answer to "What is the meaning of life?" has validity for her audience as well. In a capstone program that emphasizes experience and reflection, but does not expect an academic deliverable like a research essay or academic presentation, a well-honed essential question can serve as the guide. However, if the capstone program expects academic writing at a level appropriate for high school seniors, they will also need a research question.

A **research question** is a carefully crafted and specific question that guides an academic project in any discipline. We define a successful research question as having four qualities:

- First, a research question is **answerable**. Questions that require predicting the future or commenting on what was going on in someone's mind cannot be answered. Questions that require expertise that the student does not have (like understanding of differential equations or fluency in a new language), or for any other reason can't be answered by them within the time they have, also don't count as answerable.

- Second, a research question is **arguable**. If a question can be answered simply by looking up facts in textbooks or reference works, it won't work as the basis for a capstone, no matter how complex the answer might be, and no matter how hard the student had to work to comprehend it. Capstones are more than just independent study of what others already know.

- Third, a research question is **interesting** to the researcher. As discussed above, young researchers need a lot of support discovering what is and is not of interest to them.

- Fourth, a research question is **authentic**. If the researcher believes that she already knows the answer, the question will not work to guide the capstone project.

No one should discuss research questions without mentioning the irascible and indispensable William Badke, whose classic *Research Strategies* is as valuable for high school students as it is for Badke's intended college audience. Badke devotes an entire appendix to research questions. With brutal clarity, he divides his examples into the good, the bad, and the ugly. The good research question, for Badke, "leads to a problem-solving exercise in which information is a tool, not an end in itself."[8] The bad and the ugly lead to different forms of mere reportage. Given how difficult it can be to wean students off the idea that research consists merely in collecting and reporting on information, Badke's blunt style may help teachers convince students to help themselves by investing work at the question development stage.

It is very rare for a research question with all of these qualities listed above to fully capture the underlying motivations behind a student capstone, which should be a personal journey as well as a research or action project. Typically, good research questions feel dry to students who are on fire to change the world with their work. Reassuring students that their essential questions remain very much a part of the project can help them feel invested, even if the research question itself winds up looking disappointing to adolescent eyes. The crucial difference is that the researcher has a chance of bringing the research question to bay, while the essential questions will return to the wild at the end of the project. Experiencing the humbleness of the individual contribution to human knowledge is also part of the growing-up journey that happens in capstone.

Classifying questions using any of the above taxonomies can be difficult. Writing a good research question in particular is *extremely* difficult. Though the tasks of the project design phase (including question storming, classifying questions, and developing the one question that will guide the capstone) are all important, it is likewise important not to fetishize the taxonomies. Capstones are a culmination of the student's prior course of study, but they also challenge and extend the student's existing skill set. A student who never masters the difference between essential questions and research questions may nonetheless have a great project. At some point, the teacher may need to make a judgment call that the student's question is good enough to go on with. We've seen beautifully crafted research questions fail to deliver. Meanwhile questions that don't technically meet our criteria have nonetheless done the job of anchoring extraordinary projects.

Four qualities of a capstone research question

- Answerable
- Arguable
- Interesting
- Authentic

An open question

A good-enough question, held open over time, will also serve as a guard against the nemesis of all researchers, **confirmation bias**. Confirmation bias is the tendency to notice only data that supports a pre-existing hypothesis. Whether I am scanning a page or taking observation notes in the field, my eye picks up what I hope to find, and passes over what I am not prepared to see. In today's world of polarized and targeted media, students may need help even understanding the concept of reading and looking with an open mind. But the dangers of confirmation bias pre-date our current media environment, and threaten professional researchers as they do novices.

In text-based research, students need to understand that they are never reading all of what has been written on a topic, but only a selection, and a selection that has been formed in response to actions they have taken. Requiring that students seek out counter-arguments is one way to keep them in a questioning frame of mind. Likewise, in field-based or laboratory research, scientific methods for gathering and considering all the data produced under predetermined conditions help hold open the question. Action projects will turn out to demand humility even more than research. Though resource limitations may prevent students from meeting professional standards that allow research to be considered valid in a particular discipline, staying focused on questions rather than answers can at least prevent them from forming bad habits that will have to be unlearned later on, or from doing harm when what they intend is service— surely the very least we owe our students!

In Part 4 of this book, we propose and discuss capstone pedagogy that engages students in "real" work—that is, work that aspires to have validity beyond the walls of the school that high school seniors are preparing to leave. But it is important to remember that just sending students off campus does not guarantee "real" engagement, since mindset matters as much as environment to learning—the classroom is as real a place as any. What is real education today? If schooling at its worst consists in a fake environment in which students are rewarded for performing tasks divorced from real-world application ("doing school"), schooling at its best must tenaciously ask the question.

Notes to Chapter 4.1

Note 1, page 143: **inoculation against religious experience**—In an interview with Bill Moyer, Campbell attributes the sentence "Religion is a defense against a religious experience" to Carl Jung. The exchange was edited out of the book version of this interview series, but is accessible in the original transcript. Joseph Campbell, "Ep. 6: Joseph Campbell and the Power of Myth—'Masks of Eternity.'" BillMoyers.com, June 26, 1988.

Note 2, page 144: **an anecdote retold by Adam Phillips**—See Adam Phillips, "On Interest," *London Review of Books* 18, no. 12 (20 June 1996).

Note 3, page 144: **psychology of research**—An introduction to Kuhlthau's influential Information Search Process (ISP) model can be found on her website: www.bit.ly/3AIYyIU.

Note 4, page 145: **teaching the practice by example**—Rilke advises his correspondent "to be patient toward all that is unsolved in your heart and to try to love the questions themselves like locked rooms." The passage continues, "And the point is to live everything. Live the questions now." See page 35 in Rainer Maria Rilke, *Letters to a Young Poet* (New York: Norton, 1993).

> Du Bois opens up his relation with his reader through the famous question "How does it feel to be a problem?" The book begins with the statement that "Between me and the other world there is ever an unasked question...." See page 1 in W.E.B. Du Bois, *The Souls of Black Folk* (Mineola, NY: Dover Thrift, 2016).

> From the opening of Heidegger's essay: "Questioning builds a way ... The way is a way of thinking." See page 3 in Martin Heidegger, *The Question Concerning Technology and Other Essays* (New York: Harper Torchbooks, 1977).

Note 5, page 146: *Make Just One Change*—See Dan Rothstein and Luz Santana, *Make Just One Change: Teach Students to Ask Their Own Questions* (Cambridge, MA: Harvard Education Press, 2011). www.rightquestion.org

Note 6, page 146: *Essential Questions*—The book chapter "What Makes a Question Essential?" is posted on the ASCD website: www.bit.ly/3qXSXtE. Or see Grant Wiggins and Jay McTighe, *Essential Questions: Opening Doors to Student Understanding* (Alexandria, VA: ASCD, 2013).

Note 7, page 147: **question stems**—See page 78 in Trevor MacKenzie, *Dive Into Inquiry: Amplify Learning and Empower Student Voice* (Irvine, EdTechTeam, 2016).

Note 8, page 148: **"information is a tool, not an end in itself"**—See page 226 in William Badke, *Research Strategies: Finding Your Way Through the Information Fog* (Bloomington: iUniverse, 2011).

CHAPTER 4.2
PROJECT DESIGN

Time and attention invested in the project design phase of a capstone pay off. It is not unusual for a full quarter of the allotted time to be devoted to development and planning of the capstone project. In addition to time, scaffolding in the form of explicit tasks with clear parameters is helpful to inexperienced capstone students. Benefit comes from even a simple assignment like asking students to spend ten minutes a day either reading (wide and shallow at this phase) or talking to people about their ideas. In general, at the design phase, it is better to rush madly off in the wrong direction than to sit and do nothing. There is no "wasted work."

In this chapter, we offer a starting point for supporting students as they choose a **topic**, understand their own **positionality**, and plan ahead for task and time management through the busyness of senior year by writing a working **outline** or **map** and **timeline**. We also offer suggestions for assigning formal project **prospectuses** or **proposals**.

What counts as academic work?

The project development stage of a capstone can be understood as a complex negotiation between teacher and student about what constitutes academic work. Capstones are supposed to be personally meaningful; capstone students typically enjoy a degree of autonomy unprecedented in their previous academic careers. At the same time, capstones count as schoolwork. Often they are assessed using traditional grades and grading criteria. Even when they are not assessed with formal grades, the projects represent the school, and the school rightly exercises some control over what is and is not allowed, just as it controls what is and what is not required. To sum up, we might say that a capstone topic must have two qualities: it must be deeply interesting to the student, and it must be workable within the structures of a program. The first, only the student knows. The second, only the teacher knows. As student and teacher negotiate the project design, they are negotiating what counts as "schoolwork"—that is, what shows up as having value at school. Thus as we work through the project design phase, we are not just defining the student's topic—we are together redefining what school is.

Sometimes it is the student who pushes the envelope, challenging her teachers to grow. Just as often, teachers may need to push students with limited ideas, or simply incorrect ideas about what counts as academic work. "No book reports" was a motto in one program, but it can be difficult to explain to students that what historians or chemists *do* is not write textbook chapters about history or chemistry, much less book reports. We advocate for exposing students to peer-reviewed articles early in the process, not because these are the best way to get an overview of a topic (they are not!) but because they can be models for the type of work we expect to see from high school seniors: qualified claims about tightly focused topics, with an emphasis on analysis, not on reporting of facts.

In our view, what counts as "academic" is defined by the methods of approach, not the topic itself. In other words, almost any object or phenomenon can work as a capstone topic. What determines academic value is the way the topic is handled. (More on research methods in the next chapter.) In fact, original topics almost always lead to better projects than topics that are already familiar to the teacher. At the project design phase, it is crucial that the teacher model openness. One of the very best capstone projects we ever saw was on the topic of lawns in Albuquerque, New Mexico. It turns out that some homeowners in Albuquerque maintain green lawns at great expense in water and labor, while others xeriscape the dry earth. Both the impulse to create a little piece of New England in New Mexico and the counter-impulse to display to the neighbors that this house has a local aesthetic have fascinating histories. But when you raise the topic of "lawns in New Mexico," most students just laugh. It is very fortunate that the teacher supervising that long-ago student knew better than to dismiss an idea because it sounded weird. In fact, the "weird factor" can be a key ingredient in a superb capstone.

Furthermore, in our experience, it is often what seem to teachers like the weirdest topic choices of an emerging generation that lead to the most fascinating and valuable work. We often point out that research that ten years ago required access to an R1 research institution can now be done by a well-supported 17-year-old in her garage—or on her laptop. One consequence of that is that we are finding out what 17-year-olds do with that power. What students—even very young students—are doing can no longer be separated tidily from the work of adults. That is one of the engines behind the K–16 movement, with which high school capstones have an obvious alignment.[1] It also presents huge challenges and huge opportunities for capstone programs.

Sometimes a student will show up to the capstone program with a fabulous and ready-made topic. Just as often, a student shows up with something more suitable for an entry in Wikipedia than a capstone. (Just to be clear, we love Wikipedia, but recognize that broad overviews are best written by those with decades of experience, and least of all by newcomers to a field.) Strategies for making broad topics workable include the following:

- **Localizing:** "The 1960s" is a terrible topic, but "the 1960s in Billings, Montana" has promise.

- **Personalizing:** "Why has my country been at war throughout my whole lifetime?" is not yet a research question, but it is a better start than "US Foreign Policy since 2000."

- Previously under-analyzed **primary sources**: a high school student is unlikely to do anything new with *Mein Kampf*, but can contribute by analyzing neo-Nazi rhetoric posted in a Reddit thread during a specific time frame.

- Any **field research**: Rather than writing on graffiti in general, or even on famous examples of graffiti, the student is better off photographing local examples and analyzing those. Rather than analyzing K-pop lyrics, she is better off interviewing a few serious fans.

- Any **embodied or hands-on** experience: Though there might seem to be nothing new in spending Saturday mornings volunteering at a local food bank or taking a solo backpacking trip, in practice, the lived experience of service projects or internships—and even of simple site visits—positions students to think in new ways about topics that would be inauspicious were they to be pursued only in the library. Sometimes fresh eyes bring more to a project than the sophistication of an older generation.

Who decides what counts as academic work? Who decides what school is? Those questions should be answered differently in different contexts. **In capstone at least, we advocate for a joint negotiation that is carried out most visibly through the project design phase.** We advocate for this not only in the service of students, who deserve meaningful capstone learning experiences, but also in the service of the best academic work.

Ways to make broad topics capstone ready

- Localizing
- Personalizing
- Primary sources
- Field research
- Hands-on

Relevant history

Of course, teaching has always been a negotiation, as students who may not agree with their teachers prepare to make their own contributions. An old rhyme about Benjamin Jowett simultaneously captures and mocks the idea that the teacher alone decides what counts as school. Jowett was one of the foremost classicists and also one of the most famous teachers of 19th-century Britain, eventually rising to the position of master of Balliol College at Oxford.

Here I stand, my name is Jowett,

If there's knowledge, then I know it;

I am the master of this college,

What I know not is not knowledge.

Among the things Jowett chose not to know, that is not to acknowledge, was the acceptance of sexual love between men in the elite ancient Greek culture written about by Plato and his contemporaries. In his landmark translation of Plato as in his teaching, Jowett sought to downplay this example of a culture that was not heteronormative. Jowett's suppression of what might have been a powerfully liberating knowledge for men in Victorian Britain was part of the complex legacy left to his students, among them Walter Pater and John Addington Symonds, who looked to the Greeks to understand their own lived and acknowledged desires. Jowett was so influential that more than a century after his death, English-speaking students still often first encounter Plato in his translation. Meanwhile, the lives of men who loved other men in Jowett's 19th-century cultural milieu still rarely show up in the curriculum, even if Walt Whitman or Oscar Wilde are on the syllabus. The system in which Jowett was able to "own" Plato so completely forbade certain kinds of questions and contributed to the real suffering of real men like Pater and Wilde. And it is simultaneously true that Jowett was a powerful force for making Plato accessible not only to his own students but also to all English speakers who have not studied Greek.[2]

The version of the Balliol rhyme about Jowett quoted above makes an appearance in *Loose Canons* by Henry Louis Gates. We also owe to Gates a more precise formulation of the question "How does something get to count as knowledge?"[3] Gates asks this question in the context of a discussion of the desperate lack of Black scholars in PhD programs and professorships. What counts as knowledge is related in complex ways to who is represented in the curriculum and among the teaching faculty. At the high school level, the stakes are only higher. Despite research showing that K–12 students learn more from teachers who look like them, the national teaching force remains overwhelmingly White. While White students see themselves in the faculty, Black students and students of color more generally usually do not have the same advantage.[4] Additionally, the limited diversity in the life experiences brought to the classroom by the teaching pool does not help a school make the best possible curricular choices. In this context, empowering students to identify the topics of study meaningful to them becomes an important counterbalance in a school's overall curriculum and pedagogy. Even better, it makes at least one piece of the process visible to students and teachers alike, so that they can work on it together, in partnership rather than competition.

What counts as "academic" is defined by the method of approach, not the topic.

Shifting power, not people

Who counts? Turning over the power to decide what will be studied implies a changed understanding of the power of teachers. In schools today we sometimes see teachers feeling threatened by the rapidly declining value of content knowledge. Teachers who identify themselves with a certain body of facts fear that once those facts are dethroned or decentered, they also will lose their place at school. And it is true that teaching strategies that formerly brought career success may no longer guarantee employment into the future. But teaching itself is not threatened by the shift in what counts as academic work. On the contrary, the role of teacher seems to us more powerful and important than ever.

We noted above that well-supported 17-year-olds can now do work that previously would only have been undertaken by graduate students at elite universities. The crucial point there is the support. No matter how quick they are to learn, and no matter how robust their resources are, teens need adult support to carry out sustained projects. This support encompasses project management, dealing with the messy emotions of high-stakes work, help with the context for specific topic areas, etc. Unlike the work of content delivery, this is work that cannot be replaced with a technological substitute. It can only be provided by a human teacher in relationship with the capstone student.

Objectivity and method

A capstone colleague of ours, a brilliant physics instructor, has a practice in which students can ask him, anonymously, any questions they have about physics, his class, or anything in the universe. Louis reads each question aloud and responds for the whole class. On one occasion, the anonymous question "Will I find love?" sparked a spontaneous homily on being yourself and keeping faith. One hallmark of Louis's practice is that he takes questions meant as jokes and responds to them with a perfect and beautiful sincerity.

One day, Louis read the question "What is the likelihood that *all* scientific theories will be disproved?" Students in the back exchanged glances, and it was clear to the adult observer that the question was a humorous teenage attempt to undermine authority. Maybe even to waste some time. Louis dropped the question on his desk and looked out at his class. "That one's easy!" he said. "One hundred percent!"[5] What followed was a Popperian explanation of the scientific method. Scientists seek not to find "truth," or even "facts," but to model nature so well that they can make predictions likely to be confirmed. Science proceeds forward by attempts to *disprove* hypotheses, not to prove them. What survives repeated attempts can be called science. But only for now. In contrast to dogmatic claims about "what science says," this deeper understanding productively acknowledges the provisional nature of human knowledge.

Few misunderstandings cause as much damage as misunderstandings of objectivity. Student researchers who think that they have made themselves "objective" by an act of will are accordingly less open-minded. Meanwhile, they are misunderstanding not only their own research but also the research process itself. Objectivity is of course to be valued highly. We imperfect humans achieve some valuable measure of objectivity through method. We achieve it over time, and through the joint efforts of many. Objectivity is not achieved, as students sometimes think, by willpower: I cannot just decide to be objective. The scientific method, though often misrepresented, is one excellent example, but every academic discipline has its methods designed to increase the likelihood that the work of a researcher will be of value for more people, in more situations, and over longer periods of time.

In working with capstone students, we tend to avoid the term "objective." Instead, we ask students to think of themselves as making claims, which—if made and supported well—deserve the attention of their audience. We talk about "supporting claims" rather than "proving" anything. Claims are relational and require capstone students to think about their audiences, which has the added benefit of leading to better writing. We ask them to think about what strategies increase the likelihood that their work will be of lasting value to others as well as to themselves. And, as detailed above, we praise efforts to maintain a questioning stance deep into the project process. Capstone education includes training in method, and especially training in that highest of academic values, an awareness of the limitations of one's own knowledge.

> Few misunderstandings cause as much damage
> as misunderstandings of objectivity.

The researcher in the research

It is precisely because we are asking capstone students to produce work that is of value to others that we build in the expectation that they investigate themselves at the same time as they investigate their topics. Inquiry is a stance that entails self-awareness every bit as much as it does curiosity about the larger world. Self-reflection adds to the value of a project, rather than being a distraction.

For example, if a White male high schooler from an affluent family wants to write on hip-hop, he needs to understand the fact that he belongs to the largest consumer group to purchase that music, but not to the group whose historical experience produced the art form. He needs to understand the nature of his attraction. Is it a reaching after authenticity? A desire to get outside his bubble? Is internalized misogyny involved? A naive and false understanding of objectivity might suggest to that student that he should keep himself out of his essay. But that approach may actually increase the likelihood that his work will be unconsciously shaped by unexamined bias. Examining the interest, on the other hand, brings a positive power to the project. Tyler was a capstone student who discovered that what was problematic in his own love of hip-hop was also the raw material for a great project. Originally intending to center his project on an analysis of song lyrics, Tyler wound up shifting his attention over to understanding the fascination of White audiences for works by artists of color. He read Edward Said's *Orientalism* and Toni Morrison's *Playing in the Dark*. He didn't write the capstone essay he'd planned—he wrote a better one.

It is equally powerful to surface a positive overlap between the identity of the capstone researcher and an identity group being studied. Angelica's family has been living in central New Mexico since the days when the border between the United States and Mexico was north of Albuquerque, not south of it. Her capstone project used primary sources to connect the history of her family to the as-yet incompletely told history of this region. When Angelica says "our history has not yet been written, that is, written from our perspective," the pronoun rings. Just as in the example above, the interest cannot be taken for granted. Belonging to a particular family does not automatically confer the authority of a good research project; that still has to be earned. Both "insider" and "outsider" positions bring value to a project, as long as they are examined and made explicit. Both Tyler and Angelica started from excellent positions, and both had to work hard to convert those positions into valid academic perspectives.

Researchers use the term "**positionality**" to convey the research concept that *where I stand* shapes *what I can see*. In some fields, it is increasingly common for professional researchers to make their positionalities explicit when they publish research results. In other fields, this is not a norm. In our experience, the capstone experience is enhanced when *all* students write positionalities, regardless of the field they are working in, though many will not include a written positionality among their final deliverables. As discussed above, capstone is also a personal journey, and it is important to understand where one is starting from.

As with the skill of asking questions, the skill of identifying and deploying one's relevant positionality needs to be taught explicitly. If there is time for a full unit, students can read examples. One student favorite is "Peeling Potatoes," an essay by Greg Sarris which also serves as the prologue to Sarris's book *Keeping Slug Woman Alive: A Holistic Approach to American Indian Texts*. Sarris is an exceptional writer, and this essay is both readable for students and highly complex. Sarris's clarity about the role his own identity plays in his work helps students who need an obvious model, and they also respond positively to Sarris's honesty. (Later in the year, students can return to "Peeling Potatoes" for help thinking about their relationship to their audiences, as well as their research topics.) The preface to *The Scholar Denied: W.E.B. Du Bois and the Birth of Modern Sociology* by Aldon D. Morris similarly does a fine job making explicit how researcher positionalities shape their research and ultimately the construction of whole fields of study. (Incidentally, it can also support an introduction to the history of the social sciences for capstone students who may want to do sociological fieldwork.) A famous early positionality is in the preface to *Tell Them Who I Am: The Lives of Homeless Women* by Elliot Liebow. Liebow, a Harvard professor at the time, directly addresses the challenges that arise when a researcher occupies a position of much greater power than his research subjects. Like the examples above, Liebow is readable and interesting for high school students.[6]

Reading examples of positionalities is more effective at convincing students of their value than hearing theoretical arguments about objectivity. However, if time is short, students could start with a definition. Anthropologists Frances Maher and Mary Kay Tetreault offer one often-quoted definition of positionality:

> By positionality we mean … that gender, race, class and other aspects of our identities are markers of relational positions rather than essential qualities. Knowledge is valid when it includes an acknowledgment of the knower's specific position in any context, because changing contextual and relational factors are crucial for defining identities and our knowledge in any given situation.[7]

Once they have a definition, students will need help determining which identities might be relevant to their particular projects. Activities like the social identity wheel (widely available online), can spur thinking.

Students might also begin the process of drafting positionality statements by responding to a few questions:

- Which major identity categories (gender, race, class, etc.) might be relevant for your topic? How do you identify in each of these categories? How do the majority of your research subjects identify? In what ways do your identities make you like or unlike the group you plan to study? (Note that for high school researchers, age is almost always a relevant identity category!)

- What personal experiences have you had related to your topic? What personal beliefs do you hold related to your topic? Given those experiences and/or beliefs, what expectations do you have about how your research may unfold?

- How do you define research? What methods will you be using to conduct your research? Why have you chosen those methods? How will those methods influence what you do or don't see during the research process?

Depending on the classroom context, students may resist thinking about themselves as belonging to identity groups in ways that shape their thinking. Examples help. Modeling helps. Questioning helps. And it helps to reemphasize— and reemphasize and reemphasize—that **if the self-awareness is in place,** *every* **positionality is an asset to the research**.

Working outlines, maps, and timelines

Though the project plan does and should evolve as the project gets underway, students don't know how to start without a plan. If the capstone program is its own class and has a handbook or syllabus and scaffolded assignments, most of the planning may be done in advance by teachers. In that case, it is still worthwhile to have students work through the program expectations up front, and especially to transfer program deadlines into their personal assignment calendars. If the program has the capacity, much greater learning can be attained by having students in effect write their own scaffold, building out from a smaller number of teacher-determined program deadlines. For the sake of accountability, post the individual plan in a form accessible to all parties, including all on- and off-campus teachers and advisors as well as the student.

For a research capstone, William Badke recommends starting with a simple "preliminary outline" based on the research question.[8] This working outline simply lists the major categories of evidence that will be needed in order to answer the question. In lieu of a more elaborate outline, students who expect to write a research essay might draw a map of the final product on a template on which squares represent planned pages. This form of graphic organizer will bring home to students that they won't want to devote, for example, 15 pages of a 25-page essay to background, and thus help keep research efforts in balance.

An action capstone will likewise need a plan that includes acquiring working knowledge, contacting the site, the internship or service learning itself, and summative reflection. With off-campus partners, helping students build in lag time for communication and unforeseen conflicts on the partner's end is especially important.

Prospectuses and proposals

A prospectus is a formal piece of writing outlining a planned project. At the professional level, researchers typically prepare a prospectus to convince an institutional audience that they are qualified, in terms of both skills and knowledge, to complete the outlined project, so that the institution will want to invest time and money in them. In addition to being useful if the capstone program has a project approval process, a prospectus can serve as a reference point as the capstone student seeks input from teachers and off-campus professionals. A prospectus for a capstone centered on research might include some or all of the following elements:

- Topic
- Positionality
- Essential questions
- Research question

- Working knowledge of topic
- Research ideas
- Challenges posed by the project

An internship or service learning capstone might require a prospectus with some of the same information:

- Site and contact information
- Planned action on site
- Positionality
- Essential questions
- Working knowledge of issues, including systems understanding
- Challenges posed by the project
- Plans for reflection and sharing, if not specified by the program

Prospectuses are notoriously difficult to write, since they describe something that does not yet exist, but they have great value for getting students thinking concretely and also for helping them get practical feedback.

Shorter proposal formats can also work well, with the simplest of all consisting solely of the research question.

Sample panel proposal guidelines

These guidelines are for students in an inquiry program with a substantial action element. Students bring copies of their proposals to a panel review fair; panel meetings are friendly and supportive. Proposals are based on extensive initial work, including initial research.

Research proposal with initial list of works consulted

This concise proposal will be reviewed by a panel of faculty and staff. Because panel members will not know about any of the work you have done up to this point, your proposal must be clear, precise, and explicit.

The panel will use the following criteria when they assess your proposal:

- **The project has not already been done by others.** This does not just mean other students. If any human being ever has done the exact project described in your proposal, the panel will reject it.
- **The project reflects the unique positionality of the student researcher.** Clever project design capitalizes on your unique strengths and resources.

YOUR PROPOSAL:

1. ESSENTIAL QUESTIONS (Maximum five questions.)

These show why you care.

2. RESEARCH QUESTION (One question.)

Remember that this question should be answerable, arguable, interesting, and authentic. If you already think you know the answer, it's a bad question.

3. WHAT MAKES THIS PROJECT UNIQUE? (Answer in a maximum of five sentences.)

Among the many possibilities:

- a personal angle (a project that includes self-reflection, experiential knowledge, or personal narrative)
- a local angle ("...in Albuquerque" / "...at Bosque")
- a primary source not previously exhausted by other studies (my grandmother's journal / soap advertisements from the 1890s)
- smart fieldwork (photographing graffiti at ACME yards / interviewing car enthusiasts at Friday night meet-ups at the Sonic on Montgomery / testing catalysts for hydrogen fuel cells)

4. INITIAL LIST OF WORKS CONSULTED

Game on: how do you know they are ready?

How will you know when the projects are developed enough and the students ready to get started? If your program is selective, the application process may have already required students to get a project approved. In other programs, a formal proposal or prospectus, or both, may be required. As a school's capstone program evolves, teachers will see which sorts of design elements tend to predict success, and will correspondingly coach future students to build in those elements early. In some programs, the proposal may be evaluated by the single teacher who will then serve as the advisor for that student. In other programs, the proposal may be an opportunity to involve more of the faculty in providing input, possibly through some kind of proposal fair or live panel review (see Chapter 3.4 for a discussion of how to organize these).

Selective programs need some early gates to make sure all students admitted are qualified to work at the expected level. Programs that are graduation requirements also need an opportunity to communicate early if a project is not on track. Even keeping those realities in mind, our experience suggests that some flexibility benefits both student and program. Capstone students are often doing many of the tasks required for the first time. Proposals and prospectuses that describe a project that has only been imagined, not yet tried, are notoriously difficult to write even for experienced researchers. For students, many small failures are inevitable. Even with a comfortable amount of time allotted to the project design phase, some students will reach kick-off time without a design that meets program expectations. We have found that a soft approach works best, since students unable to check some of the early boxes may nonetheless be carried forward once they get into the heart of the work. Likewise, if a student switches topics late in the process, we do not ask them to redo all of the preparatory work to the same level.

In other words, once we've all run up and down the field a few times, it is time to start the game.

Capstone story
Niko: fast and furious

Niko knew from day one what he wanted to do his capstone project on: the modification of Japanese import cars in imitation of the *Fast & Furious* movies.

Only Niko couldn't say that. His communications were on the order of "Well, I worked at Performance Upgrades this summer" and "I like to work on my car, you know." Performance Upgrades turned out to be an auto shop. As for the type of work Niko did on his car, I would not have understood if he had said more about this, since at the time I didn't even know the difference between a supercharger and a turbo. I was a naive audience.

Niko's early text-based research yielded nearly nothing. A few peer-reviewed articles discussed the unusual treatment of race and ethnicity in the movies, something Niko said was not interesting to him, though it turned out later to be quite relevant. There was a lot of popular press on the death of Paul Walker in a car crash. An ethnographic essay on American car culture proved more helpful, at least to me, if not to Niko. The essay explained that car culture is passed on in White American society from father to son, engaging them in weekend or evening work on American-made cars, which of necessity spend most of their time in the garage, while a more practical car is used for transport. This article, also rejected by Niko as irrelevant, opened the door of communication, as Niko explained to me that the kind of car culture he liked travels peer-to-peer through a younger generation who love the *Fast & Furious* movies, a cohort as inclusive of racial and ethnic identities as the movies themselves. Participants in this form of car culture don't have enough money to own a second car: they drive to work in the car that they are also working on. And the Japanese imports? Vastly cheaper than a vintage Mustang.

Once we were talking, we were really talking. As a result, Niko began writing on what would become an engaging, flowing essay that moves from analysis of scenes in the movies, to explanations of favorite modifications, and their effect on the performance or aesthetics of a car. Eventually, Niko was ready for his fieldwork, an ethnographic study of a car meet that takes place at a Sonic restaurant on Friday nights. His interviews are woven into the essay in a beautifully natural way. In short, this became one of the most original, enjoyable, and beautiful pieces of writing I have ever received.

Niko was a good student. The impossibility of explaining his project to me early on—due to my ignorance, not his own powers of articulation—nearly sent him back into some far less interesting, more "school-y" topic that he would have certainly accomplished competently. He especially wanted to quit when the text-based research turned up nothing—that seemed understandably to Niko to be a deal-breaker for an academic project. The article on White American car culture was rejected by him because it "said the opposite" of what Niko wanted to say.

The credit I take is for not letting him quit, even though I had absolutely no idea what he was talking about. At the time, I said to another teacher, "I can see in his eyes that he has a project." What I meant was that he was clearly struggling to explain an experience. He was not making up something he wished were there, he was trying to communicate something he understood deeply in his hands, if not in his words.

The article on White car culture was a turning point, but it was not the end. In draft after draft, I had to ask Niko for more explanation. Every term thrown about at Performance Upgrades, or in the movies, required three sentences of explanation for an audience like me who barely knows how an engine works. So struggle continued, even after we both knew we were on track.

I want to draw two conclusions from this story.

The first is that realms of student experience that seem to them to belong "outside school" may be the best places for original learning. What makes a topic "academic" is in the approach, not in the who-where-when of the activity itself.

The second is that my role as a capstone teacher demands that I go into the unknown with my students, not that I be out ahead. I have never known less about a topic chosen by a student than I did about car modification. Rather than being a problem, my ignorance was in fact an asset to the project, as it drew out of Niko original feats of writing. Meanwhile, there was a sense in which I believed in the project's "school-worthiness" more than Niko did. I was sure he had something, and in the end he did.

Notes to Chapter 4.2

Note 1, page 153: **the K–16 movement**—The term "K–16" is used by various programs interested in bridging gaps between teaching and learning in grades K–12 (where pedagogy may be superior) and in university classrooms (where curriculum may be more current). The University of California's California Subject Matter Project (CSMP) is one example.

Note 2, page 154: **a cultural milieu that was not heteronormative**—For an introduction, see Lesley Higgins, "Jowett and Pater: Trafficking in Platonic Wares," *Victorian Studies* 39, no. 1 (Autumn 1993): 43–72.

Note 3, page 155: **"How does something get to count as knowledge?"**—See page 109 in Henry Louis Gates, *Loose Canons: Notes on the Culture Wars* (New York: Oxford University Press, 1992).

Note 4, page 155: **K–12 students learn more from teachers who look like them**—(See also Note 4 to Chapter 2.3.) On the demographic data, see Bruce Douglas, et al., "The Impact of White Teachers on the Academic Achievement of Black Students: An Exploratory Qualitative Analysis," *Educational Foundations* 22, no. 1–2 (Winter-Spring 2008): 47–62.

Note 5, page 156: **One hundred percent!**—Thanks to Louis Scuderi for permission to share this anecdote, as well as for contributing to the understanding expressed in this section.

Note 6, page 158: **read examples**—See the following:

> Greg Sarris, "Peeling Potatoes" in *Keeping Slug Woman Alive: A Holistic Approach to American Indian Texts* (Berkeley, CA: University of California Press, 2015), 1–14.

> Aldon D. Morris, "Preface" in *The Scholar Denied: W.E.B. Du Bois and the Birth of Modern Sociology* (Oakland: University of California Press, 2015), ix - xxiii.

> Elliot Liebow, "Preface: A Soft Beginning" in *Tell Them Who I Am: The Lives of Homeless Women* (New York: Penguin, 1993), vii–xxi.

Note 7, page 159: **definition of positionality**—See page 118 in Frances A. Maher and Mary Kay Tetreault, "Constructing Meaningful Dialogue on Difference: Feminism and Postmodernism in Anthropology and the Academy," *Anthropological Quarterly* 66, no. 3 (1993): 118–126.

> Jocie Kopfman presented on teaching positionality at the 2019 Capstone Summer Summit in Boston. In addition to suggesting some of the resources

offered here, Kopfman's presentation initiated a national discussion about the benefits of addressing positionality explicitly at the high school level. For a comprehensive overview of positionality, we also recommend H. Richard Milner IV, "Race, Culture, and Researcher Positionality: Working Through Dangers Seen, Unseen, and Unforeseen," *Educational Researcher* 36, no. 7 (2007): 388–400. DOI: 10.3102/0013189X07309471

Note 8, page 160: **"preliminary outline"**—See page 37 in William Badke, *Research Strategies: Finding Your Way Through the Information Fog* (Bloomington: iUniverse, 2011).

CHAPTER 4.3
INQUIRY: TEXT-BASED RESEARCH

Research is not finding information. Research is not even synthesizing and presenting what has been learned by others before. Rather, **research is a human process in which information, meaningless on its own, acquires value through the work of the unique mind of the researcher.** Research means understanding a field of knowledge or other human context, distinguishing quality information within that context, selecting from and interpreting that information, and presenting it to a human audience in terms of its use or meaning, as determined by the researcher. Research means sharing a unique human perspective that has been informed by a deep engagement with what other humans have learned before.

Though our definition of "research" would be unsurprising to a professional, the same word is sometimes used in K–12 settings for very different activities. The internet has made it possible for teachers to take segments of class that once might have been devoted to lecture and replace them with segments in which students gather information independently. If content delivery is the only goal, there may be no meaningful difference between the lecture and the online work. Perhaps the student working online risks acquiring information of a lower quality than might have been selected by the teacher for their lecture. Perhaps this risk is offset by the possibility opened up for student choice, since each student may study a different topic. But—developmentally appropriate as they may be for concrete thinkers at the elementary level—activities in which the gathering of information is the only goal do not constitute research in a capstone sense. As they have outgrown concrete thinking, students will have outgrown such activities by the high school years.

High school senior-year capstone programs exist in a border zone. Developmentally, seniors are more or less capable of doing work that can also be considered "college level"—and eager for greater challenge and responsibility. A high school has different resources than a college or university, but given today's open digital information landscape, there is no longer a compelling argument for holding seniors back based on their school setting. One implication is that capstone projects must not hide real-world problems behind a school-specific facsimile. In the research component of a capstone, **this means that the capstone student's research methods must be a developmentally appropriate version of the best and most current research methods used by professionals working on similar problems.** This does not mean everything must have a professional polish. It just means bringing the entirety of one's human intelligence to bear on the problem of getting the best answers available for now and qualifying any claims. It means holding the questions open and recognizing one's claims as provisional. Keeping in mind both limitations and opportunities, this chapter offers guidelines, strategies, and resources for teaching text-based research at the high school capstone level.

Research is a human process.

Student research and professional research

Changes to the information access landscape mean changes to the way research can be practiced and taught. Go back a generation and information was geographically centralized in research universities located in population centers. Access was controlled either by sheer geographic distance or by membership in that university community. The old understanding of the teacher as repository of information made a lot of sense when the teacher had spent a few years at the university storehouse before returning to her hometown to distribute more widely what she'd gathered during her time in the city. But digital information storage has rendered geographical barriers to research nearly obsolete. And the access landscape has likewise changed. Membership in the community of an R1 research university still has privileges, though instead of physically visiting the library, university faculty and students are instead logging in to databases using passwords not shared with the non-university community. But the privilege is not as clear-cut as once it was.

Unlike the older geographic barriers, barriers in the form of database paywalls shift frequently and in complex ways. Information may want to be free, but it is not having an easy time of it. Though academic publishers are invested in protecting intellectual property, researchers (who are often paid salaries by their taxpayer-supported universities, not for their publications) are more invested in open sharing. Public libraries, whose budgets pay for that database access, occupy an interesting middle ground. Though obscure to most high school teachers, the refusal of the public University of California system in 2019 to pay the private company Elsevier for continued database subscriptions rocked the world for those interested in the information landscape.[1] Elsevier had raised prices for access to research, some significant part of which was being produced on UC campuses in the first place. The decision meant that some UC researchers lost their normal means of online access to their own work and the work of colleagues whose labs were just down the hall—in this one respect, some of the best researchers in the world were no better off than a small-town high school student.

The obvious economic pressures that manifest in paywalls are not the only forces shaping the newly complex and shifting access landscape. Researchers who wanted to share and promote their own work, and access the work of others in their fields, turned out in large numbers to upload their own publications to the site Academia.edu, which had represented itself as an open-access platform. Many were later shocked to learn that Academia.edu is a for-profit company seeking to bring the dynamics of monetized social media to academic self-promotion.[2] (The .edu domain name was acquired before laws limiting its use were on the books.) But the fact remains that anyone can get an Academic.edu account and access articles without hitting a paywall—again, university researchers are no better off here than any high school student. And again, it is not precisely that information is moving freely, but rather that the sheer complexity of the access landscape creates opportunities for determined young researchers.

What we access when we access professional research

So far, we have discussed recent changes to the digital information *access* landscape. But changes to the way academic knowledge is *produced* in the first place also need consideration. The term **reproducibility crisis** refers to growing concern about the many landmark studies in some of the social sciences that cannot be reproduced. When later researchers attempt to recreate the studies, they get different results, throwing the original conclusions into doubt. One theory about the crisis is that pressure on researchers to publish positive results leads them, largely unconsciously, into the trap of confirmation bias. Another theory is that the statistical analysis practices in those fields are not adequate to distinguish significant results from noise. In an attempt to address the concern, there are movements in some fields to have researchers pre-register their experimental designs and publish entire data sets rather than just analyses. But the fact remains that the status of knowledge in those fields, as represented by peer-reviewed academic publications, has been called into question.

A note here about constructivism. We do not necessarily take the position that knowledge *per se* is constructed. However, in talking about certain fields of study, it certainly seems to us most prudent to proceed as though that were the case, since the human forces shaping what is written, published, and accessed are so visibly problematic. One need not be a constructivist to recognize that social power structures, popular media, and positionality all shape our students' search efforts, their understandings, and their eventual arguments. Additionally, students need to be aware that different academic disciplines construct and present knowledge in different ways: what is valid in one field may not be valid in another.

Does a high school capstone teacher need to know all this? Yes, we do—not in the sense that we need to know how to fix the problems ourselves, but in the sense that we need to understand what we are actually teaching when we teach research. Supervising students as they sweep up garbage data and present it as if it were divine truth—that would not be teaching at all. Real teaching depends on clarity, and without an understanding of the current research and access landscape, there is no way for teachers or their students to have clarity about what we are even trying to do.

No one knows how access to research results will be controlled in the long-term future, or by whom. No one knows how research in various fields will evolve over time. But in the immediate term, the implications for student research of the changes already underway are fascinating.

Quality over quantity

A generation ago, access to information was the primary challenge of research, and the access of younger students differed greatly from the access afforded to advanced students at research universities. Today, though access remains a complex issue, access itself is no longer the *primary* challenge for students of any age. Instead, information overload—and particularly the overload of poor-quality information—has become the greater challenge. **If students are to be using developmentally appropriate versions of professional methods, they will be looking not for *any* sources on their topic, but for the *best* sources.** Students need to be taught to value quality over quantity.

In order to discern quality, students need to understand the types of secondary sources. (The distinction between primary and secondary sources is a prerequisite for even starting a project at the high school senior level.) They must understand the difference between the various genres in which academic claims can be made and supported: an individual's blog, a popular book, a work of journalism in a respected and fact-checked publication, a peer-reviewed work of scholarship, and the consensus of an academic community. On any given question, the blog may offer the most insightful and helpful analysis, and at the same time the value of the collective wisdom of scholarship transcending the individual must be understood.

In addition to valuing quality over quantity, students must be taught to maintain an awareness that whatever they read is only a tiny selection from a vast array of information. A generation ago, it was possible for a researcher to create a complete bibliography on a topic. Given the pace of new scholarship and the speed with which it becomes available, even teams of professionals can no longer be sure that their grasp of previous work on a topic is complete. This circumstance puts intense pressure on the search process, even for young researchers. In effect, every piece of information acquired comes in response to a "ping"—a signal that the researcher has put out into the world. There is nothing neutral about text-based research today. The search process is a human process, presenting ethical as well as practical problems to the researcher.

A note on plagiarism

Our students live in a digital culture characterized more by sampling and retweeting and liking than by citation. It has proven notoriously difficult to persuade today's students that the already problematic concept of "intellectual property" has relevance for their digital lives, academic or social. Teachers in capstone programs may have more success in explaining to students the academic value of the **provenance of information**. Provenance, the record of where information comes from, drives the academic reaction to plagiarism far more than concepts of ownership. Like courts of law, which insist on a chain of custody for evidence, academic disciplines seek to ensure quality through careful citation. Because courts are trying to arrive at the truest possible account of an alleged crime, they are careful not to be distracted or deceived by low-quality information. Because academics are also trying to arrive at the best answer to a question, they make use of similarly strict rules about what can be admitted as a quality source.

Search strategies

Capstone students will obviously need to understand how to access and use the databases available to them through their school and public libraries, as well as the book catalogs. Google Scholar is another obvious place to start a search. Experienced capstone teachers know that the supposedly tech-savvy next generation may need considerable support managing targeted database searches. As mentioned above, William Badke's *Research Strategies* is an indispensable resource. Meanwhile, given the complexity of the access landscape as described above, other old and new strategies should also be taught.

One old strategy is to ask a human with knowledge in a field. Remind students that they need the best sources, not just any sources, and encourage them to depend on the wisdom of members of the older generation, who may be able not only to tell them what is the best but also to hand them a copy. Remind them that this is what professionals do. A related strategy is to find one source that is both excellent and recent and to harvest its bibliography. Tracing backward to find the sources of your sources is another time-tested professional strategy.[3]

In terms of new strategies, students should know that it has become a common practice for professional researchers to write to other researchers requesting copies of their work when that work is otherwise made inaccessible by a paywall. We obviously encourage students to be courteous and to avoid troubling professionals unnecessarily. Some researchers are on Twitter or other social media. We were shocked the first time a capstone student told us that he no longer needed help gaining access to a key source because he'd found it through social media: "The author just DM'd me," he said. But by now, we all understand that social media can also be an avenue of high-quality scholarship.

Searches and algorithms

A search algorithm is a computer protocol that generates outputs in response to inputs. Students today need to understand how computer algorithms differ from human search processes. Students especially need to understand that algorithms are not neutral, but have been written by human programmers for particular purposes. In the case of library-owned database search engines, the intended purpose should be connecting researchers with the best sources. Non-library search engines like Google are becoming increasingly important to academic research. Because Google is a private company, its searches use a proprietary algorithm. No one outside the company knows exactly how it returns the results it does. Crowdsourcing algorithms like the one used to show what "customers who bought this item also bought" on Amazon are likewise increasingly useful in academic work. Student researchers would be foolish not to benefit from these tools, but at the same time must be aware that they are seeing a selection of sources that have been gathered for purposes other than research.

Information overload feels yucky. As with the project design stage, the initial search stage of capstone brings emotion. Validating that becoming overwhelmed is normal, not a bad sign, will help young researchers stay on course. Reminding students that they are encountering only what is returned in response to the pings or signals they send out likewise helps maintain a sense of agency. Like bats using echolocation to navigate, they are flying blind in the sense that they cannot see the extent of the landscape around them. But they nonetheless can fly with confidence that they can discern enough of what they need to keep going.

Content knowledge vs. research deliverables

A significant developmental difference between the high school capstone students and the professional researchers whose methods they seek to emulate has to do with content knowledge or background in a field: the high school students don't have it. Badke uses the term "working knowledge" to refer to the understandings that are necessary to a project without being its end goal.[4] Before they can make a unique contribution, students first have to know what everybody else knows—that is, what every educated adult knows. Acquiring this information from advanced sources like peer-reviewed articles is difficult or impossible, and students should be validated in their use of encyclopedias and popular books at early stages of the capstone—just as long as they understand that these are steps, not the final work of learning. Wikipedia shines at this phase. Opportunities to integrate this early learning of "working knowledge" by teaching it to fellow students, for example, can both help with the integration and reinforce that reporting on facts is not yet the real work of the project.

The true deliverables even at the research stage of a capstone, however, should be analytical. Many capstone programs assign a set of secondary source analyses or an annotated bibliography. These emphasize what arguments each source makes, how the source supports its argument, and how it cites its own sources—thus showing an awareness of academic genre. Secondly, they show an understanding of what counts as valid in a particular field. For example, an essay about Plato's *Symposium* published in 1988 might be the cornerstone of a capstone being carried out a generation later. But a 1988 article in a biomedical field is hopelessly out of date. Finally, secondary source analyses or annotations also demonstrate students' understanding of the particular value of each source, not in general, but to their particular project. At this stage, remind students that sources with which they disagree, besides guarding against confirmation bias, have especially high value in helping them set up their own arguments. A literature review in the form of an essay is another great way for students to integrate their learning about the work of others, and in particular show their awareness that they are working in a field where others have gone before.

The heart of an inquiry project

- Primary source analysis
- Fieldwork analysis
- Scientific experiment
- Design-build
- Narrative or other creative reflection

The heart of the project

Even a capstone program that very heavily emphasizes text-based research will be doing so in order to empower the capstone student to make a better-supported contribution of their own. Though it is possible for a high school student to create a unique and original project while working exclusively with published secondary sources, this is not the best approach for most. Rather, most projects, including research-heavy projects, will be anchored in an element that we might call the "heart": the part of the project that is both most obviously unique to the student and closest to their interest.

Given the distracting and scattering effect of database work, the heart of the project likewise offers a precious element of deep and sustained concentration, a mode of work that is far more satisfying than skimming secondary sources. Analysis of a primary source can work well as the heart. Analysis of new social science data, gathered through the student's own fieldwork, can likewise be planned as the heart. A scientific experiment or hands-on demonstration can be the heart, as can a design-build project. In an action project, the lived experience of the action may be the heart. Narrative or other creative but non-fictional genres of reflection on lived experience also offer a chance for students to center their projects in a heartfelt way. We offer this reminder in this chapter not to denigrate text-based research, which can be profoundly satisfying on its own, but rather to emphasize that capstone research never means writing book reports. Instead it is an activity that makes meaning for the student and for others.

Capstone story
Anum: paint it black

"Pirates" was the first idea. Anum liked pirates. Or at least she did until the research phase of the project, when she discovered that reading history, even pirate history, still felt like school. And Anum did not like school. She spent every possible minute of her day on campus in the theater, preferably backstage or in the scene shop. "Paint it black" was a personal motto for Anum, as well as a daily practice.

When Anum's failure to turn in the required annotated bibliography led to a small crisis, she and her capstone teacher agreed that the pirate ship was sunk. A wildly colorful and wide-ranging conversation ensued. "Rigging"—both shipboard and on stage—figured largely. Anum had read *The Tempest* for English class; Ariel and company flitted through the conversation like a magical pirate stage crew.

Anum concluded that something related to drama tech was going to be her new topic. And the research phase started over.

Started over only to grind to a halt once again. Anum came to the next meeting with her capstone advisor carrying textbooks she'd borrowed from the drama tech teacher and a list of magazine articles. Nothing connected with her experience, nothing captured the joy of the *Tempest* conversation, nothing modeled the type of academic argument Anum was being asked to make.

Anum and her advisor embarked on a new search—together, this time. But even deep digging turned up only one academic source that even remotely touched on what was now emerging as a well-focused investigation of the role of drama tech in creating the magic of theater.

One was enough.

The source introduced Anum to performance theory and to the idea that actors and audience members alike perform special roles during the performance. Anum's imagination, never at a loss, was fired to beautiful thinking about the invisible ("paint it black") and therefore magical role played by stagehands in constructing the sacred space of performance. Anum's final presentation—given in a space "staged" with the tools of her trade—was a worthy and original culmination of her capstone journey.

To Anum's teacher, the project illustrated the value of text-based research even to projects that are anchored in a student's hands-on experience. The crucial academic source elevated Anum's thinking and enabled her to progress from interesting but wildly expressionistic conversation to the development of a coherent and original argument.

The project also illustrated the changing research access landscape. That source, though written in English, was an unpublished dissertation that had recently been submitted at a university on the other side of the globe. Anum and her teacher found it through Google—straight-up Google and not even Google Scholar—and not through an academic database. This was not a textbook research process—but as Anum could tell you, once the lights go down, the audience doesn't ask what's under the paint.

Notes to Chapter 4.3

Note 1, page 169: **pay the private company Elsevier**—See Brian Resnick and Julia Belluz, "The war to free science: How librarians, pirates, and funders are liberating the world's academic research from paywalls," *Vox*, July 10, 2019.

Note 2, page 169: **Academia.edu is a for-profit company**—Unlike the negotiations between the University of California and Elsevier, concerns about Academia.edu have been widely reported. For one discussion, see Sarah Bond, "Dear Scholars, Delete Your Account At Academia.Edu," *Forbes*, January 23, 2017.

Note 3, page 172: **the sources of your sources**—In some subfields or for some topics, recursively tracing the sources of *all* of one's sources eventually leads to an overview of the subfield or topic—a sense of the whole, and a confidence that the researcher knows all there is to know. For other topics, so much has been written that even professionals cannot maintain this confidence!

Note 4, page 173: **the term "working knowledge"**—See pages 27–31 in William Badke, *Research Strategies: Finding Your Way Through the Information Fog* (Bloomington: iUniverse, 2011).

CHAPTER 4.4
INQUIRY: FIELDWORK

Fieldwork is research done out in the world, beyond the controlled conditions of the library or the laboratory. Though reading text, whether in printed or electronic form, does prompt emotional and even physical responses, it is less fully embodied than fieldwork. Fieldwork engages the student researcher as a whole human being. For capstones that center inquiry, rather than off-campus experiences like internships or service work, the fieldwork component can be the crucial anchor that makes the capstone experience meaningful to the student researcher.

We define fieldwork as **embodied or experiential learning that produces new knowledge**.[1] Like text-based research, fieldwork cannot be understood simply as finding information. Rather, student field researchers understand themselves as ethical actors in the world they are also studying. Whatever their findings, they are evaluating information for its use or meaning in relation to human problems. Though it might seem that the limitations faced by researchers who are still high school students would make fieldwork comparatively more difficult to do well than text-based research, we find that the opposite is often true. The encounter with people, places, or things in the world motivates students to do their very best. And given that the encounter of *this* student with *this* part of the real world is unique, the evidence collected and claims made about it will be unique as well.

Capstone fieldwork might include interviews, qualitative and quantitative studies, surveys, ethnographies, site visits, design-build projects, technical demonstrations, and scientific experiments, among other possibilities. In short, fieldwork is an umbrella term that in a multi-disciplinary program refers to a very wide range of student activities. But the common element—that the research be embodied or experiential—guarantees other similarities and dictates that all students will need certain forms of support.

Given the messiness of work in the field, and given the time constraints on any senior-year project, failure has to be an option for the fieldwork element, even if it is not an option for overall performance in a program that is a graduation requirement. As in real life, "a good failure" can be more valuable than a trivial success. The school needs to be prepared to support the student whose excellent plan may yield no usable results. If there is formal assessment, it is important that it focus on the following: a well-considered plan, responsiveness and appropriate behavior in the field, and honest writing up of results—or any lack thereof. Capstone projects build habits for the future, and pressuring students to report successes that many are unlikely to achieve can only build bad habits or lead to dishonesty. Students will also need considerable help with the project management aspects of fieldwork. Few students will understand just how far in advance they will need to plan, especially if their fieldwork design depends on other people.

In this chapter, we provide practical suggestions and resources for getting students thinking about fieldwork. Additionally, we offer guidance for schools in teaching ethical research practices which mitigate some of the risks associated with off-campus student learning.

> We define fieldwork as embodied or experiential learning
> that produces new knowledge.

Why fieldwork?

Though student fieldwork sometimes fails to produce much in the way of data, it nearly always leads to enormous learning. Consider the following questions that we might ask ourselves as teachers: Do our students understand science as a body of previously established facts, or are they learning the scientific method and process of discovery? Do our students understand the difference between primary and secondary sources in the humanities? Are they able to analyze, interpret, or engage each in appropriately distinct ways? Do our students know the difference between qualitative and quantitative analysis in the social sciences? The difference between descriptive and inferential statistics? In setting up a study, are they able to choose an appropriate number of variables and come up with ways to measure each? What are their skills when it comes to numerical data analysis? What about the visual display of data? Do they know when a histogram offers the best communication, and when a bar graph is to be preferred? Perhaps most importantly, are they critical readers of research done by others, able to evaluate the claims made as trustworthy or not?

Not one of the concepts indicated above is beyond the reach even of younger high school students. But if we are honest about our overall school curriculum, many of us would hesitate to answer "yes" to some or all of these questions. In our experience, high school seniors are more likely to acquire deep understandings of methodological concepts like these when they use them in a capstone project, rather than just through reading about them. For example, a student who has spent several hours in a booth at McDonald's observing counter interactions and categorizing the customer behavior as "polite" or "rude" will know full well how often he hesitated before marking one or the other. He will then understand that data sets he encounters in print have likewise been produced by humans who must have had many moments of uncertainty before they place their checkmark in one of the predetermined boxes. Experiencing how knowledge is constructed in even one of the disciplines can help them become more skillful readers of scholarship in all disciplines.

Research in the social sciences

If you are fortunate, your capstone teaching team may include a teacher trained in research in the social sciences. However, it may be that social science research methods are a gap, while more teachers feel ready to supervise work in the sciences or humanities. Given how many capstone students may want to run surveys or conduct interviews, any such gap on the teaching team would need to be addressed. As a start, both teachers and students need to be clear on the difference between quantitative and qualitative work in the social sciences. Like the difference between primary and secondary sources, this difference is crucial for project design. Understanding it is a prerequisite for capstone.

For students who want to do any **quantitative** studies, the math department may be willing to provide support, both with calculation and with the visual display of numerical data. (Even easily accessed programs like Excel are able to produce excellent visuals.) Since student-gathered data sets will inevitably be small, it is imperative that students understand that they are working in the realm of descriptive and not inferential statistics. They will be making claims about their data, not generalizing from it. For example, a capstone student might be able to report that 87% of her classmates believe that the school's physical education requirement is too strict. She cannot support a claim that high school students in general dislike physical education.

Qualitative study is a gold mine for capstone fieldwork. Qualitative work in the social sciences includes solo interviews and small interview sets, biographies, site visits, focus groups, case studies, and ethnographies. The skills that high school seniors bring to their projects likely lend themselves better to in-depth work with very small sample sizes. Carefully interviewing five peers might lead to far more interesting results than surveying one hundred. (Even students who are doing quantitative work might be encouraged to include one open-ended question at the end of a survey, as the results are likely to be a valuable supplement to the numbers collected.) An essay mentioned above, "Peeling Potatoes" by Greg Sarris, works well to introduce qualitative fieldwork and ethnography by example. For precepts, we also highly recommend the chapter on ethnographic research in Pavel Zemliansky's undergraduate textbook, *Methods of Discovery: A Guide to Research Writing.*[2] Readable and engaging for high school students, this chapter will help them generate ideas about people, places, and things relevant to their projects and conduct the fieldwork once designed.

Zemliansky also gives a brief introduction to the concept of "thick description." Though this concept will take on its largest importance at the writing phase, it needs to be introduced early to ensure that students take adequate notes while in the field. As developed by anthropologist Clifford Geertz in his 1973 *Interpretation of Cultures*, the concept of "thick description" recognizes the way individual ethnographic observations are embedded in a whole scene which also needs to be interpreted. Most of what is interesting in a student's field experience cannot be captured by checkmarks; Geertz validates for students in advance that the *whole* of their experience will be of value.

A second concept from anthropology is likewise essential for capstone researchers doing qualitative study and introduced by Zemliansky. The term "participant-observer" describes the necessarily awkward role of the researcher who cannot avoid becoming part of the situation she is studying. The researcher in the field needs to maintain self-awareness. This is of course necessary for her safety. But it is also because the researcher's real-time reactions are also relevant data that may upon later reflection lead to insights that otherwise might be lost. Thirdly, the researcher's self-awareness as a participant is also crucial to maintaining ethical behavior throughout the research process. We will discuss ethics in more detail below, but for now note that no good comes of allowing students to think that there is a dichotomy between behaving well towards others, including research subjects, and collecting "objective" data. Ethical research gets better results, and ethical research starts with understanding that as a human who moves in space, I cannot make myself "disappear" out of a field setting.

The concept of the participant-observer can be better introduced to students who have already considered their positionalities in relation to their projects.

The relevance of the positionality to the research may in fact be better understood by capstone students who are planning fieldwork. It is easy for students to understand, for example, that interview subjects are likely to give different answers to questions depending on the identities of the interviewer. Older women are unlikely to be as comfortable telling a teenage boy about their experiences of motherhood as they would if talking to another older woman. But teens who vape are more likely to give honest information to another teen than to an adult. There is much to gain in having students think about fieldwork opportunities in which they have an *advantage* over older researchers, despite their inexperience.

Written plan

Because students do need so much support for off-campus work, and because work in the field can be dangerous, we would expect a written plan to be submitted, with approval required before any action is taken off campus. Such plans would likely include:

- The overall research question for the capstone as a whole
- If different, the question that the fieldwork will seek to answer
- The action plan:
  - Who? Names or criteria for all human subjects, including how they will be contacted, etc.
  - When? Deadlines for all actions, including experiments, surveys, interviews, etc.
  - Where? Locations for all actions, including experiments, meetings, etc.
  - All additional details: for example, if anyone is to be interviewed, the exact questions will be provided
- Pertinence: an explanation of *how* a successful execution of the plan will help answer the fieldwork and/or research questions
- A preliminary note of possible ethical issues involving animals or humans, including risks to the researcher
- A positionality

With fieldwork, keep in mind that anything that can go wrong with a plan has a high probability of doing so. Also keep in mind that the sheer life experience of adult teachers will enable them to foresee trouble that is not anticipated by students. When you are reviewing fieldwork plans, it is a good time to let your imagination for possible disasters run wild. Even if a student's plan is approved, it won't hurt to ask the question "What will you do if…?" When all goes well, it won't hurt you, the teacher, to have your pessimism mocked. When it doesn't go well, the student may be spared danger, or just disappointment: "Well, we knew that was a possibility…" is a reassuring thing to be able to say later when the plan has failed.

Teaching ethical research

Research is a powerful intervention in the world. Even text-based research projects without an explicit action component exist in this world, not outside it, and must be understood as interventions with real-world consequences. If your capstone has students doing any research at all, it is *your* ethical responsibility to teach *them* about ethical research practices. This is as true for text-based research as for field research, though the consequences of unethical behavior may be more immediately visible in the second case. At a minimum, students need to understand that research is a relationship. As explained by Suzanne Blum Malley and Ames Hawkins in *Engaging Communities: Writing Ethnographic Research*, previous learning experiences may have led students to approach textual sources with a consumer or ownership mindset.[3] When we empower students to do research involving living human beings, it is imperative that we counter consumer mindsets proactively. In our experience, student researchers rise to the trust we place in them—as long as we provide appropriate instruction and support.

A multi-disciplinary capstone program will sponsor projects in many fields, and each of those fields may have its own ethical practices. As with fieldwork instruction, however, all students can benefit from considering the general ethical standards relating to research on human subjects. The American Anthropological Association posts excellent resources on its website. We recommend as required reading for all students the chapter "Framing Ethical Research" from *Engaging Communities*. This fine undergraduate text presents a shortened version of the AAA ethical standards in a form very suitable for high school students. This textbook is available online as an open access resource, but for convenience we quote the four principles summarized by Blum Malley and Hawkins here:

1. Show respect for the people you are researching at all times, during [both] the data collection process and the writing process.

2. Make sure that your research does not "harm the safety, dignity, or privacy of the people" you are working with.

3. Inform the people you are working with of your project and what it entails. Ask for consent [from the] community to conduct your research and determine in advance whether or not people want to remain anonymous or receive recognition.

4. Plan to share your writing and representation of the community with its members.[4]

In addition to exposure to ethical principles, students will need support at the practical level. Examples communicate more clearly than rules. Because students are doing a version of what professionals do, examples—of forms for gaining informed consent, for instance—are easy to find online.

The goal of instruction in research ethics is not to enable students to eliminate all risk to participants, audiences, or the researchers themselves. Rather, students need to understand first that risk exists, and second that risks associated with a particular plan must be weighed against the likely value of the research results. High school seniors are ill-equipped by prior education and life experience to imagine the possibilities for harm intrinsic in research work. Questions about a sensitive issue may trigger a trauma response in an unprepared interview subject. Information that seems innocuous to the researcher may be viewed as damning by other audiences with whom it is shared. During a study, a student researcher might acquire information they are not equipped to manage— for example, evidence of a crime. Misrepresenting human sources, perhaps through insufficient care rather than ill intent, can have consequences far beyond what the researcher imagined. The possibility of harm to the researcher is also present. Many risks intrinsic to a plan can be mitigated, others tolerated.

The school's ethical responsibility

Some risks cannot be tolerated, either because the worst-case scenario is just too bad, or often simply because the likely value of the results is too small. A capstone is a school project and capstone researchers are students. At the end of the day, the decision about whether a risk can be tolerated must belong to the school, and not to the student. Even this reality, rather than disempowering the student researcher, can be part of the program's instruction. In the professional world, as in schools, individual researchers do not get to make risk-reward calculations by themselves. Instead, that work is done by the sponsoring organization's institutional review board or IRB.[5]

Institutions (including universities, government organizations and private businesses) that support research have an IRB to ensure that no unethical practices occur within their organizations. An IRB reviews research on human subjects, including interviews, qualitative or quantitative studies and surveys, ethnographies, and some site visits. (An institutional animal care and use committee, or IACUC, reviews research on animals, including domestic animals and pets.)

We want to emphasize this point. A capstone is a school project. The school is responsible for actions taken by the student while conducting research off campus. Capstone programs sponsor a wide range of projects in any given year; we are not talking about a one-off independent study here. **In sending capstone students to do research off campus, schools take on an ethical responsibility that must be met systematically, and not only on a case-by-case basis.** Though instruction is essential, offering instruction in research ethics does not by itself absolve the school of its responsibilities. In other words, **your high school capstone program really does need its own ethics review process.**

Ethical review in the high school context

In the university world, in a government laboratory, or in the R&D division of a private company, the IRB is a formal body. Researchers submit written proposals and may hear back only whether they have been approved or rejected. In a high school, the reviewing group more likely consists of an informal committee of teachers, only a few of whom may have much research experience. The collective life experience of a team of ordinary adults is usually more than adequate to spot potential problems missed by the student researcher. If a few members of the teacher-staffed panel are trained to help improve the fieldwork design, then all the better. Instead of an impersonal review process, meeting in person facilitates communication and also adds to the learning for the student, whether they pass the review or not. The review itself is a learning occasion, a friendly and supportive conversation.

Having a plan rejected by the IRB can be upsetting to students. In our experience, most students are ultimately able to recognize that the school has an IRB because it takes students seriously and recognizes their power to have an impact in the world. One common reason for an IRB to reject a plan has to do with time-wasting. For example, a survey that is so badly designed that it cannot answer the student's research question will simply waste the time of those who respond to it. At a school where many students are doing capstone research, the accumulated burden of many badly designed surveys would not be trivial. Wasting the time of research subjects is a small harm, but if there is no benefit to be had, there is no reason for the school to tolerate it—and in fact, the student may learn more from being treated as a responsible ethical agent by the IRB than he would from carrying out the flawed plan.

How does the program decide which student projects involving human subjects need IRB reviews, and which can just be approved by the student's capstone advisor? In practice, an IRB review is probably not necessary when the subjects to be interviewed are adults who have spoken publicly on the topic before (e.g. interviewing an executive about business or a teacher about education) and/ or when there are no special vulnerabilities or stigmas associated with the topic. An IRB review is a good idea to protect both student researchers and subjects when the study involves any vulnerable population, including anyone under the age of 18, and/or addresses any potentially controversial topic. Research that involves students going to unfamiliar locations may also need a review. Additionally, a review would be strongly recommended when there is a possibility that the student researcher might want to publish the study later. Of course, students who pursue research through an institution other than their own school, a nearby university for example, would be covered by that institution's IRB.

Students who will be meeting with the IRB should submit the following information in advance:

- A sensible study design that is likely to elicit relevant data, including all the information requested at the fieldwork proposal stage (see above)

- Evidence of preparation to avoid wasting subject time (e.g. student should have adequate working knowledge of subject area; student should have practiced any recording technology; study is designed to elicit only meaningful data, rather than "fishing"; etc.)

- A discussion of possible risks to the researcher and/or to subjects, and of any other possible negative impacts of the study, accompanied by an explanation of how the researcher plans to mitigate these risks

- Method for obtaining informed consent, including a script

- Plans for secure storage of data obtained, plans for preserving anonymity if that has been promised to study subjects, and plans for secure destruction of data after the study is complete

The adult members of the IRB will then consider whether the student has thought of all risks, and if so, whether the likely value of the data obtained outweighs those risks. Though the student should take notes of suggestions made during the IRB meeting, it can also be helpful to have the student's capstone advisor present in a listening role. In the likely event that the IRB approves the project conditionally, the capstone advisor can be the one to follow up with the student and make sure requested changes to the plans are made.

Informed consent

Informed consent will go a long way to reassure the school that a student's project is ethical. The level of formality in the informed consent process will depend on the project. Informed consent can be verbal or written. For written consent, the form participants sign should include information about whether their input will be anonymous or connected with their name. It should also explain how input will be collected, stored, and used, and whether it will be destroyed at the end of the study. (If participants are told that they will be anonymous, all data must be stored with identifying numbers rather than names from the outset. Additionally, if the student researcher knows the names—in the case of interviews rather than surveys, for example—she must commit never to discuss them.) There should be a warning about any potentially triggering topics that may be introduced by the researcher. If participants will be photographed or recorded, that needs to be specified as well. Lastly, participants should be reminded that they can withdraw consent at any time. If subjects are under the age of 18, the consent of parents/guardians may be needed as well.

At one end of the spectrum from informal to high-stakes consent, imagine a project in which a student has filmed three different advertisements for a local coffee shop. There is nothing in the films likely to be upsetting to an ordinary person. Though it is not a central part of the project, the student wants to include some audience reactions in his presentation. This student might get consent for an informal focus group by saying "Hey, are you willing to watch my ads and tell me what you think? I won't record you, but I will be talking about your reactions when I present my capstone project." A verbal yes to this question should suffice. Meanwhile, a student interviewing her basketball teammates about their experience recovering from concussions will probably want signed consent from parents/guardians. Though the students themselves may have been very open in public about their experiences prior to the study ever starting, the fact remains that they are discussing personal medical information with a researcher. At the other end of the spectrum, it very occasionally happens that students propose fieldwork that seeks to raise traumatic issues, rather than just running a risk of unintentionally encountering them. In that case, it would be the IRB's responsibility to reject the proposal. Just because potential participants might be willing to consent does not make some conversations a good idea.

Learning for students and for schools

As is often noted, we live in a culture in which the maturity and capacity of teenagers is often underestimated. Teens sometimes say that they like their after-school jobs better than they like school itself, in part because they are given real responsibilities in the workplace. Challenging students likewise to take on real responsibilities at school can bring enormous satisfaction and pride as well as learning. It is not necessary that a capstone program overformalize its ethics instruction or review practices. Just like professionals, student researchers will make mistakes. When that happens, the program will support the students as they put repairing the damage above other considerations. The goal here is not perfection, nor even professional polish. Rather the goal is to ensure that both students and teachers in the capstone reflect on the real-world impacts of capstone inquiry and action and mobilize their own intrinsic compassion and judgment. Again, in our experience, people rise to the trust we place in them, as long as instruction and support are in place.

Our schools confine students to desks for far too much of the day. Fieldwork can elicit enthusiasm and diligent effort from students who do not thrive in traditional classrooms. Fieldwork also offers excellent opportunities for helping young students understand research as a human process. Often, the experience of working with field data leads to dramatically better work in the text-based part of the project as well. Even plagiarism prevention can be assisted through the field component of a capstone project, since students may find it easy to understand the ethical imperative to avoid misrepresenting an interview subject, for example, and then be able to transfer that understanding to text. Though not the first element to implement in a new capstone program, fieldwork is a highly valuable element that can help a program thrive.

Examples of capstone student proposals and the IRB response:

- A student proposing to survey peers about vaping acknowledged a risk of getting subjects in trouble with their parents or schools. Her plan was approved with the inclusion of careful steps to maintain the anonymity of those responding to the survey.

- A student proposing to interview athletes about their body image acknowledged that her questions might trigger an emotional reaction, and also that she might encounter serious mental health issues. Her plan was approved after she made arrangements with the school counselor to provide support if needed. The counselor also reviewed all her questions in advance. Her informed consent process reminded participants of their option to withdraw at any time.

- A female student proposed to engage members of an incel community on Reddit. Despite her plans to remain anonymous, her proposal was denied because of the IRB panel's concerns for her safety.

- A student proposed to replicate some of Asch's studies of social conformity with her peers. Her proposal was denied because neither she nor the panel could figure out how to mitigate the likely negative impact of conducting the studies, which at least bordered on manipulation, in a small closed community like her school.

- A student proposed to interview people suffering from schizophrenia. Her proposal was approved because the interview subjects were adult activists who have spoken publicly about their experience with the disease, and because the interviews were arranged through a trusted adult family member of the student.

Notes to Chapter 4.4

Note 1, page 177: **experiential learning**—At the high school level, fieldwork can be understood as a scaled-back version of what professional researchers do—hence the phrase "produces new knowledge" in our definition, though the knowledge produced may be limited and local, not publishable. An equally powerful lens for thinking about the fieldwork component of a capstone is Alice and David Kolb's experiential learning theory, which we discuss at length in Chapter 4.7. In the first case, the emphasis is on the deliverable, while if we use the second lens, we focus on the student's learning.

Note 2, page 180: **Pavel Zemliansky's undergraduate textbook,** *Methods of Discovery*—This excellent and widely used resource is available in its entirety online: www.bit.ly/36Cndks.

Note 3, page 182: **"Framing Ethical Research"**—This resource is likewise open access online. See Suzanne Blum Malley and Ames Hawkins, "Chapter 2: Framing Ethical Research" in *Engaging Communities: Writing Ethnographic Research* (Open-access book. December 31, 2015). www.engagingcommunities.org

Note 4, page 183: **the four principles**—Our quotation of these four is from the online text. See Suzanne Blum Malley and Ames Hawkins, "Chapter 2: Framing Ethical Research" in *Engaging Communities: Writing Ethnographic Research* (Open-access book. December 31, 2015). www.engagingcommunities.org

Note 5, page 183: **institutional review board**—We owe our understanding of the importance, benefit, and feasibility of IRBs or similar review panels at the high school level to Dan Shaw, who for many years guided the ethics review for Bosque School's capstone senior thesis. Though specific formulations (and any mistakes) are our own, we thank Dan for shaping our understanding of how to teach ethics as intrinsic to quality research in any field.

CHAPTER 4.5
ACTION: SERVICE AND INTERNSHIPS

Learning by doing is intrinsic to capstone, with nearly all high school programs at least offering an off-campus action element. That off-campus engagement may take the form of service (through community engagement or service learning) or work (though internships). Off-campus learning always entails logistical challenges for schools, which retain responsibility for the safety and learning of students even when they are not on campus. For capstone programs, the challenges may be even greater, since the personalization of capstone education leads to each student being in a different location—in a large program, there can be a lot of strands to keep free of tangles. Chapter 3.6 addresses how adults organize to address these challenges.

Even with excellent adult infrastructure in place, however, a greater responsibility also falls on the participating capstone students. Students appear off campus as ambassadors of the school; their behavior reflects back on the school community and impacts chances for future students to be accepted in similar placements. Meanwhile, students are likely to encounter new experiences off campus, some of which may overwhelm their previously developed coping strategies. Both the fact that the student's external behavior will reflect on the school and the fact that internally he may feel challenged in new ways suggest the importance of supporting students through all action elements of a capstone. In this chapter, we will consider what preparation and support students need before making contact with a service or work site, during the project, and in their summative reflection.

Capstone seeks to help students move beyond limitations associated with the *role* of "high school student." Both community engagement and internships force students to navigate multiple new roles at the same time as they still carry some of the responsibilities of the student role. Action projects offer an opportunity for students to problem-solve and learn self-advocacy as they explore roles that will only become more important in their future lives. Community engagement projects help students understand their roles as citizens in a democracy. Depending on past exposure, they may start the project thinking of "citizen" as a relatively passive role; the capstone can provide opportunities to experience active participation in democracy as a role that goes beyond paying taxes and voting.[1] Internships are similarly rich in opportunity, as they help students understand their future roles as skilled workers, whether as technicians/ artisans or as professionals. Like citizenship, work roles are deeply meaningful to adults in ways students may not understand without direct experience. Despite the challenges they present for program management, the deep learning that comes from action elements in capstone makes them well worth the effort.

In preparing students for off-campus learning, as in managing adults in the program, attention to equity is essential. Both service work and internships are unpaid, and some students can afford to give time while others cannot. A very few capstone programs are stipended, but most depend on the program leaders to consider whether action elements are equally accessible to all interested capstone students. Access is not the only equity issue. Students come to school with widely varied life experiences and identities, and these may influence how they experience the encounter with the off-campus setting. Awareness of systems—as well as nuanced attention to individual needs—at the preparation and reflection stages increases the likelihood of more benefit for more students in any action learning element of the capstone.

Social justice: teaching systems and framing service

School programs that match students with local service organizations used to be referred to as "community service." Now more favored terms include "service learning," "community engagement," "social entrepreneurship" and "social innovation." The very evolution of the terminology points to awareness that the *framing* of school-community partnerships already has impacts. Whether an entire capstone program centers service work, or whether a service focus is chosen by a smaller cohort of students or by a few individuals, the capstone program will want to carefully consider the way it frames the service element in the capstone for students.[2]

We will take the most widely used term as our starting point. Capstone teachers unfamiliar with **service learning** may find it helpful to think of it as occupying an intersection between classroom learning, experiential learning, and community service. The National Youth Leadership Council defines service learning as "an approach to teaching and learning in which students use academic and civic knowledge and skills to address genuine community needs."[3] Unlike community service or volunteer work that takes place independent of schooling, the learning of the participating student is a major goal of the service-learning partnership. Unlike other forms of school-directed learning, including classroom instruction and student research, advancing the goals set by the community organization is likewise intrinsic to the service learning partnership. Different forms of service learning weigh these two goals differently, but the tension between them is always present and often productive. At a minimum, service learning typically includes (1) classroom-based and/or text-based learning in advance of or alongside the interaction between students and community; (2) the interaction or service itself; and (3) reflection on the part of the students, possibly including self-reflection and/or an impact study. As in experiential learning, the student reflection is considered an essential element, not an afterthought.

As actually practiced in American schools, service learning has been criticized. At its worst, service learning might lead neither to real learning nor to real service, instead consisting in an empty performance that actually tends to reinforce and perpetuate injustice.[4] When, as is often the case, the students are primarily White and privileged in other ways, and the partner sites located in communities of color, even the implicit or explicit framing of the students as already able to provide service, with the community partner seen through a deficit lens as only in need—both damaging false assumptions—can reinforce racial stereotypes, while failing to set the partnership up to lead either to learning or to valuable work.[5]

For this reason, schools have sought to rethink programs in alignment with the principles of "**critical service learning**." As articulated by Tania D. Mitchell in a landmark literature review, traditional service learning "emphasizes service learning without attention to systems of inequality," while critical service learning seeks to "deconstruct systems of power so the need for service and the inequalities that create and sustain them are dismantled."[6] Critical service learning works against assumptions about roles in the school-community partnership, which is reframed as reciprocal. Specifically, Mitchell's review uncovers three widely held principles of the critical approach: "a social change orientation, working to redistribute power, and developing authentic relationships."[7]

The principles brought forward by Mitchell in this review lend themselves readily to capstone. A "social change orientation" means understanding that the causes of injustice are systemic or structural, and not a matter of individual choices. Because capstone students have the benefit of time for study, their opportunity to understand the context of their work is enhanced. "Working to redistribute power" includes attending to the ways in which power is exercised in the student-community interaction and rethinking stereotyping assumptions about roles. The capstone structure, with its looser connection to traditional schooling, positions the capstone student to reach for a better understanding of the multiple roles to be played out in the partnership. "Developing authentic relationships" would in a capstone context include prioritizing people above the student's perceived understanding of the tasks dictated by school. Again, the capstone program's unique structure supports learners in thinking beyond their roles as students.

Supporting service-centered capstones has overlap with supporting research capstones and especially ethnographic research or research on human subjects. As in ethnographic research, or any research on human subjects, the student's work understanding his own positionality will be crucial to any value created for others or for the student himself. The capstone student needs to understand his own participation in the systems that create and maintain the inequality and injustice. One potentially transformative element of a critical service learning approach is explicit attention to race, and especially to the operation of Whiteness in service learning. The capstone advisor does not need to have a position on the relative salience of race and of socioeconomics in order to see that conversations through the lens of race are likely to lead to learning. Where White students are comfortable discussing socioeconomics, but not comfortable reflecting on their own participation in racialized dynamics, that very discomfort signals the opportunity for learning. Capstone advisors and students alike will find "Service Learning as a Pedagogy of Whiteness" by Tania D. Mitchell illuminating alongside any resources on positive racial identity development.[8] As we stress in our chapters on research, *every* positionality brings value to the capstone, as long as the self-awareness is developing in the course of the project.

Service learning in capstone

What distinguishes service-centered *capstones* from student participation in service learning *programs* is that the projects are individual, intrinsically motivated, and sustained. Though the project will probably happen in the context of pre-existing relationships between adults at the school and adults in the community, the initiative for contact will either start with the capstone student or be taken over early on. Depending on the scope of the sponsoring capstone program, the student may have significantly more time for learning in advance of the service itself, and for reflection after the fact. Because of the student's individual interest, and also because of the greater time available, the pre-interaction learning of the capstone student can be significantly more in depth than in a service learning program required of all. Developmentally, high school seniors are eager for contact with a broader world and ready for the responsibilities entailed. Service learning and senior-year capstone can work beautifully together.

Instruction for capstone students whose projects will center on service learning would include context and positionality:

- understanding the local, regional, national, or global histories that led to the injustice being created in the first place
- understanding the systems that perpetuate the injustice in an ongoing way
- positionality: understanding my own ongoing participation in those systems

Instruction would also include method and practices:

- etiquette: arriving on time, listening stance, responsiveness, how to write a courteous email, etc.
- commitment to prioritizing people and relationships above school tasks, etc.

Instruction would include reflection:

- reflection, including the positionality, in advance of interaction in the community
- ongoing reflection accompanying the interaction
- summative reflection, probably incorporated into a final project deliverable

Preparing students for community engagement: understanding histories and systems

Imagine two capstone students, Ray and Lori, starting their senior year of high school in Tulsa, Oklahoma. Ray hopes to pursue an internship with Habitat for Humanity. Before even approaching his local branch, Ray would want to understand the local and national context for the housing needs he hopes to help address. For local context, he might start by studying the Greenwood Massacre. For national context, he might read Ta-Nehisi Coates's famous essay "The Case for Reparations" and *The Color of Law* by Richard Rothstein. Lori meanwhile is interested in environmentalism. She plans to explore volunteer opportunities by contacting the OK Earth Coalition. In order to understand the systemic basis of her local community needs, Lori would want a thorough grounding in settler colonialism generally. Given her local context, she might want to learn specifically about the Trail of Tears. She would want to know about the principles of environmental justice drafted at the First National People of Color Environmental Leadership Summit in 1991.

Both Ray and Lori would want to complete initial research and reading *before* making their initial contact. They would want to reflect on the fact that in making initial contact in the community, they are asking for help as much as offering to provide it. In making contact, they will be asking for the time of adult professionals who are not their teachers and who have work to do other than teaching them. Students may need to be reminded that courtesy and respect for the time of the expert community organizers or nonprofit workers starts with not expecting them to teach material that the students can easily find online. As the project evolves, the capstone student is likely to receive lots of instruction from those outside experts, but that should have a foundation to build on. In keeping with the principles of critical service learning, capstone students should at a minimum have a knowledge base that equips them to move beyond naive assumptions about "needs" that divorce them from the histories and present-day systems that create and perpetuate them in the first place.

The school's community engagement or service learning director can provide resources to help students understand the perspective of the community partners on work with students. The chapter "Principles for Success in Service Learning—the Three Cs" by Dadit Hidayat, Samuel Pratsch, and Randy Stoecker can be read by capstone students to help them see the difference between their presence in the usual venues of their life—school, activities, or home—and their presence in a community organization site.[9] As Hidayat and his coauthors note, community organizations may have low expectations when inviting students in as partners. It won't hurt the capstone student to know that and to feel challenged to create something better. High school seniors often bloom in settings, like after-school jobs, where they are expected to show up as adults. The capstone program will want to help them see the opportunity in responsibility.

Reflection and service learning

One core principle of service learning, as opposed to community service, is reflection. Action does not automatically lead to learning. Rather, learning arises out of reflection on action. Reflection in general will be discussed more completely in Chapter 4.7; here we note only a few aspects of reflection that are specific to service. First, given the structure of service learning outlined above, multiple-entry journaling can be an effective method for ongoing reflection. Bringle and Hatcher, who are helpful on both the theory and practice of reflection in service learning, offer a range of journaling strategies, including several multi-entry approaches. For example, a journal entry might consist of relatively immediate reactions, followed by a second layer of reflection in which the student links events and reactions to histories and systems, as understood through the student's reading.[10] The school's service learning director can provide prompts for student writing that might be applicable in the capstone context as well.

Second, in a capstone, the ongoing reflection is likely to culminate in a summative reflection that might be delivered as a narrative in a presentation or developed as a section in a long essay. The capstone student who is working in a framework of critical service learning will be aware that evidence of systemic change is not likely to be visible inside the timeframe of her senior year of high school; she will shape her narrative accordingly. The narrative may instead focus on her learning or possible learning outcomes for her audience. Depending on whether the service learning element is required or optional, different capstone programs will structure ongoing and summative reflection in different ways.

The benefits and challenges of internships

Like community engagement, career internships place students off campus and out of sight of their teachers. Internships, however, bring a very different set of opportunities and challenges. Internships are quintessential career experiences for budding skilled workers. Students have the opportunity to live the life of an adult who is successful in an area that interests them. They get a taste of what it is like to use the particular skill set for a job and to interact with people who do the work daily. Some students even get to produce authentic work, like getting authorship on a published article.

As discussed in Chapter 3.5, maintaining an internship program requires substantial work with adults on and off campus. The program will require a constant supply of supervisors at the various internship sites. There are also numerous oversight issues as students leave campus to travel to institutions where they work in an environment that is very different from school. Meanwhile, there are challenges in preparing students for the internship experience as well, and in supporting their learning during and after their work on site.

So far we have referenced programs in which the internships occur during the school year with organizational support from teachers. There are other models in which students and their families take the initiative to arrange a placement during a school vacation. In these cases, students shoulder the responsibility of finding both people to work with and time for the work. These are actually fairly common, given the challenges inherent in teachers running internships during the school year. Vacation internships arranged by students or families can work as well in a capstone as placements during the school year, as long as expectations are documented and communication with teachers before and after the summer is excellent.

Preparing students for the workplace: etiquette and boundaries

Internships are special kinds of capstones in many ways. Notable among them is that most of a student's time is spent off campus and away from the purview of teachers. Because the students are school ambassadors, care should be taken when approving students to take on this role, with so much of their time being independent and unsupervised by teachers. Students instead are overseen by their supervisors on location, and if updates are sent to teachers, there is a lag between the event and the reporting. Preparing students for this experience is essential. In addition to instruction for students, expectations for all parties—students, teachers, and off-site supervisors—must be explicit and documented, since neither the student nor the off-site supervisor may have the capstone teacher's big-picture understanding of the context for the internship. We address related issues in Chapter 3.5.

Students need to act like professionals to get the most out of their internships. The capstone internship may be the first time they have had to consider professionalism and adult etiquette. Their best behavior is essential, not only to ensure a good experience but also to keep the supervisor interested in the program and likely to accept more students in the future—quite a lot is on the line when students venture into organizations by themselves. Students need to do the following:

- Be punctual.
- Communicate on time and use proper grammar.
- Keep in touch with their capstone teacher about their activities.
- Complete their school assignments on time.
- Be proactive when they have to cancel a visit, contacting all important people.

- Be their own advocate.

The first visit is a special opportunity for everyone to meet, review expectations, and preview what will occur on site. It is helpful to have a brief agenda, to work through the essential elements of the appointment, because this may be the only time the teacher gets to participate. The content of this agenda is outlined in Chapter 3.5. The school's expectations will figure prominently in this meeting—one could call this the "healthy boundaries" moment. Teachers can make the most of this moment, including anything extra to give students a full picture of the future, like a tour of the facility with introductions to any possible co-supervisors.

Keeping up with what transpires off campus is a resulting necessity. Many internships are weekly happenings, and life can intervene to cancel some of them along the way—vacations, weather, conflicting schedules, etc. If teachers are not careful, a surprising amount of time can pass with students doing "nothing" for valid reasons. Just imagine running internships during the holiday season—many unavoidable interruptions ensue. As in any good curriculum, scaffolding is the solution. Teachers need to plan for regular updates to keep up with these external events. These can be simple posts about what recently happened, or reflections on the goals of the program, or some other relevant aspect of a capstone program. These posts make for wonderful additions to digital portfolios, where they are easily checked by teachers working back on campus. They are terrific opportunities for students to reflect on their experience, maximizing their learning, as we discuss in Chapter 4.7.

Internships offer students some of their most concrete experiences of failure. Students gain a direct view of what failure looks like in the real world, a topic we explore further in Chapter 4.8. They learn how often it happens and develop a sense of how to negotiate through it. Capstone prepares students for real life like no other program, and the clarification of what failure is and how professionals cope is a prime example. Related to this, internships can also provide the invaluable experience of deciding what students do *not* wish to do in the future. They learn all that comes from the tenure, and save much time, energy, and emotion by moving away from it as they edge closer to college and beyond. That is another great gift of capstone.

Navigating roles and boundaries

Imagine an example to illustrate the important points on internships. Mary has been matched with a professor of biotechnology at a local university. Her capstone teacher has sent students to this laboratory before and has a good working relationship with the principal investigator, who runs a large lab. The professor pairs Mary with a graduate student to do the actual work in the lab. During the first visit, Mary travels with her capstone teacher for their first meeting. The teacher prepares a short agenda, including the essential elements of the internship. They do introductions, exchange contact information, learn about the opportunity in the lab, go over what assignments the student will need to do at school, review the school's behavior code, and even get a tour of the lab. (Note: some labs may have students work on confidential information that should not be shared publicly, like research ideas, data or pictures. It is essential that students honor the sharing rules of the lab.) Mary travels to the lab all on her own the following week, using school-provided transportation. After a couple of months of successful work, the graduate student texts Mary about spending extra time working at the lab. Mary is honored and excited but really does not have the time in her schedule to accept the offer, a fact that she brings up during a regular meeting with her capstone teacher. After a conversation, the capstone teacher then contacts the professor, who was unaware of the suggested expansion of time and recognizes the challenge for the student. The professor reviews the behavior code with the graduate student, who politely rescinds the offer, and Mary continues her work as originally planned.

General plans for establishing projects off campus

- A **planning meeting** with a **thorough agenda,**
- which establishes **lines of communication**
- and features the school's **expectations of behavior.**

Notes to Chapter 4.5

Note 1, page 192: **roles as citizens**—For an excellent discussion, see Joel Westheimer and Joseph Kahne, "What Kind of Citizen? The Politics of Educating for Democracy," *American Educational Research Journal* 41, no. 2 (Summer 2004): 237–269.

Note 2, page 192: **it frames the service element**—The understanding presented in this section on community engagement was developed with the help of Anna Rutins, who supported our learning over many years, including suggesting most of the sources quoted here.

Note 3, page 193: **National Youth Leadership Council**—www.bit.ly/3kjhXKC

Note 4, page 193: **reinforce and perpetuate inequality**—For an overview of recent critiques, see Tania D. Mitchell, "Traditional vs. Critical Service-Learning: Engaging the Literature to Differentiate Two Models," *Michigan Journal of Community Service Learning* 14 (Spring 2008): 50–65.

Note 5, page 193: **even the implicit or explicit framing**—The quotation is on page 614 in Tania D. Mitchell, "Service Learning as a Pedagogy of Whiteness," *Equity and Excellence in Education* 45, no. 4 (2012): 612–629.

Note 6, page 193: **"deconstruct systems of power"**—See page 50 in Tania D. Mitchell, "Traditional vs. Critical Service-Learning: Engaging the Literature to Differentiate Two Models," *Michigan Journal of Community Service Learning* 14 (Spring 2008): 50–65.

Note 7, page 193: **three widely held principles of the critical approach**—See page 50 in Tania D. Mitchell, "Traditional vs. Critical Service-Learning: Engaging the Literature to Differentiate Two Models," *Michigan Journal of Community Service Learning* 14 (Spring 2008): 50–65.

Note 8, page 194: **"Pedagogy of Whiteness"**—See Tania D. Mitchell, "Service Learning as a Pedagogy of Whiteness," *Equity and Excellence in Education* 45, no. 4 (2012): 612–629.

Note 9, page 196: **their presence in a community organization site**—This source includes many quotations from nonprofit workers detailing the difficulties from their perspective of working with students. See D. Hidayat, S. Pratsch, and R. Stoecker, "Principles for success in service learning—the three Cs" in *The unheard voices: Community organizations and service learning*, eds. R. Stoecker, E.S. Tryon, and A. Hilgendorf (Philadelphia, PA: Temple University Press, 2009), 146–161.

Note 10, page 197: **several multi-entry approaches**—See Robert G. Bringle and Julie A. Hatcher, "Reflection in Service Learning: Making Meaning of Experience," *Evaluation/Reflection* 23 (1999): 179–185.

CHAPTER 4.6
ACTION: DESIGN AND BUILD

Students making things: an idea beautiful in its simplicity.

In a sustained capstone, a design-build or maker element often becomes the heart of the project—the element that takes it to the next level. Like fieldwork, service learning, and internships, design-build or maker elements engage students in ways that may have been missing from their previous experience of school. What all these elements have in common is an embodied experience outside the usual classroom space. What distinguishes design-build or maker elements as action elements in the capstone is the experience and the goal of making a *thing*. The thing made, the product, brings its own objective logic to the learning. Having an outcome that the student can see and touch introduces a satisfaction beyond audience appreciation or teacher assessment. Students find the making journey memorable and compelling as well, and the object made may later serve as a memento of a special experience. We especially love design-build and maker projects which allow the school to honor and make visible the success of students for whom the book-learning side of school has been a disappointment.

In this chapter, we discuss different ways to think about design-build and maker elements in capstone programs, and point out a few widely accessible resources for supporting students who choose this option.

Design thinking

The term "**design thinking**" dates back at least to the 1970s, but credit for the recent popularity of the term in the K–12 world is probably due to the Hasso-Plattner Institute of Design at Stanford—known now as the Stanford "d.school" (d for design, of course). Materials offered online at the d.school website are not only free but also genuinely accessible to students in the sense that they are easily understood with little or no teacher support. Rather than offering theoretical explanations or histories, the d.school resources get students engaged immediately in learning by doing. In a school setting in which one capstone teacher may be supervising many different types of projects, the fact that these materials can be used by students without teacher support is no small recommendation.

Design thinking takes a solutions-based approach in the sense that work is organized around a problem and a user who needs it solved. The user's experience of the solution is paramount, offering an assessment and feedback that are again independent of the capstone teacher's supervision.

One version of the d.school materials presents the design thinking process in five steps: **empathize**, **define**, **ideate**, **prototype** and **test**.[1] To empathize, students can interview their intended users about the problem, which in this case is the core issue of a capstone project. From these interviews, the problem is identified and defined. Next, ideas are developed to solve the problem, with simplicity and boldness valued. Prototyping comes afterwards, to build out the solution. Testing is the next stage, in which everything comes full circle, and the solution is shared with the users. Users provide vital information to the capstone student during this part of the cycle. In the spirit of entrepreneurship, where design thinking is popular, a pitch—or a very brief summary of the idea, an "elevator pitch"—is often assigned.

The design thinking process is iterative, with prototypes being redesigned based on user input. The process articulated in the d.school materials is robust enough to anchor a very substantial capstone, with iterations of prototyping, ideating, and testing leading to better and better builds over the course of the year. The final build can be assessed as the project's main deliverable, and the intended users take the place of an authentic audience. Alternately, a presentation and pitch to a new audience may be the final deliverable. The inevitable resistance of materials guarantees challenge and the need for problem-solving and perseverance. Though not the only way to structure a capstone, design thinking offers a beautiful fit for most of the goals that typically motivate schools to launch capstone programs in the first place.

Students making things: an idea beautiful in its simplicity.

Design for people

Though this chapter focuses on hands-on building of physical objects, it is important to note that design thinking as articulated by the d.school and others does not have to be aimed at the making of a material object. Outside of schools, the term shows up often in software development, where the UX (user experience) of a website guides design and redesign in the sense of coding and recoding. The product is virtual, not material.

Even in projects that will result in a physical product, the human-centered or user-centered phases of design thinking, including initial interviewing and user testing, can predominate over the build phases, in a sense constituting the real work of the project. In these cases, the build phases are secondary and may not proceed beyond prototyping before the project is considered complete.

Understanding the overwhelming importance of the inquiry phases in some design projects helps us see that design thinking has considerable overlap with ethnographic fieldwork. It follows that many of the principles of ethical qualitative research methods discussed in Chapter 4.4 apply equally here. If students intend to work with any vulnerable population in the user role, teaching research ethics will be as important as it would be if the goal were research rather than building.

Design thinking also can have overlap with community engagement or service learning in a capstone. The article "Design Thinking for Social Innovation" by Tim Brown and Jocelyn Wyatt illustrates the approach with examples from around the globe.[2] When the designer's cultural context differs from the user's, self-aware and skilled inquiry has heightened importance. Perhaps more easily accessed by American students is the organization Makers Making Change, which helps students interested in hands-on building identify needs that they can fill locally.[3]

In its iterative and intrinsically reflective nature, design thinking also bears resemblance to the experiential learning cycle articulated by Kolb and Kolb. Design thinking focuses on the user, and experiential learning theory on the student, but both models offer a structure in which doing alternates with integration of learning.

In short, one of the beauties of design-build projects is the way they balance listening to people with making things. In design-build, inquiry and action can never be separated.

Capstone story
Olivia: building a garden

Olivia was on a mission. From the outdoor-friendly state of Oregon, she had the combined interests of reconnecting people with their environment and with architecture. She wished to make these resources available to her fellow students in some fashion. Olivia was primed for a capstone project.

Olivia had her eye on an underused area on campus: an outdoor space that held occasional school events. It had fallen into disrepair over the years, with cracking masonry and weed-filled joints, and prickly ivy overtaking sitting spots. It had potential and needed lots of work and resources.

It was pitch time for capstone projects at her school. Olivia was among the first to approach the lunch table established for brainstorming proposals. "I want to renovate the outdoor area, creating a green space, connecting people with the environment, and improving relationships in our community."

Where to start? Renovations are giant projects where design meets planning, funding, infrastructure and maintenance. This was a daunting proposal, but this was a determined student.

Exploratory questions revealed that the space had lots of potential. The facilities manager was keen on the idea of an adjacent area for classroom activities and general student use. Olivia had already identified an alumnus who was eager to help design and fundraise. It was time to take this project proposal seriously.

Olivia got her space after years of effort and a surprising number of approvals. She had to arrange meetings to secure permission from a couple of administrative departments (principal, facilities, etc.), lock up funding for the renovation, and collect feedback from all intended users. Persistent effort, creative problem-solving, and many partners allowed her to realize her dreams. Her multi-use garden remains a popular spot on campus to this day.

Thinking with your hands

All of that said, in our experience the most compelling capstone experiences for students do involve the hands-on work of *making real things*. Most transformative are the projects which go beyond prototyping to culminate in a final object that can be judged independently of the maker and their process.

What is the source of the transformations we have observed? We remember these students: Anne, who sewed a kimono using traditional methods; Mauricio, who built a straw-bale dog house; Olivia, who designed and built a garden courtyard on her school grounds; Rob, who built a gaming computer. Not being sure why these experiences were so compelling, we speculate. Perhaps the type of whole-body thinking entered into in the course of the making process was grounding for students in an increasingly distracted world. School is often associated with book learning—that is, the type of learning that can happen for a student seated at a school desk in a classroom. This type of learning is relatively disembodied. Meanwhile, the understanding of embodied cognition suggests that our bodies are as involved in what we call "thinking" as our brains. Thinking with our hands is not just a metaphor.

Though most schools heavily prioritize book learning (and screen learning) over hands-on learning, it is important to note that in the 21st-century workplace, humans who can think with their hands continue to be valued. In *Dancing with Robots*, their study of employment trends in the digital era, Frank Levy and Richard Murnane identify three categories of work that continues to be done by humans and not robots: "solving unstructured problems, working with new information, and carrying out non-routine mechanical tasks."[4] The third of these categories requires thinking human hands.

Levy and Murnane give numerous examples. Care for children and the elderly requires sophisticated skill sets that integrate head, heart, and hands. Computers will never feed a baby as well as a person. Health care likewise includes elements that cannot be computerized. Though car manufacture can be largely routinized (completing the process started with Henry Ford's production line), troubleshooting breakdowns on the line itself continues to require humans with strategies in their heads and skills in their hands. Likewise, though car *manufacture* can be done by robots, car *repair* continues to demand diagnostic and problem-solving qualities that depend on the flexibility of a human being.

Some of the work listed above has been historically undervalued and underpaid in America, though Levy and Murnane's work suggests that this may change. Meanwhile we will also note that other work that has been historically valued very highly likewise requires thinking hands. All experimental science involves an understanding of materials and material processes that depends on the hands as much as the head. Ad hoc problem-solving is integral to modern science. Consider, for example, research conducted on high-energy particle accelerators like the one at Fermilab outside Chicago. Research teams may wait months for a tiny window of time on site. If something in their equipment breaks, there is no time for fancy solutions. Rather, a skilled team member is more likely to rig a quick fix using duct tape or tin foil. The skills of that team member may resemble the skills of an auto mechanic as much as they do the skills of a theoretical physicist, and they are just as integral to the success of cutting-edge modern science.

Soulcraft

A very different argument for the value of hands-on learning sees it through the lens of **craft**. The publication of *Shop Class as Soulcraft* in 2009 is one landmark in the maker movement that has led to maker spaces and innovation labs in schools across the country—shop class reimagined as well as renamed. Craft work is hands-on work directed toward making objects that are unique and beautiful, but also useful. The author of *Shop Class as Soulcraft*, Matthew Crawford, argues for a renaissance in craft work for reasons that will be familiar to proponents of liberal arts education: "[C]raftsmanship might be defined simply as the desire to do something well, for its own sake."[5]

Crawford values the way that a craft worker becomes a creator rather than a consumer, enabling a resistance against some of the pressures of the larger culture of capitalism. Again, his argument will be familiar to teachers in traditional academic fields. Humanities teachers, for example, ask students to create media in part to equip them to think independently in a cultural environment of potentially overwhelming media influences. The act of making helps the maker to understand that the products or media he encounters in the world are constructed, and not inevitably or naturally as they are.

In a capstone program, the craft approach will lead to very different experiences and understandings from the design-build approach. If design-build practitioners may be primarily "people people" and prototypers, leaving the actual manufacture of the end product designed to others, craft workers are just the opposite. Craft workers may even skip the design phase entirely, allowing materials and not people to guide the making. Acquiring true skill in any craft will take much longer than the one year of the capstone, so the craft student will not have a simple narrative to tell at the end of the year. She will not be able to say, "I learned to weld, and now I am a welder." Highly skilled welders have many years of learning behind them, not one. Instead, the rewards of capstone craft work may be more subtle.

Resources for capstone makers

Unlike design-build projects that emphasize the design phases, maker projects understood through a craft lens may require considerable resources. In the absence of school support in the form of skilled adult guidance, materials, tools, and space, the program will face an equity issue, since some students will have access to what they need through friends and family, while others will not. Another equity issue has to do with gender: the maker movement has been critiqued for a failure to include girls and women. Given these realities, a capstone program that sponsors maker projects will want to start with intentional framing designed to make the option feel real to all interested students. And the program leaders will want to invest in some creative identification of resources—people, materials, tools, and workspaces—as well.

If your school has an innovation lab, maker space, shop, or robotics lab, the director of that space is the likely first resource. Physics and chemistry teachers likewise are familiar with hands-on methods, as are teachers in the drama tech department. At most schools, however, the best adult support for design-build projects may be unknown unless a call is made to seek out teaching or non-teaching staff whose skills may be expressed on weekends in their garages rather than at school. We've seen members of a school's facilities crew, for example, shine as support for special design-build projects.

For program leaders interested in building their own capacity, *The Maker's Manual* is a fine starting point.[6] *Make* magazine is likewise a resource, and instruction videos available for free online can provide specialized instruction, once the capstone student has initial adult support. If the school does not have its own maker space, the capstone program leaders may be able to locate public fabrication labs or shops that offer time and equipment for a reasonable fee.

Notes to Chapter 4.6

Note 1, page 204: **empathize, define, ideate, prototype and test**—See the information-rich website from the d.school. Here is a good starting page: www.stanford.io/3hG0QRB

Note 2, page 205: **"Design Thinking for Social Innovation"**—See Tim Brown and Jocelyn Wyatt, "Design Thinking for Social Innovation," *Stanford Social Innovation Review* (Winter 2010): 30–35.

Note 3, page 205: **Makers Making Change**—See www.makersmakingchange.com.

Note 4, page 207: **"solving unstructured problems, working with new information, and carrying out non-routine mechanical tasks"**—See the report written by Levy and Murnane for the think tank Third Way. Frank Levy and Richard Murnane, *Dancing with Robots: Human Skills for Computerized Work* (Third Way), July 17, 2013.

Note 5, page 208: **"the desire to do something well, for its own sake"**—The quotation is from page 9 of the 2006 essay, which has the same name as Crawford's later book: Matthew B. Crawford, "Shop Class as Soulcraft," *New Atlantis* (Summer 2006): 7–24.

Note 6, page 209: ***The Maker's Manual***—See Andrea Maietta and Paolo Aliverti, *The Maker's Manual: A Practical Guide to the New Industrial Revolution* (San Francisco: Maker Media, 2015).

CHAPTER 4.7
REFLECTION

Much of a young person's career in school is focused on end products. What grade did you get? What was your personal best of the season? What course did you get into next year? Concentrating solely on the outcome of an experience ignores many opportunities for learning—and really misses the point of school. What do we adults remember about our past years in school? We are more likely to recall relationships and events rather than benchmarks that summarize achievement in school, in the sense of "What was the final accomplishment?" There is little risk that outcomes will receive too little attention in the capstone program (see our discussion of "deliverables" in Chapters 4.10 and 4.11), but we all need to work harder at opening up opportunities for learning that emerge when students attend to the process.

Reflection is an effective way to rebalance the relationship between process and outcomes. It is a major element of most successful capstone programs. In our home classrooms, we know that one of the secrets to teaching is meeting students where they are. When we determine what a student knows, their preferred learning mode, and what has worked for them in the past, we can craft lessons that allow students to learn in a lasting way. In other words, formative assessment informs future instruction. In a capstone program, much of the meta-analysis of learning usually done by teachers is turned over to the students themselves. Reflection takes the place of formative assessment, allowing students to understand themselves as learners in the capstone context and design better and better evolutions of their projects—better both in the sense of leading to great outcomes and in the sense of facilitating more learning.

Reflection provides a mine of valuable ideas and connections. Even when things are going well, stopping to look back at what has passed and considering the different ways forward—especially when done with a small team of like-minded peers and teachers—reveals opportunities that rarely appear without planned moments of consideration. Zooming through a forest, focused on bagging an impressive peak, can be a wasted outing, because one missed a side trail to a life-changing vista. A second trip, at a more considered pace, can fix this problem, allowing a person a chance to see the grand view, and alter his plans for the season, to experience more, similarly inspirational moments.

Reflection and experiential education

Teachers who use the term "reflection" are often drawing on the model of experiential education developed by Alice and David Kolb, itself based on the work of Kurt Lewin, John Dewey, and Jean Piaget. Experiential learning theory (ELT) was established with the publication of David Kolb's *Experiential Learning: Experience as a Source of Learning and Development* in 1984. This landmark work, cited in literally *tens of thousands* of later studies, was reissued in 2015 with updates, while recent generations of teachers have been introduced to experiential education through David and Alice Kolb's 2017 *The Experiential Educator: Principles and Practices of Experiential Learning*. Teachers whose backgrounds are in traditional classroom disciplines are likely to find any of these books illuminating as they design or evolve their capstone programs.

The experiential learning cycle articulated by Kolb and Kolb rotates through four stages. Concrete experience (CE) is the initial and immediate stage. Reflective observation (RO) lifts immediate experience into the field of awareness where learning can begin. Abstract conceptualization (AC) begins the making of connections which allow learning to transfer into future contexts. Active experimentation (AE) tests conceptualization, preparing for a new round.[1] In the later books, Kolb and Kolb emphasize the iterative and integrative nature of experiential learning by refiguring the cycle as a spiral. They also reemphasize a hallmark of the experiential model of learning: its holistic focus on the learner, rather than on the transfer and recall of information. "The most important aspect of the learning cycle is that it describes the learning process as a recursive circle or spiral as opposed to the linear, traditional information-transmission model of learning used in most education where information transferred from the teacher to the learner is stored in declarative memory for later recall."[2] Whether or not they explicitly identify with ELT, most capstone programs nonetheless rely on understandings that are helpfully articulated by it.

As David Kolb notes in the introduction to the updated edition of *Experiential Learning*, the term "experiential" refers to the whole cycle, and not only to its first stage. Though educators sometimes use the phrase "experiential learning" when speaking simply of off-campus or hands-on activity,[3] without the subsequent stages, Kolb makes clear that this is a mistaken approach. "Experiential" is a way of understanding learning per se; it does not even exclude learning from text, though it does emphasize direct embodied experience alongside traditional book learning. Nor does the Kolb model suggest that learning happens through activity alone. Rather, as Kolb says, "Learning is the process by which knowledge is created through the transformation of experience."[4] For capstone educators not already familiar with ELT, perhaps its greatest gift is its clear emphasis on the role of **reflection** in transforming experience into learning. Though students will reflect informally whether we ask them to or not, ELT argues persuasively for the gains that come with building in structured reflection. The reminder is all the more welcome for capstone as the current structure of traditional schooling can make it difficult for teachers to make sufficient space for reflection.

Reflection effectively rebalances the relationship between process and outcomes.

Reflection in capstone

Many students may arrive at capstone having in effect been trained in traditional classes to dislike reflection. Our obsession with items to place in our virtual trophy case of educational experiences devalues this beautiful practice. With the exception of those wonderful classes that journal or take the time to be mindful in other ways, most courses feel like a rush to the final exam, the next class, and ultimately the best college. It is no wonder that students resist reflection. Capstone teachers need to scaffold reflection in their programs, creating meaningful moments to consider the past, with direct connections and benefits to course objectives. While students may not fully appreciate the benefits of reflection until the end of a capstone project, many will be enlightened sooner, gaining a powerful new skill in their educational toolbox.

Reflection is essential to capstone for at least two reasons. First, the personalized nature of capstone creates an interesting working dynamic, in which checking in can only be done via reflection. Unlike in a team setting, where partners provide the essential feedback needed to spur on a project or offer a course correction, the individualized nature of capstone relies on reflection for this invaluable internal data. Pausing and scanning the landscape for signs of progress and looming challenges can only be done with the introspection that comes with reflection. Second, **reflection catalyzes learning in a unique learning environment**. In the innovative capstone space, traditional assessments are untenable—some programs grade projects but none test students in the traditional sense—creating a need for another way to stimulate and gauge learning.

At the start, middle, and end, capstone works best when reflection is embedded in the curriculum. One simple reason is that students often take on ambitious projects in capstone, and therefore frequently meet significant challenges. These are real, hard problems that take time and retrospection to resolve. Only then can students find a way forward, continually navigating the smooth and choppy sections of their project. Furthermore, reflection is crucial for the kinds of 21st-century learning most valued in capstone. Without reflection, learning becomes automated and meaningless, just importing data and exporting answers that may or may not have real meaning.

Types and modalities of capstone reflection

Whenever reflection is employed, it can helpfully be broken down into three types for capstone. **Personal reflection or self-reflection** includes the student in his project. This includes his history, experience, and motivation to complete the work. As a personalized experience, these attributes are important drivers and deserve attention when reflecting on any aspect of the project. Equally crucial if the capstone includes research or community engagement, personal reflection is essential for understanding positionality. **Process reflection** refers to metacognition about activities that are used to gather information, make decisions, and categorize action items. Given the individual nature of most capstone projects, the student's individual understanding of process becomes determinative. **Retrospection or summative reflection** is the final kind of reflection, occurring after the project is completed. As we explain later in this chapter, this is a rich moment reflecting on all that has transpired during a capstone project, and gaining power from the approaching ritual of graduation from high school.

Structured (as opposed to informal) reflection includes writing activities (journals and logs, identity memos, blogs, and quick activities in response to writing prompts) and conversational activities (one-on-one with capstone advisors, peer cohorts, class discussions, and one-time discussion activities like wagon wheels or fishbowls). We discuss an example of each below.

Like any long-term project, a routine is vital to reflection. Students need regular assignments with clear guidelines to prompt them to consider their projects, investigating what transpired and keeping an eye on upcoming activities in the future. Classes with scheduled time can create many of these events and do the work together with students. Teachers need to balance the actual work done with reflection time, because students will not have much to reflect on if this kind of writing or conversation happens too often. Four times in a semester is a good baseline in a year-long program. There is obviously lots of leeway according to the type of program and amount of work done in each one.

Teachers should make the written reflections meaningful by discussing them after students write out their ideas. Deliberative processes require steps that are followed and repeated in a disciplined way. Sitting down to talk about what was learned is a clear way to hold everyone accountable for this important practice. The joint meeting may bring about considerations (which crystallize during the conversation) that were not quite resolved in the reflection written just by the student. This collaborative moment importantly starts with a solo consideration, then moves to a two-person discussion in which bigger ideas may emerge, as they always do in capstone.

Another important aspect of writing is the full documentation that it creates, which is invaluable at the end of the program. Final presentations should include a mixture of experiences and outcomes that can be too numerous to remember. With regular posts collected in a portfolio, this information is easily located, and serves several needs. It fulfills the reflection component of the presentation and provides excellent testimonials for public relations, to name two benefits. To advertise just what capstone can accomplish, teachers can use these reflections, with permission of the students, to share quotes for school publications. The power of capstone is best conveyed in the words of the students themselves. A body of reflective writing is invaluable in this regard.

The conversational learning cycle

Kolb and Kolb introduce the "conversational learning cycle" in *The Experiential Educator.*[5] The cycle follows their established four-part experiential learning cycle consisting of concrete experience (CO), reflective observation (RO), abstract conceptualization (AC), and active experimentation (AE). To this cycle is matched the two steps of the conversational learning cycle: speaking and listening. The Kolbs' diagram for the combination of these cycles is shown below.

Conversational learning cycle with experiential learning cycle	
Student 1	Student 2
Speaking (AC, AE)	Listening (CE, RO)
Listening (CE, RO)	Speaking (AC, AE)

In the capstone classroom, this can be simply employed in groups of two, where each student takes turns speaking about their project and listening to their partner do the same. This process guides each student through the two conversational activities, which Kolb and Kolb refer to as "reading" and "flexing." Reading is when a student gets feedback from their partner and creates perceptions that come from the conversation, and flexing is when a student makes intentions and acts upon them.

The conversational learning cycle will create many ideas related to a student's capstone project which feed into classroom activities planned by their teacher. Regular assignments are a good example. Timed properly, the conversation will produce information that can be used as material for capstone homework. This is an effective plan to combine different types of learning. An example is a conversation (verbal learning) and the particular assignment, like a written portfolio post (written learning).

Journaling

Teachers who consciously incorporate formal reflection at all are most likely to use journaling. As pointed out by education researchers Janet Dyment and Timothy O'Connell, journaling is not an innate skill: it has to be taught, and not just assigned. In the absence of instruction, students are likely to write *descriptions* of experiences, rather than using writing as a means of *reflection* on experience.[6] Dyment and O'Connell suggest making the purpose and expectations of the journaling assignment explicit and teaching students about reflection by introducing them to one or more theories and sharing examples. They also suggest that responses from a trusted reader, probably the teacher, are conducive to more meaningful student work. Additionally, they point out that journaling can be done before a significant experience (anticipation), at the time of the experience (as soon as possible, for remembering details), or after (reflection). The types of multiple-entry journals recommended by Bringle and Hatcher (see Chapter 4.5) are based on the recognition that experience shows up differently depending on our distance from it.[7] Multiple-entry journals typically have an initial entry that is more descriptive, and one or more later entries that discuss the same material either through the lens of related reading (about systems and histories, for example), or from a personal angle.

Reflection in the beginning

In the rush to begin exciting capstone projects, students often develop a fixed mindset, which needs to be addressed right at the beginning of the school year.[8] Their ideas are usually broad and complex, and they quickly become focused on all of the interesting aspects of their potential work and eager to jump right into the deep end of the pool. Teachers need to meet this flurry of interest with foundational plans to begin the year in proper form. Students need to refine their ideas, identify exactly what they will work on, and plan out the first few steps. This ensures that they will head out on the correct path on their capstone journey.

Questions to reflect on at the beginning
• Consider the current title of your project. What are the major goals of your project that fit into this title? In terms of concepts and/or products, what are you hoping to accomplish by the end?   • What motivates you to take on this project? What experiences have you had that are relevant?   • Who is your intended audience? How will you structure your project to meet the interests of your audience?   • What is your connection to your audience? How will this influence your project?

Centering students and their ideas, choosing the most important ones to explore, is the nature of capstone work at the beginning. Any activities that achieve this goal are worth the time at the beginning of a project. Documentation is a critical part of the process, not only to systematize the selection process but also to record all of the possible pathways, should another option be required in the future. Writing out all of this information creates a wonderful collection of ideas for reflection, as well as the final student presentation.

Collaboration is an integral part of any classes about starting capstone projects. Gathering people who are engaged in capstone will always produce ideas that are applicable and interesting. Combining students into small teams to shape their central idea is an excellent use of class time, because it does so in a productive way, it allows the capstone students to bond, and it gives all the students the sense of their shared experiences. This last point is important as the path they choose will be littered with rocks and roots, demanding periods of extra effort to make continued progress.

Reflection in the middle

We are proponents of at least one major deadline in the middle of the year as a full check-in with capstone projects. Without a clear moment to assess the larger aspects of the project, students run the risk of entering uncharted lands, without a map or a compass for the second half of the work. Given how many moving parts can be involved in a project, it is critical to completely assess how things are going sometime in the middle of the year. In a year-long project, we like the "50% by February" rule. This seems to be a great month to run a status update, comparing the original goals and timeline with reality, and planning out the final portion of the school year, always keeping in mind how increasingly busy schools get in the run up to the end of the year.

Questions to reflect on in the middle
• What parts of your project have you been the most pleased with during the first half of your project?
• What challenges did you experience and how did you resolve them?
• Looking back to your original aims, and considering all the work that you have done, are these goals still relevant? If so, what kind of modification might they need?
• Do you have enough time to complete all the steps that you are planning on? If not, which ones are most important that you need to finish?

This meeting in the center of the academic year is an opportunity to reinforce some capstone tenets. First, change is part of the process and should be embraced. Not only is it acceptable to modify plans in the winter months but it is also usually the smartest thing to do. Sticking with the original plan may actually be the worst option. Even students that are working largely according to plan will change things up as they progress through the year. Second, some projects need a reboot in the middle of the year, fully restructuring the plan in order to salvage the original intent. It can be challenging managing capstone projects and students, and surprisingly easy for one to slip through the cracks and enter dangerous territory, in which it is questionable if the student may continue or has enough time to do so. A checkpoint through which everyone must pass will catch these situations in time to do the necessary work to resurrect a project—in schools where capstone is optional, this may be a time to cancel the project altogether in a mutually agreeable way. Lastly, reinforcing the point about the busy spring calendar, February is the last full month before vacations interrupt the flow of courses and special events consume more and more of our school time—like capstone presentations at the end of the year!

A reboot should follow the first principles of a project. Return to the September plan and reassess the value of each component. Once there is agreement on what should remain, students and teachers can reassemble the pieces, deriving another solution for the revised intentions. This kind of total overhaul takes less time than one imagines, and creates a new way forward that is invigorating, making it worth the invested energy and effort. Remember that it deals with a situation that was steadily eroding the student's goals and enthusiasm. This reformulation creates a profound release and renewed vigor in the project, creating a spark that should keep the student going right up until the end of the course.

Programs with class time can harness the power of conversational learning—outlined above—paired with reflection. Reflection can be easily done at the end of a planned lesson, especially one that uses other students to generate topic ideas. Teachers can organize students into small groups and give them some discussion points. This can be as straightforward as asking students to summarize recent work, identify moments of challenge, and then explain how they navigated these experiences. This has a two-fold effect. Processing personal experiences to explain them to others is a metacognitive act which triggers understanding and learning. A student will gain insight just by laying out the experiences to others. Additionally, the combined wisdom of the group will generate novel ideas that everyone benefits from, in direct or indirect ways. Students can make use of direct feedback from others about their project, or remember other insights that relate to their work in tangential ways. Both forms of ideas are beneficial and only accomplished in a group dynamic.

Changing plans before disaster strikes is an invaluable life lesson. It can be hard to do with a project that is dear to a student's heart, like many events in our lives. Doing the challenging work of assessment and evolution is possible in capstone with the right curriculum and teacher. The benefits of learning this within the world of capstone, and then embodying this as they grow older, is a major opportunity for capstone students. This illustrates for them the value of a growth mindset and the benefit of using it in as many situations as possible.[9] Forming this life experience in high school is worth the time and effort.

Merging these ideas about middle-of-project with reflection, these moments of change are replete with experiences for reflection. Just like life, the only thing one can be certain of is change. Capstone plans will be modified as long as the program lasts, continually adapting to the current conditions, and each redirection is a reflection opportunity. (One could almost be overwhelmed with the number of chances to consider the evolution of a project.) Second only to the end, this time in the center of the calendar is a rich moment to assess the path of the project.

Reflection at the end

If retraining students to practice authentic reflection is a necessary chore, it can be quite enjoyable when done at the end of a capstone project. Sitting down to remember all that transpired during a project is one of the most rewarding aspects of capstone. Like a good story, capstone experiences have an inspirational start, plenty of plot twists during the year, and truly impressive final products. Completed while basking in the afterglow of a successful presentation, reflection at the end is a meaningful and proud moment for students—it's the best time to reflect. The nervous energy of presentation day is gone, leaving just the invaluable experience to consider, as well as all the ensuing congratulations from the school community. Audience members, students and adults, are consistently surprised at the depth and caliber of capstone projects demonstrated at the end of the year. Their expressions of interest and congratulations provide all the spark capstone students need to understand what they have honestly accomplished.

Questions to reflect on at the end
• What were the highlights of your project, including experiences and outcomes?
• What surprised you about your work on your project?
• Thinking about the students who will join this program next year, and your experience, what advice would you give them?
• Who should you thank for helping you with your project?

Fun work still requires a lesson plan. Teachers should set aside time at the very end of the program for the important final reflections. Guiding questions are wonderful prompts to focus students on key points throughout the year, including the beginning and middle and any other notable calendar dates unique to the program. A word count signals the depth of reflection. Asking for a certain number of words gives a student a sense of how much they should consider and then write. Lastly, teacher feedback on culminating reflections honors their importance, letting the student know that what they had to say was understood and appreciated.

From these personal reflections come invaluable insights. They tell teachers what worked and point to future improvements, even when they are complete surprises. They are the source of terrific quotes that can be used to publicize the program to the school community. Most importantly, they are concrete examples of the power of capstone, and provide the accolades that capstone teachers deserve to hear and consider. The distance students have traveled by the end of the program is impressive indeed, and clearly written in these final reflections.

Notes to Chapter 4.7

Note 1, page 212: **experiential learning cycle**—This material is widely reproduced online, or see page 33 in David Kolb, *Experiential Learning. Experience as the Source of Learning and Development*. First Edition (Englewood Cliffs, NJ: Prentice Hall, 1984).

Note 2, page 212: **"a recursive circle or spiral"**—See page 33 in Alice Y. Kolb and David A. Kolb, *The Experiential Educator: Principles and Practices of Experiential Learning* (Kaunakakai, HI: Experience Based Learning Systems Inc, 2017).

Note 3, page 212: **the term "experiential" refers to the whole cycle**—See page xviii in David Kolb, *Experiential Learning. Experience as the Source of Learning and Development*. Second Edition (Upper Saddle River, NJ: Pearson, 2015).

Note 4, page 213: **"the transformation of experience"**—See page 38 in David Kolb, *Experiential Learning. Experience as the Source of Learning and Development*. First Edition (Englewood Cliffs, NJ: Prentice Hall, 1984).

Note 5, page 215: **their conversational learning cycle**—See pages 190–193 in Alice Y. Kolb and David A. Kolb, *The Experiential Educator: Principles and Practices of Experiential Learning* (Kaunakakai, HI: Experience Based Learning Systems Inc, 2017).

Note 6, page 216: **journaling is not an innate skill**—See page 234 for the initial point. For the recommendations, see pages 234–243 in Janet E. Dyment and Timothy S. O'Connell, "The Quality of Reflection in Student Journals: A Review of Limiting and Enabling Factors," *Innovative Higher Education* 35, no. 4 (August 2010): 233–244.

Note 7, page 216: **multiple-entry journals**—See Robert G. Bringle and Julie A. Hatcher, "Reflection in Service Learning: Making Meaning of Experience," *Evaluation/Reflection* 23 (1999): 179–185.

Note 8, page 216: **develop a fixed mindset**—See Carol Dweck, *Mindset: A New Psychology of Success* (New York: Ballantine, 2006).

Note 9, page 219: **the value of a growth mindset**—See Carol Dweck, *Mindset: A New Psychology of Success* (New York: Ballantine, 2006).

CHAPTER 4.8
FAILURE IS AN OPTION

Failure is one of those things that adults know more about than teens just by virtue of having been around longer. The topic of failure inevitably brings along the topic of the student-teacher relationship. We care about our students as human beings whose stories cannot be captured on a transcript. We don't want to see our students fail. But sometimes, more than that, we don't want to see them miss out on failure. Much as our own past failures may burn in memory, we also value what those failures brought into our lives. Schools understandably want to protect young people from too much adult reality. And yet different human beings outgrow the artificial containers schools provide at different points. We don't always get it right. One of the best opportunities a capstone program can offer its students may be the opportunity to fail. At least, we know that many of the programs represented in the National Capstone Consortium do very intentionally make failure an option, and that the teachers from these programs talk about each year's most spectacular or special failures with the same interest and enthusiasm as its successes.

So, what exactly does it mean to allow failure to be an option in your capstone program? First, let's consider what it looks like when failure is *not* an option. If the consequences for failure are draconian, it is not truly an option. If the capstone is a graduation requirement, we want to see it functioning as a culmination, not a gate: the goal of capstone is not to introduce a high-stakes hazard at the end of the race. In the case of capstone graduation requirements, failure is not an option, and as the end of the year looms, we will see students and teachers alike scrambling for a minimal appearance of completion. But if there are no consequences at all, failure is still not really an option, at least not in any sense that would allow it to constitute a learning opportunity. In some programs, capstone is an opt-in and short-term activity, with a low bar for entry, low expectations, and no repercussions at all when a student withdraws. Opting out is just opting out, and is not registered as failure.

But in between "everyone must pass" and "opt in or not, it's all the same to us," there are many ways in which capstone programs allow space for the option of failure and the learning that can accompany it. One program we know of is expected of all graduating seniors, and acknowledged with a certificate from the student's advisor, but not assessed or required for graduation. Failure is an option, and when it happens it is likewise acknowledged with a nuanced message from the advisor: "Yes, we see that you did not do your capstone." In the context of a strong student-advisor relationship, that message can be enough to initiate some learning from the failure. In other capstone programs, some elements may be required, in that the students are held back until they perform at some minimum level, while other elements are expected, but not required in the same sense. In other words, failure in these elements will be registered or acknowledged, but the student may nonetheless proceed with the rest of the project and toward graduation. Thus, for these elements, failure is an option.

"Good failures" and "bad failures"

A break-out session at the National Capstone Consortium 2017 summer summit considered the topic of failure. Initiated and led by first-time attendee Erik, the session was one of the most insightful and enjoyable we've ever attended.[1] In the course of the lively discussion, a consensus emerged. The capstone teachers represented strongly approved of and wanted to support students who took risks, even when their projects did not yield conventionally successful outcomes. One type of failure, we agreed on that day, is a failure against the traditional measures of school and yet not a failure in our eyes. Those "good failures" are the projects that go big, engage the student, involve a lot of activity, and in the end yield little in the way of concrete deliverables. One thing that distinguishes, or should distinguish, a school from a workplace is our freedom to acknowledge big learning even in the absence of a product that can be appreciated by outsiders. Meanwhile, the teachers present that day expressed dismay at the frequency of "cake-mix" capstones—projects that take no risks and might just as well be done as part of a conventionally structured class. This second type of failure, the "bad failure," encompasses the projects that take the opportunity offered by a capstone program and convert it back into the terms they know. These projects check all the boxes. They take the scaffolding meant as a support and turn it into pure limitation. The program structure should function like an endoskeleton, holding up the body and allowing it to move freely, not like a constraining exoskeleton, limiting growth. But the "bad failure" projects allow program assignments to become the only shape the project has. They turn capstone back into school at its worst.

For example, teachers that day preferred messy but original essays to book reports. They preferred experiments that were big experiences for the students, but produced no data, to tidy demonstrations. They preferred the projects that challenged them to grade creatively to those situations where, as they said, "We had to give it an A," meaning that it met all the assessment criteria—but in a way that made them wish they'd asked for something else!

The early failure and the pivot

In a year-long program, early failures often prepare the way for later successes. Jake was a few months into his research when he found a master's thesis that essentially had done "his" project, a study of a long-running children's television show. Though Jake's original project design has already been clever, the discovery forced him to shift to an ultimately more interesting and current focus on the show's expansion to a global audience. Jake wound up developing his Spanish by analyzing episodes of a Spanish-language spin-off of the original show. Similar examples of early obstacles leading to better projects abound.

There are even cases in which an early failure in some sense *becomes* the new project. In the fascinating book *Adapt: Why Success Always Starts With Failure*, Tim Harford explores the idea that success has far less to do with excellent planning, or willpower, or resources, and far more to do with *responsiveness* than we usually think.[2] In Chapter 4.1, we discussed the idea that interest is what happens when something in you meets something in the world. Likewise, a project might be what happens when your plans for the world come up against and engage the world's plans for you. In a learning context, it's not necessarily so bad to find out that the world had bigger plans than you did. Harford notes a disconcerting study of expertise which registered experts doing better than novice participants at tasks set by the researchers—but not very much better.[3] When we marvel at what high school students accomplish in capstone programs, we might consider whether their capacity for failure—that is, to see that plans made under other circumstances are no longer working and adapt— might be one of their greatest assets. As beginners, they bring what Shunryu Suzuki called a beginner's mind to their work: open, responsive, accepting, adaptable, alive to possibility.[4]

> A program structure functions like an endoskeleton, holding up the body and allowing it to move freely, not like a constraining exoskeleton, limiting growth.

Judgment on stage

Failure and success are judgments delivered and accepted in public. A few years ago, when books and articles about embracing failure were all the rage, one theory offered was that failure provided an opportunity for "fairly merciless self-examination"—following, of course, the merciless examination of the larger public.[5] If embraced, the theory suggests, failure allows learning from judgment. Popular culture gives us many examples in which viewers like to watch as harsh judgments are rendered; there is no shortage of participants willing to entertain us in this way. Shows like *The Great British Baking Show* and *Forged in Fire* put contestants in absurdly difficult conditions and then publicly judge the inevitable failures. On *The Great British Baking Show*, amateur bakers attack a series of challenges involving odd ingredients and recipe constraints; the results need to look and taste as if produced with all the resources and time in the world. On *Forged in Fire*, amateur smiths forge knives using strange combinations of metals; those who succeed at making anything with an edge see their work tested by being bashed against rocks, bent in blade-bending machines, and only after several rounds of abuse being used to cut some tough material like silk or bamboo. After testing, the judges on either show pronounce their sentences upon the cakes or knives and then—in true reality-television fashion—one of the contestants is sent home. Though many failures are unavoidable under these contrived circumstances, the judgment theory of learning from failure suggests that the popularity of these shows is not just about schadenfreude, or pleasure in someone else's pain. Rather, there is something invigorating in the clarity of judgments that are blunt, but not capricious, and that are made about products and not people. Above all, there is something inspiring about watching bakers and knifesmiths *learning* on camera.

Given the public ritual aspect of capstone programs, it is perhaps not surprising that failure would be a topic of such great fascination for capstone teachers. Failure in capstone programs tends to be more public than failure in other academic settings. At the very least, a student's absence from an exhibition is likely to prompt speculation. Capstone failure is also permanent. You can't "retake" your senior capstone as you retake a math class. But, as the warmth and joyful quality of that 2017 summer summit conversation conveyed, there is nothing shameful in any of this. When the judges on *Forged in Fire* send smiths home, they always shake their hands first. There is a respect intrinsic to the offering of an opportunity to fail. You have to be considered worthy of it. Correspondingly, being a spectator to failure can bring the feeling of compassion and the thought "There but for the grace of God go I." In other words, failure can also be ritualistic in that it is community-building. It can even be cathartic. In a capstone program that cultivates mutually supportive student interactions, teachers see students reaching out to struggling peers. In a program where the paths to success are visibly varied, the negative impacts of competition are mitigated, and ambition for accomplishment does not have to undermine relationships.

Failure and grades

Failure and success are judgments that are made in a context: they are judged against standards. If the capstone is graded, those standards will be determined at least in part by the teachers giving the grades. Unlike television judges of baking or forging, teacher-judges of student work are operating in a system that brings deeply entrenched assumptions and expectations. Capstone teachers can't just make up an utterly new grading system, innovatively reframing success and failure, and expect either students or the school registrar to go along. In other words, we acknowledge that capstone programs do not exist in a vacuum. Housed in schools, and often transcripted as well as assessed, they are subject to habits and expectations that are too deeply ingrained to be overcome in one year or one career. The regretful teacher comment quoted earlier reflects the dilemma: "We had to give it an A." Capstone belongs to schooling, and no capstone program is going to resolve all of the tensions inherent in schooling. Rather, through trial and error, capstone program leaders who choose to grade at all will over time evolve a system that at least avoids dampening energies the program is trying to encourage. We are happy to be able to add that even in programs that do grade their capstones, standards of judgment that are tied to traditional grading practices may still be offset by the ritual or public performance aspect of the capstone, especially if the program culminates in an exhibition with an authentic audience. Experience suggests that it is possible to grade and still have a program in which projects are largely driven by intrinsic motivation; we discuss capstone grading strategies in more detail in Chapter 4.9.

Especially revealing of the ways in which success and failure are measured against teacher judgment and the usual rules of school are the projects that snatch success from the jaws of expected failure—that come through under what seemed the most improbable of circumstances. For a teacher, there is no lesson so sobering as seeing a project that you *did not believe in* come through with panache, earning appreciation from others with more faith than you. There was the student whose work had been erratic all year and who forgot to prepare for her last-chance presentation slot. After tears in the hallway, she pulled it together, stood up without notes or slides, and knocked it out of the park. She had been learning all year, even though she hadn't been turning in much evidence of that fact. Then there was the student who had ignored the standard advice to focus his topic and effectively done three shallow research projects rather than one good one. Again, against all probability, the three illuminated one another to produce an unexpected insight. Lesson learned—by the teacher, this time.

Varied paths to success

Though we know to value failure when it happens, capstone teachers generally expect to see a lot of success. This is because it is possible in the capstone framework to design for *more* success for *more* students. We think of capstone programs as drawing on the philosophy of "universal design" in architecture. The field of universal design shifts attention from the supposed ability or disability of individuals to the accessibility or inaccessibility of their designed environments. Unnecessary staircases impede free movement on wheels, but a well-placed ramp allows all to enter. Kitchen cabinets set needlessly high in a wall are out of convenient reach for some, but storage kept closer to counter level works for both taller and shorter cooks. Round knobs require grip strength, but lever door handles can be opened with any hand—or, if preferred, with an elbow. Universal design seeks to create flexible spaces that invite diverse users. Universal design takes responsibility for an environment that is built by particular people for particular purposes, not natural and inevitable.

As the designers of learning environments, teachers have much to gain from access thinking. The architecture of learning at most schools so obviously favors some types of learners over others. Success or failure are determined by the learning space more than by the choices of individual students moving within that space. Capstone programs offer teachers the chance to change the space in ways that change lives. It would take a book much longer than this one to list all of the students we have seen thrive in capstone after years of rarely or never being able to claim success at school. One strategy in program design that supports the success of all students is the valuing of the home knowledge, whether familial or cultural, usually excluded from the school setting. Another is incorporating off-campus or embodied learning where students less comfortable with text-based modes can shine. Another is offering a menu of ways to demonstrate learning, allowing students to choose their deliverables. If a chain is only as strong as its weakest link, a capstone project does not have to be a chain. It can be a web, complete with woven strands that independently support the larger structure—failure of one thread does not impact the entire web. In other words, a successful program design can offer many very different paths to and definitions of success.[6]

Questioning failure

No topic in this book calls us back to the core capstone principle that "expertise is emergent" more than the topic of failure. We have many questions about capstone failures and how they are defined in our schools:

- Is failure desirable or deplorable?
- Who decides what counts as a failure and what does not?
- When does failure lead to learning, and when is it pure loss?
- How closely should a capstone program's definitions of success and failure track the definitions offered in more traditional programs at the same school?
- When should the focus of the capstone teaching team be on the individual student who has failed, and when should the team be looking at the program systems or structures within which that student shows up as failing?
- What is lost to a program when failure is not an option?

We are not attempting to answer these questions for other capstone educators. Rather, we testify that we have found value in discussion of such questions at the end of each year with our program teams and with colleagues nationally at the capstone summit.

Capstone story
Julia: science under the microscope

As her senior year got underway, Julia was excited to have secured a promise from a professor at a nearby university to help her engage in a level of research far beyond what could be supported at her high school's capstone program. Julia's program normally kept student projects on campus, and was especially cautious about capstone students making arrangements for off-campus work without there being a pre-existing connection to teachers at the school. And indeed, this was to prove a case that justified her school's usual caution. Without actually telling Julia that he had changed his mind, the professor soon stopped answering Julia's emails and showing up for the meetings they had scheduled at his lab.

Julia's project was being advised by two capstone teachers with research experience at the university level. They advised polite perseverance, reminding Julia that the university had a different schedule and that the professor was probably unaware that she at least needed to complete her part of the work before her high school graduation date. But as the months went by, perseverance got Julia nowhere, and the unpleasantness of the experience was compounded when she heard by chance of some sexist remarks made by the professor about another female student only a year older than she was.

Julia was puzzled by the professor's rudeness—but also by the lack of surprise on the part of her high school capstone advisors. They commiserated but were not outraged: that's just how it is in universities. Lots of professors treat their students badly. And yes, if you are a young woman contemplating a research career, you do have to be prepared to protect yourself from sexist attitudes and behaviors. There were a lot of conversations about how advancement in the university research world works, and the personal toughness required to get through many programs. These conversations were hard on everyone.

Julia was eventually able to complete a small part of the research she had initially planned, and could have written a satisfactory final report on her data alone. Instead, Julia delivered a superb essay, simultaneously entertaining and poignant, recounting and reflecting on the entirety of her experience in the lab at the nearby university. In short, she recognized that the value of her experience had to do not only with learning some science but also with learning about the institutional culture of science. The essay was nuanced and fair—even generous—though it also cast some light on the statistics about the underwhelming percentage of PhDs awarded to women in fields like the one that Julia plans to go into. Planned as a science project, Julia's final deliverable had a value and a depth far beyond what anyone had envisioned at the start of the year.

Julia graduated and went on to study at a different university where we hope the professors are uniformly conscientious about their teaching and utterly free of bias. But experience suggests her capstone won't be the last obstacle of this sort Julia faces. For us, her project raised difficult but important questions about how to prepare students to make the world a better place, and how to prepare them to survive and succeed in the world as it is.

Notes to Chapter 4.8

Note 1, page 224: **Initiated and led by first-time attendee** Unlike other professional organizations to which we have belonged, the National Capstone Consortium operates on a peer-to-peer model. Our summit is partly planned in advance by participants, but also includes "unconference" sessions led by any member with an idea.

Note 2, page 225: ***Adapt***—See Tim Harford, *Adapt: Why Success Always Starts With Failure* (New York: Farrar, Strauss, and Giroux, 2011).

Note 3, page 225: **a disconcerting study of expertise**—Harford gives a detailed account of a study conducted by psychologist Philip Tetlock. Tetlock asked hundreds of political scientists, economists, and other professionals to make concrete predictions, and then waited to see if these were proven correct. The professionals performed only slightly better than a control group of undergraduates. See pages 6–8 in Harford.

Note 4, page 225: **beginner's mind**—The famous quotation: "In the beginner's mind, there are many possibilities; in the expert's mind there are few." See page 21 in Shunryu Suzuki, *Zen Mind, Beginner's Mind* (New York: Weatherhill, 1970).

Note 5, page 226: **"fairly merciless self-examination"**—See Camille Sweeney and Josh Gosfieldjan, "Secret Ingredient for Success," *The New York Times*, January 19, 2013.

Note 6, page 229: **different paths to and definitions of success**—Todd Rose explains how American schools came to offer only the one narrow path to success in the first place. See pages 39–58 in Todd Rose, *The End of Average: How We Succeed in a World That Values Sameness* (New York: HarperOne, 2015).

CHAPTER 4.9
TO GRADE OR NOT TO GRADE?

To grade or not to grade? The question may be quite easily answered. If the capstone resembles other school activities that are not graded at your school, don't grade it either. If the capstone resembles academic classes at your school, then go ahead and grade it too. How to grade? If you do decide to grade your capstone, then this question may be easily answered as well. Grade the capstone the same way your school grades other classes. Probably, these are the only possible answers to these questions. It will take more than one capstone program to change habits and beliefs that have been entrenched in American education for more than a century. Nonetheless, the questions themselves are not without interest for capstone educators.

Capstone programs often launch with the explicit goal of moving teaching and learning at a school beyond hide-bound structures and practices. In other words, capstone belongs to a larger movement of school reform in American education. Grading belongs to what educators are hoping to see reformed. The A–F grading system became nearly universal in American high schools by the middle of the 20th century after being aligned with the percentage system and the four-point scale. Now, nearly universally, an A corresponds to a 4.0 and to 90% or above.[1] The A–F grading system has close connections to the Carnegie Unit credit system established even earlier—in the first decade of the 20th century.[2] Also nearly universal in American high schools and colleges, the Carnegie system designates the credit hour as the measurable unit of learning or achievement. From inception and by design, the Carnegie system and A–F grading create a transcript that makes a student's learning *fungible*, that is exchangeable across institutions. Crucial moments in the lives of our students are made possible by this fungibility. Transfer students depend on it. Most visibly for capstone programs, the current college admissions process requires high school transcripts that are legible as equivalent, regardless of the school where the credits were earned. Also worth remembering is the fact that the essential arguments being made for and against the credit unit and A–F systems today were already being made more than a century ago. Whether or not they have become hide-bound with time, the systems we capstone educators are trying to reform *out* were once reformed *in* by educators with many of the same concerns we feel so urgently now.

As we have noted elsewhere, capstone is forward designed, not backward planned. With backward planning, teachers set goals and then design activities through which students will meet those goals. Capstone programs are instead designed to position students to exceed any goals that could possibly be set by teachers. We literally cannot know what they are going to do with the substantial resources of time and access we place at their disposal. In other words, capstone is designed to elicit work that deserves to be witnessed or celebrated as much as evaluated. Meanwhile any decision to grade your capstone will embed it in systems that are beyond the control of the program, and also of the school. Capstone teachers cannot decide by themselves what grades *should* mean, since students and families understand that what matters is what they *do* mean—to college admissions officers in particular.

But students and teachers are creative and resilient. Those planning a capstone program already know how to navigate the pressures that shape life and learning at their own school. As they also know, credit and grading systems flexibly serve many functions in and between schools: capstone educators have proven time and time again that it is possible to balance the apparent contradictions between an innovative capstone and traditional grading. Paradoxically, a capstone program might win more freedom and space for innovation by choosing to conform to the school's existing grading system than by going into battle with it. There are upsides to grading your capstone as well as downsides.

To grade or not to grade?

To grade or not to grade? Let's consider our initial question more pragmatically.

From a practical point of view, an upside to grading the capstone is that doing so will immediately embed it horizontally and vertically in the existing structure of the school in terms easily understood by students, families, and teachers alike. This decision will align the capstone with the realities of education as it exists and is experienced by students. On any given day, students have choices to make about how they apportion their time. Given the realities, a graded capstone may be better positioned to make demands on this most precious student resource.

Imagine the situation of capstone student Kayla, a senior in Richmond, Virginia who loves history. By senior year, Kayla has exhausted the humanities electives at her school and is taking advantage of an optional capstone class to get just a bit more history into her schedule. While taking a global studies elective as a junior, Kayla developed an interest in African diaspora and marronage. Her global studies teacher helped her secure a capstone internship at the Black History Museum and Cultural Center of Virginia. Meanwhile, Kayla's college application process focuses on large public universities, where her test scores and grades will count more than essays and recommendations. Furthermore, Kayla's internship forced her to cut back hours at her afterschool job. Her parents were supportive and agreed to make up the difference in Kayla's college savings fund. Kayla loves her hours at the museum, but she also feels strongly that she has responsibilities that go beyond her internship.

In this imagined situation, Kayla *wants* to spend precious hours following up on reading suggestions from the curator at the museum and writing to unfold her own blossoming understanding of how history works. The museum presents people of African descent as agents of their own history. This differs from what she encountered, for example, in the US history survey she took alongside global studies last year. Because Kayla's capstone is a class for which she is supposed to be reading and writing, she has protected time to do what she wants to do anyway. Her capstone teachers validate that it takes more time to absorb complex ideas about agency and representation than it does to memorize facts from a textbook. Likewise, they validate that the emotions Kayla experiences as she examines her own positionality in relation to her project are expected in the research process. That the school is crediting the time she spends learning about marronage demonstrates that the topic counts as academic, rather than existing in opposition to a dominant curriculum; on her transcript, Kayla's A in capstone counts the same as her A in US history. Were the capstone not graded, Kayla would still be benefitting from the internship. However, because the capstone is a graded and transcripted class, she is able to have a fuller experience than would otherwise have been likely. In effect, the capstone becomes more visibly *a part of school*, rather than competing with "real school" for Kayla's very precious time.

There are equally good arguments against grading your capstone program. If the upsides of grading a capstone have to do with getting into alignment with external educational realities, the downsides have more to do with what is internal. Again from a practical point of view, the downsides of grading have to do with motivation. Intrinsic motivation in young people, as has been widely recognized, can easily be lost in systems of extrinsic rewards and punishments.[3] One of the most consistent and visible opponents of grading, as of all overemphasis on competition, is Alfie Kohn. Kohn considers grading "problematic by its very nature," no matter what system is used,[4] most of all because it undermines intrinsic motivation. Building on the work of Carol Dweck and others, Kohn further argues that a student's focus on achievement or outcomes, as manifested in grades, may undermine their engagement in the learning process entirely.

A capstone program that is not graded might instead focus on cultivating other forms of motivation. The term "intrinsic motivation" (like "passion") may evoke an unenthusiastic response from students who have heard it mainly from adults who are disappointed in their efforts. A non-coercive strategy for interesting students in the concept of intrinsic motivation is to have them consider Mihaly Csikszentmihalyi's concept of "flow." Developed by Csikszéntmihalyi over a period of many decades and still being researched, the flow state is "the subjective experience of engaging just-manageable challenges by tackling a series of goals, continuously processing feedback about progress, and adjusting action based on this feedback." Flow is both enjoyable and highly productive. Nearly all students we've talked to can recall some experience of a flow state, though they often mention sports or music rather than academics. Consider asking students to imagine how they might design and execute their capstones to create the conditions for flow, which include "challenges, or opportunities for action, that stretch (neither overmatching nor underutilizing) existing skills" and "clear proximal goals and immediate feedback."[5] Students find flow enjoyable and are intrigued by the possibility of actively seeking to cultivate it. This strategy enlists students as allies as the program faces the challenge of supporting intrinsically motivated work in an institutional school setting.

As a counter-example to Kayla, let's imagine Miles, a student in an ungraded internship capstone at a high school across town. Though a straight-A student, Milo has been discontented with his academic work. He shocked his parents last summer by announcing that he might take a gap year after graduation rather than going straight on to college; he says he thinks he is burned out. Milo's program has placed him at a local business, a tennis academy that trains elite athletes while also serving the community with an inexpensive youth program that includes a tutoring and mentoring component. Miles coaches the youth players and also tutors math. Later in the year, he begins spending more and more of his hours in the business office, helping with accounts and program planning. Tennis is a thriving sport in Richmond, and Milo becomes interested in the strategies required for the business to stay competitive in its market. Overall, the ungraded capstone feels to Milo like a break from school, rather than an added class.

But the capstone does of course have a school component. Milo's learning is supported with a reflection component carried out in a cohort of other seniors, most of whom are also in his college planning seminar. He has to give several presentations and is surprised at how much he has learned about the business side of tennis. Both the hours spent on site and the conversations with peers in his cohort help Milo start to think about some different possibilities for his future. He begins talking to his parents about studying business next year. Meanwhile, the tennis academy offers him a paid job, and the conversation about the gap year becomes a positive exploration of possibilities rather than a source of tension at home.

Finally, a desire to be part of a group experience shared with capstone peers can also provide motivation that is extrinsic, but not as fraught as the motivation of grades. A program culture that supports peer-to-peer sharing will tend to grow this social motivation or positive peer pressure. The desire to impress an authentic adult audience at the capstone exhibition likewise offers an extrinsic motivation that we value. If the program is so well established at the school that younger students look ahead to capstone as their moment in an ongoing celebration of the school community, that sense of ritual too will motivate. In short, there are ways other than grades to connect your program horizontally and vertically into the life of the school. All in all, the experience of the Capstone Consortium demonstrates that it is not necessary to grade in order to inspire a very high level of commitment and engagement from capstone students.

Students and teachers are creative and resilient.

How to grade?

If your program does decide to grade capstone work, there remain many options to consider. As mentioned above, students and families will come to the program with a prior understanding of the meaning of grades in the college admissions process. We recommend that capstone programs honor that understanding by keeping the capstone grading system in reasonable alignment with what students already understand. At least, communication about departures from their expectations need to be clear.

Working in alignment with an A–F system, capstone teachers still have many options. One strategy is to explain the capstone class as teaching and assessing skills relating to inquiry and action. Each capstone assignment is explained as a skills demonstration and assessed from the same point of view. For example, an annotated bibliography would be assessed as a demonstration of skills in reading and analysis, while an interview with an expert would be assessed for previously identified interpersonal skills like writing a professional email. Throughout the year, a distinction is maintained between the skills demonstrations on the one hand and the learning or the project on the other; the project exceeds any of its particular manifestations. A student who changes topics mid-year would not be expected to repeat earlier demonstrations, since their purpose was related to the skill rather than to the project per se. A program that grades in this way can even have major final deliverables that are not graded at all. A distinct but related strategy is portfolio grading. Students are invited to try a wide range of assignments over the course of each grading period, receiving formative feedback on their attempts. At the end of the period, students revise, polish, and curate their best work and submit it for a summative portfolio review. Pass/no pass systems are also common in capstone.

Any capstone grading system must keep in mind that capstone students will be trying many of the skills required for the first time. In general, capstone students are experiencing a degree of freedom that may be unprecedented in their previous academic experience. Developmentally, as well due to inexperience, high school seniors may have less ability than adults to manage a long-term independent project and especially to anticipate obstacles and delays. Given these realities, many of the "best practices" of grading today become even more vital. **Scaffolding** can be provided through a handbook or assignment sequence. If the program has the capacity, teaching students to build their own assignment sequence, including setting their own deadlines, can lead to very powerful learning. **Differentiation** is a natural fit for capstone, becoming both more necessary and easier to accomplish than in a typical class. **Formative feedback** is likewise even more important in capstone than in classes more familiar to students. Because so much of what they are doing is new to students, early guidance has more impact. Keeping in mind the development and experience of high school seniors, capstones will overall want to avoid any combination of high-stakes grading with low structure. The amazing work done by capstone students happens as much because of greater support as because of greater freedom.

Capstone can work as well with standards-based assessment as with traditional A–F systems. Indeed, at some schools, the entire capstone project is understood as a performance assessment reflecting the student's whole high school career. A report of the Learning Policy Institute advocated for summative performance assessments and graduation portfolios as a promising alternative to traditional transcripts.[6] The authors of the report hope that a turn to performance assessments might support a more fundamental shift toward teaching and assessing 21st-century skills. In the independent-school world, the Mastery Transcript Consortium likewise advocates for a system of mastery credits supported by an electronic portfolio. The student work described in this book is of the type imagined for such a mastery portfolio. Meanwhile, the organizational learning that happens in a capstone program, as teachers attend to emergent expertise in partnership with their students, aligns naturally with the development of a school's unique mastery credits. The overlap between these efforts and capstone as we understand it is very considerable. Advocacy for education policy is beyond the scope of this book, which aims to support teachers starting programs. However, if you are at a school already engaged with the performance assessment or mastery transcript movements—in other words, if you have support from your school administration—you have an exciting opportunity to participate in the development of new systems of assessment. As with other aspects of the program, piloting and iterating in grading allow the capstone team to absorb what they learn in partnership with their students.

Whatever grading system you choose—or use by default—keep in mind that capstone frequently exceeds what is assessed. The goal is to grade fairly without sapping energies that the program is trying to increase. Motivations other than grades remain a major factor for students even in a graded program. Likewise, the ritual function of the program in the life of the school supports it through a structure that is independent of assessment. Do your best to grade well, if you grade at all, but don't mistake what you grade for the program itself.

Norming

If the capstone is graded, there will need to be a high level of alignment. Particularly a cross-disciplinary team will need considerable time for norming. We also recommend rubrics: whatever their value for students, they greatly assist communication within the teaching team. A standard method for norming has the whole team read three samples—a high, a middle, and a low—and complete a rubric and assign a grade for each. Then sharing and conversation follows. It need not be a problem when one teacher gave one student a B+ while another said B−, as long as there is an open conversation about the reasons for each choice. In our experience, over time, individuals in a high-functioning team will norm themselves toward the group average. Another strategy to keep grading fair across teachers on the team is to use a shared gradebook visible to all. A formatted online spreadsheet into which all teachers enter all assignment grades, and from which all teachers export all final grades, aligns with the principle that "transparency takes care of accountability." If I have said in a meeting that I am willing to grade a proposal element more strictly than I was first inclined, all my colleagues will be able to see whether I backslid later. Normal variation in students will mean that different teachers may have different averages. However, transparency will again assist in an organic norming. If my colleague's final average for all his students in the capstone hovers around 88% three years running, but mine is consistently below 85%, we should talk about that. Reviewing teacher averages for individual assignments and for final, transcripted grades should be a routine part of the running of the program. Again, the key is conversation to understand the thinking behind any grading that falls far from the group norm. In a capstone program, it often happens that there is no director, or that the director is not the supervisor of teachers on the team, who instead report to department chairs in their home academic departments. The combination of a fluid, collaborative structure with a high-stakes function like grading is not intrinsically problematic, but it does heighten the need for transparency and communication.

Rubrics

As mentioned above, rubrics are helpful for communication within the cross-disciplinary teaching team. They likewise can helpfully bridge the distance between a school's traditional grading scheme and less traditional assessment goals introduced by the program by communicating new expectations to students. We offer three examples below.

Sample proposal rubric (concision and clarity)
This proposal rubric communicates to students the need for a concise and clear style in a proposal that is to be reviewed by busy adults, who may be volunteering time as part of a panel, "speed dating" review, or other approval process.

	project design	initial works consulted	proposal format
A	Exceptional project design positions researcher for the next phase of the project.	Appropriately focused bibliography of high-quality sources demonstrates researcher's readiness for the next phase of project.	Proposal conveys project design with exceptional clarity.
B	The project is unique and feasible. The project reflects the position of the researcher.	Bibliography includes the required range of sources. Sources are high quality and on topic.	The language of the proposal is clear, concise, and correct. Entries in the Works Consulted are complete and in perfect MLA format.
C	A project in this area has potential; however, *the project design may be imprecise or unclear.*	Bibliography includes the required range of sources. *Overall quality of sources may be weak, or too many sources may be off topic.*	The language of the proposal is clear, *but may include a few minor errors.* Entries in the Works Consulted are complete and in MLA format, *containing at most a few minor errors.*
D	*Proposal does not yet define a clear project.*	*Bibliography may be incomplete or off topic.*	*Proposal may be hard to understand. Entries in the Works Consulted may be incomplete or contain significant errors.*

Sample fieldwork rubric (making space for failure)

This is a cross-disciplinary rubric for grading "fieldwork," defined as "embodied learning that produces new knowledge," and usually consisting of surveys, qualitative studies, site visits, or scientific experiments. Note that this rubric communicates to students that it is possible to earn an A even if the fieldwork fails to produce any data. The rubric avoids incentivizing unethical research practices.

	written plan	in the field	written analysis
A	Ingenious design opens possibility of eliciting new knowledge.	Student's initiative and responsiveness maximize the field experience.	Insightful analysis manifests the use or meaning of the data or experience.
B	Clear, concise written plan revised with input and approved before beginning fieldwork. Plan includes self-reflection, ethical review, methods (including any technical needs), and goals, all in a discipline-appropriate way. Written plan is pertinent to the student's overall thesis project.	Student conducts fieldwork in a safe and ethical manner. Student conducts fieldwork with proper method and documentation. Student responds to unexpected events in the field, maintaining an open, inquiring approach.	Write-up of the analysis is discipline-appropriate. Analysis demonstrates awareness of the limitations of any data collected and respect for any human or animal subjects. If appropriate, analysis prepares student to show pertinence of fieldwork to student's overall thesis.
C	Written plan is complete, *but some elements may be vague or unclear.*	Student conducts fieldwork in a safe and ethical manner, *but may use compromised methods or fail to document work.*	Analysis exists, *but may demonstrate room for growth in understanding of data or experience and its meaning.*
D	*Major elements may be incoherent or missing. Plan may be completed too late to allow for full field experience.*	*Fieldwork may be shallow or incomplete, or scheduled too late to allow for full analysis.*	*Analysis may be shallow, erroneous, or incomplete.*

Sample presentation rubric (preparing for an adult audience)
Students have experience with academic expectations. They likewise have ideas about presentation styles from sources (YouTube, political speeches, etc.) that may or may not be appropriate to the capstone. They typically come to the program without much experience presenting in-depth research work. This rubric communicates that both academic substance and presentation polish will be valued equally by the adult professional audience attending the final capstone exhibition.

Criteria	Excellent	Good	Average	Fair	Poor
Argument: Thesis is arguable (a reasonable person could disagree) and framed in a civil way (people who might disagree feel that they are addressed fairly); credible support for thesis is presented.	5	4	3	2	1
Clarity and sophistication: Topic is clearly introduced; presenter's position (argument) is perfectly clear; parts of presentation follow logically and smoothly; complex material is presented in a way that makes it accessible and interesting.	5	4	3	2	1
Preparation and mechanics: Presenter begins without delay and takes exactly 18 to 20 minutes; presentation is free of distractions and interruptions; visuals or handouts are managed efficiently; the audience's time is treated with respect.	5	4	3	2	1
Engaged delivery: Presenter stands up straight, faces audience and makes eye contact; voice is clear and audible; presenter's manner demonstrates that s/he is serious and interested in topic; the audience is made to feel engaged.	5	4	3	2	1
Overall rating of presentation:	5	4	3	2	1

Notes to Chapter 4.9

Note 1, page 233: **The A–F grading system**—See page 15 in Jack Schneider and Ethan Hutt, "Making the grade: a history of the A–F marking scheme," *Journal of Curriculum Studies* (2013). DOI: 10.1080/00220272.2013.790480

Note 2, page 233: **Carnegie Unit credit system**—See pages 62–63 in James M. Heffernan, "The Credibility of the Credit Hour: The History, Use, and Shortcomings of the Credit System," *The Journal of Higher Education* 44, no. 1 (January 1973): 61- 72. For an excellent short history, see also Ethan Hutt, "A Brief History of the Student Record" (Ithaka S + R), September 6, 2016.

Note 3, page 236: **systems of extrinsic rewards**—For a general literature review, see Allan Wigfield, Jacquelynne S. Eccles and Daniel Rodriguez, "The Development of Children's Motivation in School Contexts," *Review of Research in Education* 23 (1998): 73–118. For a longer discussion of intrinsic motivation, see also Chapter 3.1 in this book.

Note 4, page 236: **"problematic by its very nature"**—See page 145 in Alfie Kohn, "The Case Against Grades," *Counterpoints* 451 (2013): 143–153.

Note 5, page 236: **flow**—Csikszentmihalyi's best-known book is *Flow*. Our quotations come from page 90 of a short article that is suitable for sharing with students: J. Nakamura and M. Csikszentmihalyi, "The concept of flow" in *Handbook of positive psychology*, ed. C. R. Snyder and S. J. Lopez (Oxford: Oxford University Press, 2002), 89–105.

Note 6, page 238: **performance assessments**—R. Guha, T. Wagner, L. Darling-Hammond, T. Taylor, and D. Curtis, *The promise of performance assessments: Innovations in high school learning and college admission* (Palo Alto, CA: Learning Policy Institute, 2018).

CHAPTER 4.10
DELIVERABLES

There is an inherent tension in every capstone project. On the one hand, the capstone is a personal journey made at a time of enormous transition in the life of a young person. On the other hand, the goal of the journey is a further stage of maturity—one that includes readiness for the adult experience of having your products judged, independent of you as a person and independent of your journey. Whether formally graded and transcripted or not, most capstones incorporate both process elements and one or more final "deliverables." A program goal is to make the tension between these productive.

Capstone deliverables include formal end products like papers and presentations that can be graded on rubrics (with limited reference to the process or the person that produced them), or even assessed by authentic audiences (to whom the person and their process may be completely unknown). There is no doubt that the quality of final deliverables is enhanced when the learning involves embodied, transformative, and/or off-campus experiences. At the same time, those rich experiences are never fully "captured" in the deliverable. The advising capstone teachers will observe much that cannot be registered on rubrics. All of that said, producing "deliverables" that are judged on their own merits is an experience that brings its own learning and can also be a source of great satisfaction and pride for the capstone student.

The concept of the capstone deliverable demands a further word on assessment. As discussed in the previous chapter, some capstone programs assign grades and some do not. In general, high-stakes, all-or-nothing grading systems do not lend themselves to supporting projects that are also personal journeys for the participating students, no matter how much reflection was built into early stages. Scaffolding formative assessments that build in sequence toward major deliverables helps. If your program will be assigning traditional grades, portfolio systems are likewise worth considering. Depending on project design, different students might choose to include different elements in their portfolio, so that each student is assessed on the most relevant and successful work. If the capstone is a graduation requirement, programs will also want to avoid setting up gates too near the end: neither the students nor the schools need that stress.

Deliverables

- Action project with impact study
- Artwork or performance
- Scientific poster
- Design-build product
- Personal narrative
- Digital portfolio
- Research essay
- Presentation

Writing is thinking

Writing is a form of thinking. People can think things in writing that they can't think without it. They can sustain thoughts over time, so that the initial strands develop into webs of thought that are stronger and more expansive. They can catch flaws in their thinking and correct them. They can catch happy moments of genius, and allow those moments to anchor hours of more mundane production. Given the power of writing to take thinking to the next level, it is the rare capstone program that will not include some form of writing as a core element—whether as an ongoing mode of reflection on the experience, or as a deliverable.

Just as writing adds something essential to a capstone program, so capstone can add something enriching to a school's teaching of writing. Teaching writing when the students have something to say—well, that is a whole different ball game. This is especially true when what the students have to say is complicated and requires careful setting up, forcing them to develop their skills. And it is especially true when they care deeply about being understood. Their belief in the value of the project drives them to communicate it with the greatest clarity possible.

In the teaching of writing, *pretense* shows up when *interest* leaves the room. Pretense is what you get when students feel they have nothing to say, and are writing anyway, just to turn something in. It happens when the material they are writing about is uninteresting to them—often because it is drastically inappropriate developmentally. Students' brains do develop between the spring of the senior year of high school and the fall of the first year of college, but hardly to a degree that justifies limiting their challenging reading in high school to op-ed pieces out of newspapers when they will be reading Plato or Martha Nussbaum a few months later. In our experience, students often produce much better writing when engaging texts or concepts that they are struggling to understand than when they are bored by easy material. When they have to think, they do. Since capstone programs ask students to use developmentally appropriate versions of professional research methods, rather than understanding research as collecting encyclopedia articles or reference works, they catapult most students into appropriately high levels of challenge even during the text-based part of the capstone. Add in embodied experiences that challenge students to understand and process their own observations and reactions, and you have set the stage for the best writing these students have ever done.

"Instantly we know whose words are loaded with life, and whose not,"[1] Ralph Waldo Emerson says. We know because we feel while reading the same excitement that the writer felt while writing. Good writing has a quality of discovery that arises when the writer is working something out as they write. Capstone offers an opportunity to get more students into a state of high interest, high motivation, and high challenge. That's a game-changer for their writing as it is for their projects.

Depending on the design of the program, capstone writing might fall into a wide range of genres, from creative to narrative to journalistic to argumentative—each genre structures thinking in its own way, and each can be "loaded with life." In the remainder of this chapter, we focus on academic argument as the genre most commonly taught in inquiry-based capstone programs.

21st-century skills

In our research chapter, we suggested that research is a human process, one in which information, meaningless on its own, acquires value through the work of the unique mind of the researcher. Just as research is a human process, so is research-based writing. In fact, though this book has separate chapters for each, in practice, research and writing are interwoven processes. Understanding emerges during writing, rather than pre-dating it, and new understanding leads to new interests for the research and reading elements of the project. Whether or not students use the personal voice ("I"), the unique human perspectives they bring to their projects will essentially shape the value that they are creating for their readers.

In our research chapter, we also noted that the changing access landscape of digitized information implies new challenges and opportunities for capstone research. Likewise, advancements in technology imply challenges and opportunities for capstone writing. On September 8, 2020, the newspaper *The Guardian* published an op-ed piece that was written, as the paper said, by a robot. As we touched on in Chapter 2.2, the writing was generated by GPT-3 (Generative Pre-trained Transformer 3) technology that had been developed by a private company named OpenAI. OpenAI made aspects of its technology accessible to the public via an API (application programming interface). In less technical language, the article was written by software able to gather information from natural language sentences created by humans (it was able to "read") and use what it gathered to create natural language sentences that are in turn interpretable by humans (it was able to "write"). The natural language text at the disposal of the API for its "research" included the entirety of Wikipedia, along with a subset of the internet.[2] Though the op-ed piece was a terrific publicity stunt, and though GPT-3 was hailed as a breakthrough technology, the underlying principle is not new and we can expect natural language processing software to continue to improve by leaps and bounds. More and more information will be digitized and searchable, and software will be better and better at gathering information and reporting on it. In other words, it is already the case that gathering and reporting does not, by itself, constitute human work.

Here's the good news. A robot can gather digitized information, even out of natural-language sources, but it cannot actually *read*. It can relay information in natural-language reports, but it cannot actually *write*. Those remain activities of purpose or meaning, therefore human activities. So, the upshot is that capstone teachers and students are free to focus on what was always the fun part: understanding the use or meaning of information in human contexts and making arguments about that use or meaning for the benefit of human audiences.

Evidence-based argument

Sometimes near the start of the year, students in an English class may ask if they are "allowed to say 'I'" in their essays. Their question reveals the contortions to which years of "schooling," years of studying fake school genres, have subjected us. At its best, a school-specific genre like the "five-paragraph essay" can teach a student how to construct an argument, with a claim backed up by evidence, and every link between evidence and claim explained, in a way influentially articulated by Stephen Toulmin a generation ago. What we see more often now is a mindless parody, in which some key term is introduced and repeated over and over, until you are sure it is dead. If you ask the student whether she actually thinks her thesis is true, she may even laugh. It's not supposed to be true—it's school! Needless to say, the five-paragraph essay does not say "I." Instead, it too often starts with disowning knowledge.

We take the view that a researcher who is aware of her positionality is more likely, not less likely, to produce work that is of value to others. But this is not because we view writing as "expression." Rather, writing is a matter of relationships. Whether or not a piece of writing includes first-person pronouns is less important than the researcher's self-awareness and efforts to ensure that her work has value to her readers. The concept of a relationship with readers can help capstone students connect their "I" to forms of writing that, though they may be less rigid than the five-paragraph essay, still follow recognizable genre conventions of academic writing. Readers have an easier time of it when a text follows genre conventions that they recognize. So there is a balance to be struck in keeping the writing "alive" while also giving readers the familiar structures that facilitate their understanding.

A full writing curriculum that prepares students to write developmentally appropriate evidence-based arguments requires more than one year, and is likewise beyond the scope of a capstone book. However, if your capstone program is multi-disciplinary and centers academic writing, we do recommend reviewing and re-emphasizing a few helpful models.

The first is the Toulmin model, which we consider as relevant now as when Toulmin's *The Uses of Argument* came out in 1958. In alignment with Toulmin, we seek to steer students away from the Scylla and Charybdis of relativism and fundamentalism in their thinking. Instead, students are making claims that deserve consideration from others because of the way they are supported and reasoned. The Toulmin model helps students understand that in addition to making claims and providing evidence for them, they are also responsible for "warrants": explanations of *how* their evidence supports their claims. In a humanities paper, this might be called the "interpretation" or the "analysis," or possibly students will recognize the equally serviceable term "quote sandwich." In a lab report, we are talking about the "discussion." In science education generally, the CER or claim-evidence-reasoning structure is likewise aligned with the Toulmin model. When capstone students with projects in different disciplines are working together in cohorts or classes, it helps to have a common terminology equally applicable to all. What matters is not whether capstone teachers introduce Toulmin or use the CER language but that students understand that they are constructing arguments for readers, not just expressing themselves or tossing out ungrounded opinions. Additionally, for developmental reasons, high school students still need help learning to write strong warrants for their claims.[3]

The second model we recommend comes out of the undergraduate writing textbook *They Say, I Say: The Moves that Matter in Academic Writing* by Gerald Graff and Cathy Birkenstein. This excellent book demystifies academic writing by explaining it as a long-running conversation in which the search for truth is advanced through "moves" of agreement, challenge, and more nuanced engagement with the ideas of previous writers. Research-based writing is writing in context. Each new piece of academic writing enters the pre-existing conversation—no topic is so original that it has no relevant history. The fundamental concept is so simple that we have seen it taught successfully to seventh graders using single-page graphic organizers: "Tell me what they say, then tell me what you say." Yet even high school seniors are easily overwhelmed by the arguments of others and fail to view their sources as contributions to a conversation in which they too have a voice. Like the concept of warrants, the concept of connecting what "I say" to what "they say" can help young writers make huge improvements in an astonishingly short time.[4]

The 1234 technique offers a further specification of the "they say, I say" model that works well in a multi-disciplinary capstone. This is a technique for integrating quotations from sophisticated secondary sources. Typically, high school seniors have practice quoting primary sources, but are not clear about how their integration of secondary sources should be different. The technique works as follows:

1. Introduction: who is the source? What is the original context for the words the student is about to re-apply? What is the source's **overall** point? (at least half a sentence; probably one or more full sentences)

2. Secondary source quotation

3. Explication: **restatement of secondary source point in the student's own words** (at least one full sentence; probably more)

4. Application: how does this secondary source apply or relate to **the student's** work (at least one full sentence; often much more; often located in a new paragraph)

Obviously, only interesting quotations from sources making arguments deserve this level of attention. The assumption is that the sources are making arguments, not just reporting information. But for those anchoring secondary sources that may be helping the capstone student frame the whole project, the 1234 can be illuminating. It articulates what mature academics *do*; capstone students see *why* academics engage sources this closely as they find their own thinking raised to higher levels. This technique is especially helpful for projects that pair established theoretical sources with new primary-source material. For example, one student used the theory of identities presented in Amartya Sen's *Identity & Violence* in a study of Marjane Satrapi's *Persepolis*. That is a completely original pairing, but with the help of this technique, the student was able to make clear how the theory presented by Sen illuminated aspects of Satrapi's graphic novel. Another excellent capstone analyzed Barbie dolls through the lens of arguments about the representation of women made by John Berger in *Ways of Seeing*. In both cases, the primary source analysis was new and original to the students, but elevated by engagement with an established theoretical model.

> Good writing has a quality of discovery that arises when the writer is working something out as they write.

Scaffolding capstone writing

If your capstone is a year-long program that emphasizes inquiry and expects an evidence-based argument as a major deliverable, you may find yourself in the position of asking students to produce the longest piece they have ever written—possibly by a wide margin. The principles for scaffolding a long piece of writing will be familiar to any writing teacher at your school. Assignments spread out over the course of the year might include some of the following for a general project:

- Question storm
- Positionality
- Prospectus
- Secondary source analyses or literature review
- Preliminary analysis (scientific analysis, causal analysis, historical analysis, primary source analysis, secondary source analysis, etc.)
- Main argument
- Counterargument with refutation or partial concession
- Conclusion

For inquiry-based science capstones, the elements of a scientific paper might offer an alternate assignment sequence:

- Introduction
- Hypothesis
- Methods
- Results
- Conclusions

Some capstone programs supporting science projects ask for a written deliverable that is more like a science master's thesis than a peer-reviewed article. In that case, a much longer history and discussion of the topic might precede the sections explaining the experiment or demonstration conducted by the capstone student for the project.

In addition to scaffolded assignments leading to a final, formal deliverable, process writing is always of value. In a project that may evolve as the year goes on, process writing may even offer the added bonus of producing material that later becomes part of that final deliverable.

A word about the concept of the "preliminary analysis": because student researchers are processing all that content knowledge that more mature researchers can take for granted, they are particularly susceptible to writing in a report mode early on in the process. However, putting off *all* the written analysis to the last month or so of a program can create unnecessary stress. One solution is to ask students to outline or plot in a graphic organizer the whole of their essay, but write only a preliminary part of it early on. This early writing then becomes the first body section of the final essay, following on from the introduction but preceding what later will become the heart of the argument.

This strategy can work with nearly any topic. In a humanities essay that will later be centered on a primary source, the preliminary work might be an analysis of the historical context in which that source was first produced. In a science essay that will later argue for research into alternative automobile fuels, the preliminary work might be an argument about the unsustainability of current fuel sources. In each case, the "preliminary analysis" evolves naturally from early research. Often the claims made early on, far from being earth-shattering, lift the material only a short step above mere reporting into a relatively shallow analysis. Nonetheless, the writing is not to be understood as "just facts" or "just background": a claim is made and supported. Adopting the voice of argument early, and developing some material that can be inserted into the final essay, usually proves to be helpful later in the process. In contrast to this, asking students to draft an entire research essay inside a few weeks after months of learning can create an unhelpful level of stress.

Examples of an initial writing deliverable in the form of a preliminary analysis:

Scientific analysis

A capstone advocating research into T cells as most likely to lead to a cure for cancer might begin with a preliminary analysis of the causes of cancer.

Causal analysis

A capstone arguing that the American diet contains too much animal protein might need to start with an analysis of the complex factors that shape why we eat what we do.

Historical analysis

A capstone on political writing in *Teen Vogue* might benefit from an analysis of political writing in American women's magazines from their rise early in the 20th century.

Major primary source analysis

A capstone on the military-industrial complex might depend on an in-depth analysis of Eisenhower's famous speech predicting its rise.

Major secondary source analysis

As in the example above, an analysis of Amartya Sen's argument in *Identity & Violence* might set up later work on Marjane Satrapi's graphic novel *Persepolis* and its historical context.

Other deliverables

The possibilities for formal, final deliverables are not exhausted by written pieces, nor by presentations, which we discuss in the next chapter. Each capstone program fits the unique school that houses it. A science-specific program might culminate in an exhibition of capstone posters with the same elements one would see in the poster hall at a scientific conference. At an art school, the capstone might have a creative piece or performance as its sole deliverable. A school committed to community engagement might ask students to submit an impact study for their action project. A program emphasizing the capstone journey over academic elements might take a personal narrative as its sole deliverable; these might be attractively printed and bound as part of the capstone ritual. What matters is that the deliverables fit the unique program that best serves that school.

Notes to Chapter 4.10

Note 1, page 247: **"loaded with life"**—The quotation is from Emerson's essay "The American Scholar." See page 48 in Ralph Waldo Emerson, *Five Essays on Man and Nature* (Arlington Heights, IL: Crofts Classics, 1954).

Note 2, page 248: **GPT-3**—See "A Robot Wrote This Entire Article. Are You Scared Yet, Human? | GPT-3," *The Guardian* (Guardian News and Media), September 8, 2020.

Note 3, page 250: **the Toulmin Model**—Though we list the original text here, this model is a staple of composition programs and student-friendly versions are easily found on the web. Or see Stephen Toulmin, *The Uses of Argument* (Cambridge: Cambridge University Press, 1958).

Note 4, page 250: **They Say, I Say**—See Gerald Graff and Cathy Birkenstein, *They Say, I Say: The Moves That Matter in Academic Writing* (New York: Norton, 2010).

CHAPTER 4.11
PRESENTATIONS

In the capstone programs we know nationally, the deliverable most commonly asked of students is a presentation. Even in extensive programs that also ask for research essays, or process blogs, or off-campus work, or even all of these—still, the presentation often seems to become the centerpiece of the program. Perhaps it is that even in a digital age, there remains nothing more powerful than a human speaking to other humans. Perhaps it is the way that the school events at which capstone students present their work for the year offer a ritual that is craved by the whole community—the students themselves, their teachers, and their families. Certainly, presentations reach a larger audience than written deliverables, and thus promote the program as well as the individual student work. For whatever reason, capstone programs that don't culminate in some celebratory presentation event are rare.

Capstone presentations are like no other presentations. The performative quality of what is often the last academic obligation of a capstone student's high school career lends power to the occasion of the capstone exhibition. The presenter (capstone student), audience (family, peers, and public), and hosting community (the school) are each positioned for a unique role as they come together to carry out this ritual. The presenter, a soon-to-be-former student, takes a hard-earned place as the expert in the room. Adults, both family members and teachers, now become the listeners, making way for those they once guided. The school, whose daily routines usually perform very different structures of power and expertise, now hosts an event that celebrates the power and knowledge of students. **The specialness and uniqueness of capstone presentation events dictate thoughtful, intentional preparation of students** and care for the event design itself (as discussed in Chapter 3.6).

As with other forms of capstone instruction, the teaching of presentation skills happens in a pre-existing landscape of student expectations and impressions.

What students think when they hear "presentation" may be the style of a favorite teenage influencer's YouTube channel. It may be the style of a political speech. Or students may think that the style of a TED Talk is the "normal" way to give a presentation. In any case, whether the school expects all students to present in the same style or is open to options, the parameters need to be made clear to students well in advance of the big day.

Especially if the presentations will take place in classrooms, students may also be thinking (for better or worse) of the style of lecturing teachers as they envision their own capstone presentations. The program may need to clarify for some students that a one-time presentation given as the culmination of a year's work to a one-time audience is significantly more formal than an ordinary lecture given by a teacher to a class of students he sees every week. Likewise, unless the school does an extraordinary job teaching presentation skills to students over many years, prior experience may have set a lower bar than is appropriate for a public capstone exhibition. Again, parameters, including minimum expectations, need to be clear in advance.

It is a good thing that the excitement of the public audience impresses capstone students much more than teacher approval as represented by grades. (By the way, capstone programs generally do not grade presentations as they are delivered to a public audience. If a presentation grade is a part of the program assessment, it is given earlier at a practice stage.) Though we are glad that capstone students are moving beyond seeking teacher approval, teachers nonetheless can be helpful in pointing out what presentation strategies are likely to appeal to an audience composed mainly of adults. Students who are at an age to care greatly for the opinion of peers may design a presentation that they think will impress them. But the super-casual or ironic style of some teen video channels may not land well with audiences of adults. Students may not understand that jokes or even technological gimmicks in combination with serious topics may feel inappropriate to many adults. Students may also need help understanding that adults are not in school all day, are quite willing to sit and listen for long periods of time, and have long attention spans. It is important that students giving practice presentations get feedback not only from peers but also from adult teachers more likely to know how the adult audiences at the exhibition will react.

On the big stage

While teaching presentation skills, it is also important to remember how very high-stakes capstone events can feel to students. The timing falls near graduation, with moving out of the family home on the horizon. The audience may include the triple threat of teachers, family members, and peers, each of whom brings its own different and even conflicting expectations. The student may have strong feelings about the project itself, and a desire to do it justice. Just the sheer idea of public speaking may by itself be enough to make this a dreaded event. Even students who feel great about all of the factors above may find that overwhelming excitement feels a lot like overwhelming anxiety. We validate that the emotions are normal, and also make the crucial point that many experienced and excellent public speakers routinely experience physiological symptoms like sweating and shaking. Far from being bad signs, these are merely the responses of a healthy body to a clutch moment. Do what the experts do: wear a dark top or jacket and either hold a sturdy podium or don't touch anything that will shake with you! And know that secretly sweaty experts deliver flawless presentations every day. For once, it really is how you look, and not how you feel, that counts.

Inexperienced presenters also need reminding that during their presentation, they are actually the *only* ones who don't have anything to worry about. They are the only ones who know what is going to happen in the next half hour! It can reduce anxiety to have students practice behaving like hosts. The very act of greeting members of the audience as they arrive and welcoming them into the space demonstrates to the audience that the student owns the space. It is the student who is at home; all others are guests. For that same reason, you may want to refrain from having teachers introduce capstone student presenters: it empowers them more to just let it be their show from the start. If possible, enabling each capstone presenter to "set the stage"—that is, alter the physical space according to a plan made in advance—can be empowering. One student might play music as the audience enters. Another might have chairs arranged in a way designed to make space for a demonstration. Within the bounds of what is practical, such strategies can calm nerves and cultivate a sense of ownership that translates into a compelling delivery.

If your program can afford to bring in an outside person to deliver a workshop on presentation, that is likewise an opportunity to build student confidence as well as skill. If that is not an option, consider soliciting the support of the school's drama department. Presenting is not the same as acting, but what actors know about holding space, projecting voice, and connecting with audiences is all relevant for a capstone presentation.

Sample presentation guidelines

These guidelines are for students in an action-based capstone that emphasizes narrating the capstone journey at the presentation stage. At this school, students make presentation slides, record their presentation, then take part in a panel discussion in a small group of students with similar project topics. Recordings are made available to the community to watch before attending panel discussions, and are very useful for other purposes in the school.

Presentation guidelines

Presentations

Students will record screencasts of their presentations before the exhibition day. After audience members have watched their videos, students will be available for live video meetings for questions and answers.

Students should plan on presentations that last about ten minutes, and to be present for Q&A meetings. Detailed schedules will be announced soon. Once information is available, students are encouraged to invite family members and anyone connected to their projects to attend.

Our special event day is in May, date to be determined.

Guidelines

Each student will create a Google Slides presentation. Remember that you are the presenter and the expert on your topic. Your slideshow is there only to complement what you are saying, not replace what you are saying.

Keep your slides simple. Add an image or two and a couple of words. You can type lots of notes in the speaker notes and talk about them.

Required elements

- Title of project, name of student, year at school
- Background information
- Relevant information that provides the basis of the project. Begin with your annotated bibliography. These slides don't need a lot of text, but something to support what you are saying.
- What was your past experience on this topic?
- What inspired you to take on this project?
- What were you hoping to accomplish during your year of work?
- Overview of project
  - What events occurred during your project?
  - What was your projected process at the beginning of the project?
  - Pictures of student "in action." Several images of student completing project, from both early and late stages of the experience. The more pictures the better!

- Provide a caption for each picture.
- Be sure that your images are thoughtfully laid out, not floating in space.
- What was your key product at the end?

- Reflection on the project
  - What were the challenges? Be honest, but don't let this overwhelm your message.
  - What were the successes? What would be the next steps if you were to continue?
  - Again, these slides don't need a lot of text, but something to support what you are saying.

- References
  - Use APA format for all citations. You need at least two.
  - When using images or media that is not your own, be sure to cite those as well!

Recording guidelines

- Use an external microphone to record good audio instead of using the built-in mic.
- We suggest you use Screencastify because it adds your videos right to Google Drive for easy sharing.

Authentic audiences (a note on authentically bad behavior)

The point of authentic audiences is that they are real. And unfortunately, real people sometimes behave badly. It may even happen that some adults attending the capstone exhibition are uncomfortable with the elevation of the student to the position of expert, and their own "demotion" to the role of listener and learner. They may unconsciously try to return things to the status quo with strategies that disrupt the student's plan. In our view, the successful performance of the capstone ritual positioning student as expert is ultimately of benefit to all. To that end, capstone students need to be prepared to handle authentic audiences and their occasional bad behavior.

Students need to be ready to *field* audience questions that they don't want to *answer.* It can even be quite fun to imagine nightmare questions and then share strategies exercising the speaker's prerogative from the podium. "You do *not* have to call on your father" is an important message. If students are really nervous, they may want to have a friend in the audience with a question ready to ask in case Dad is ever the only one with his hand up. If a question-and-answer segment is planned at all, students should be prepared for deflection of the following types of "questions" at a minimum:

- **The question that is really a chance for the adult to grandstand and use air time.** "Thank you, thank you, so fascinating, I see we have another question in the back!" If the adult goes on, the capstone student can move to another part of the room, make eye contact with the next questioner and just talk over the adult until they stop.

- **The bizarrely specific question that is actually the adult showing off that they know stuff too!** "So interesting, thank you for the question! I really wanted to look at the many breakfast foods enjoyed by delegates to the Constitutional Convention, but it was just (raise voice here and articulate distinctly) *beyond the scope of my project.*" Here the student should again transfer eye contact to the next questioner and move on.

- **The question that reveals something the student probably should have addressed, but didn't.** Rather than being embarrassed, the student can express understanding that the point is real. "Oh, that is really important." Here the student may pause and make a note to self. "Can you stay after so I can get the exact reference?" Then the student should again immediately move on (possibly to a friend who can be relied on for a friendly question)—and when the session ends, approach the adult, who hopefully will be gracious. Even though the adult may genuinely want to teach, this is the student's moment to be the expert. We do not advise students that they are obliged to cede the floor, even to adult experts on their topic.

- **The openly hostile question.** Here, we advise students to act like politicians, and address instead some question of their own invention, while ignoring the one actually asked. "Don't you think the Supreme Court made the wrong decision?" can be deflected rather than addressed. "Aaaahhh, mmmhh, as I detailed in my opening section, the separation of powers was a main topic of discussion in 1787. The delegates foresaw the challenges." Or "It's so interesting that this fell to the judiciary branch, since it might not have if the president had acted differently the year before." ("Ah" and "um," which presenters want to avoid during the main presentation are great for holding onto the speaking space so that the hostile questioner cannot continue.) We acknowledge that this is a slippery move, not worthy of real academic discourse. But if an adult tries to start a fight at a student presentation, we again don't think that the student is obliged to engage.

Actually practicing these various deflections can reduce anxiety. Students are savvy and understand that sympathetic members of the audience will see what they are up to when they deflect. In fact, students don't need instruction so much as they may need permission. After all, we are suggesting that *they* decide what will and will not be discussed in spaces where for many years those decisions have belonged to adults. Now we are telling them that those same adults don't get to dictate what *they* do with *their* capstone presentation time. Again, given that most students are already familiar with deflection, in general adult moderators are disempowering and rarely needed. However, it is also a good idea to have a teacher stationed in the room during presentations, with the understanding that they will only intervene if the presenting student signals a wish for support.

All of these nightmare scenarios point to the shift in power represented when a capstone student is positioned as the expert and gives a presentation to an authentic audience that includes adults. Some adults may want to put the student in what they think is the student's place. Others may fall into an opposite trap, and show insensitivity to the fact that a high school senior with expertise in a topic is not the same as a full-fledged professional. Program teachers cannot control what adult audiences will do. Given this reality, we send an empowering message when we put students in front of these audiences: "You are ready to handle whatever happens. You've earned this."

Capstone story
Martin: photojournalism and the ADA

In a sense, Martin's capstone was shaped by anticipation of his final presentation from the moment he decided on his topic: photojournalism and the disability rights movement in the years leading up to the passage of the Americans with Disabilities Act in 1990.

Martin was a passionate photographer and budding activist, so photojournalism was a natural choice. But this topic was not only personal but also familial and communal. Martin wanted his project to honor his uncle Mark, an activist with cerebral palsy who had participated in bus-access protests in the same town where Martin's family still lived. A picture of Mark blocking a bus in his wheelchair had appeared in the local paper. Mark's death the following year had left his family with a welter of emotions. A generation later, the community conflict long since resolved by the ADA, the emotions from that time nonetheless still lived on.

The positionality statement that accompanied Martin's project proposal surfaced further issues. As an able-bodied young man, Martin understood that he had a lot to learn about visual representation and the empowerment or disempowerment of disability-rights activists.

At the time of its appearance, Martin's father had been embarrassed by the picture of Mark that had been published. He felt that the journalist—who also still lived nearby—had exploited Mark and the family, evoking pity rather than creating an understanding of the transportation issue. Martin's grandmother disagreed. She felt that the photograph was a part of Mark's legacy as an activist. Whatever form Martin's personal learning journey took, he was going to have to navigate his family's views on the night of the presentation, and he was going to have to do so in front of an audience that included strangers as well as friends.

Not surprisingly, a project that had begun as a historical study evolved into an investigation of the ethics of visual representation. On the night of his capstone presentation, Martin found himself in front of a packed room. Family, friends, and community were there to experience what he had chosen to share.

Recognizing that his project had multiple goals, Martin had planned carefully. He had come to recognize that the ongoing family conversation about Mark's legacy needed more space than would be offered on the night. With his grandmother's and father's support, he had planned a dinner in Mark's honor for the following weekend.

Meanwhile, his goal for his public audience was education. Though his research had focused on the local conflict, Martin chose to present the more distanced national history and to do so using already well-known images by Tom Olin, rather than the emotionally laden image that had motivated his own work. When it came time to put the local story into the context he had created, Martin used a single image of Mark, one taken at the family dinner table many years before.

Martin's authenticity produced a warm and engaged atmosphere in the room. During the question-and-answer segment, Martin's grandmother spoke about her son and about her own memories of the early years of ADAPT. A few of Martin's friends stayed after to ask her and Martin's father about that time. The small size of the audience, the mingling of family, friends, and public in one space, and the conversation across generations all contributed to a meaningful community experience. At the end of it, Martin felt that his capstone was complete, but his work of understanding the role and responsibilities of photojournalism— the public sharing of powerful moments—was only beginning.

Be prepared, be confident

All of that said, students may not understand just how much planning and preparation it takes to deliver a high quality presentation. As with other parts of the process, scaffolding increases the likelihood that more students will enjoy the experience, do justice to their own work, and reflect well on the program. At a minimum, students who are going to face a fully public audience deserve a formal practice in front of a significant live audience. The "dress rehearsal" presentation is also an appropriate time for assessment, if the program is going to do that. It is also a great opportunity to film.

In order to provide modeling and instruction, capstone teachers need to remember that different presentation styles lend themselves to different aims. Edward Tufte famously blamed the 2003 Space Shuttle disaster on PowerPoint presentations, and specifically on the reliance on bullets to relay information that needed the clarity of full sentences.[1] No human lives should depend on your capstone's presentation styles, but Tufte does make a crucial point about the limitations of certain modes of communication.

A program that allows students choice in their modes of presentation might teach and model some selection of the following representative styles. As advocated in Garr Reynolds's *Presentation Zen: Simple Ideas on Presentation Design and Delivery*, a clean style, possibly removing all words from slides in favor of powerful images, can be an effective counter to the "noise" of the day, allowing audiences to absorb a deeper message. The compelling narrative style known to most of us from TED Talks is well explained by the consulting team known as Stand & Deliver (Peter Meyers and Shann Nix) in their book *As We Speak: How to Make Your Point and Have It Stick*. The capstone journey itself often makes for a powerful TED-style story. Students who care deeply about communicating a complex message and having it retained would do well to learn about the science of learning. An excellent resource surprisingly relevant for schools is Bruce R. Gabrielle's *Speaking PowerPoint: The New Language of Business*. Gabrielle's advice for ordering evidence, chunking information, and foregrounding key points applies to academic material as well as to business. (We even know teachers who made changes to lecture slide decks based on research presented by Gabrielle that audiences retain complex points longer if they read them off slides in the form of complete sentences. Tufte would probably approve as well.) Nancy Duarte's *Slide:ology: The Art and Science of Creating Great Presentations* is good on the visual communication of concepts. And a very small number of students might choose to imitate an academic conference style by delivering a well-rehearsed reading of a script. At a normal speaking rate, eight double-spaced pages translates to 20 minutes of presentation time. This option serves students who write very well and have a highly nuanced argument to make. Lastly, even in a capstone event that is advertised as an exhibition of presentations, some students might do well to incorporate interactive elements, or even offer audiences a fully interactive session. Teachers know how difficult it is to nail down the timing for activities with unpredictable live audiences, and will offer these students extra support for the significantly greater preparation required.[2]

Though we have listed a number of resources above, and YouTube of course offers an endless supply of further advice, the motivation students feel to wow their audiences means that capstone instruction at the presentation stage can have a more grassroots form. Ask students to list all the many forms of presentation they know, and to say what they like and don't like about each. Consider having groups of students watch and critique a few recorded presentations together. Create a process in which students are sharing drafts early and learning from each other's best moves.

Notes to Chapter 4.11

Note 1, page 263: **reliance on bullets to relay information**—See Edward Tufte, "The Cognitive Style of Powerpoint: Pitching Out Corrupts Within" in *Beautiful Evidence* (Cheshire, CT: Graphics Press LLC, 2006), 156–185.

Note 2, page 263: **representative styles**—See: Nancy Duarte, *Slide:ology: The Art and Science of Creating Great Presentations* (Sebastopol, CA: O'Reilly Media, 2008); Bruce R. Gabrielle, *Speaking PowerPoint: The New Language of Business* (Insight Publishing, 2010); Peter Meyers and Shann Nix, *As We Speak: How To Make Your Point and Have It Stick* (New York: Atria, 2012); and Garr Reynolds, *Presentation Zen: Simple Ideas on Presentation Design and Delivery* (Berkeley, CA: New Riders, 2012).

CONCLUSION

American education is at a crossroads. Titanic forces are pushing and pulling our schools in all directions, demanding innovation at all levels of learning. Students and teachers need solutions that:

- align with the best thinking from our educational philosophers
- are available to all types of students
- are adaptable to differing degrees of school resources
- make the best use of teachers' ingenuity
- meet the needs of the modern students and their future careers

Capstone authentically accommodates all of these needs, and belongs in any school that is transforming into a true 21st-century learning environment—away from the realm of rote learning and standardization—along with other programs that employ innovative learning curricula. Capstone takes the vision and energy of teachers, makes it available to students in an experiential learning setting, and effectively harnesses the resources from their school and its surrounding community. All capstone constituents are transformed by the program as they participate in the journey and the culminating event associated with each project, and realize the power of this modern educational curriculum in the process. Capstone truly changes students, teachers, and ultimately schools. Its potential is enormous and available to everyone. Many schools have realized this and adopted the program in specialized forms, and the movement is growing.

Capstone belongs to a powerful kind of learning that follows forward design. Programs that use this approach are student-centered, and are flexible and open-ended at all levels. Teachers and students work together in a fashion that is more like workplace interaction and less similar to the kind of learning that is common in our schools today. Forward design is categorically not backward design, and it is also not standardized or dictated by external entities in any way. It makes the best use of the creative energy of teachers—and the students that they are focused on—and places them at the center of making and shaping the modern courses that our students require. Capstone demonstrates the potential of forward design in a way that should catch the attention of all educators as they create the programming for the future of our schools. It is an excellent model to adopt as it easily embodies the mission statements and strategic initiatives of these evolving schools.

As we have laid out in this book for capstone projects, forward design broadly begins with the student and a focused set of milestones that are identified at the beginning. Teachers and students work together toward those set points, adjusting as necessary along the way. There is a clear endpoint in mind at the outset, but most projects change during the school year and become something a little different along the way. Some students even blow right past their milestones and attain new heights of learning, to the delight and surprise of everyone involved. The final target is something to aim for like a guiding star on a long journey. It exists for general navigation, remaining on the horizon no matter how far one travels. This allows a student to reach a destination, all the while focusing on the meaning and learning of the journey instead of just mindlessly checking off tasks as they progress. Forward design projects start with a realistic goal and timetable, and are then aimed in a direction in adaptable ways, so that fortuitous factors can be considered as they appear along the path.

We have seen capstone in a myriad of types of schools including all possible combinations of independent, public, small, large, affluent, limited resources, etc.—a complete matrix would indeed be large and complex. Each program is perfectly dovetailed into the educational needs of the school, filling a space that is unique to the school and joined firmly by capstone. Capstone is a growing movement by any measure, and yet an opportunity gap remains. Programs across the country exist in isolation, constructing programs on their own. Many of the issues in our schools are handily addressed by capstone programming— see our points on 21st-century skills in Chapter 2.1, for example. The growing capstone movement will benefit from common philosophy and community. We aim to develop a capstone way of thinking with this book—both in terms of best practices strategies—and to refer readers to the National Capstone Consortium, where they can join an active and rich educational community.

Capstone is very popular throughout the country, taking on slightly different names across the states. Many programs fit our definition of capstone and use different terms to identify it, with "performance assessment" being among the most common. Most schools operate on their own, making their own curriculum and shaping capstone to fit the needs of their school and its specific needs. A few states are taking steps to formalize capstone, organizing their schools and districts, providing guidance and resources to foster its development. Among the states on this track, Connecticut and Colorado stand out, for example. We applaud this scale of capstone and expect the trend to continue as educators learn about capstone, observe its potential, and see what students are accomplishing in these pro-capstone states. The pipeline that runs from high school to college and/or career is a compelling reason to explore the capstone option. Capstone not only allows students to learn in a personal way but also demonstrates the skills that colleges and workplaces are looking for in terms of learning and motivation and prepares them for a career, unlike most other courses on their transcript. This is why we think the capstone movement is in its infancy.

The flexible nature of capstone programming, its grassroots development, and the creative potential of the synergy of teachers and students, continues to push the boundaries of what is possible. As in our forest metaphor, with intricate relationships and emergent properties, capstone follows an evolutionary process. Forward design is simple and powerful, creating experiences that are astoundingly inventive and successful. As observed in nature, natural selection creates adaptations that seem too complicated to be believed, but cannot be dismissed because we do understand the underlying mechanism and events.[1] In a school environment populated with a diversity of ideas, containing sufficient resources and energy, students can complete similarly amazing goals in capstone. The phenomenon should only grow as schools, districts and states provide more support for capstone.

We have observed that capstone has impressed everyone who has interacted with the program wherever we have looked. Students value the agency that they gain in a program that is designed just for them. The associated choice and available resources allow them to attain meaningful goals at a level that is uncommon in their other courses. Teachers gain educational power because they are the best people at school to create and ramp up these programs, as they know the most about how to work with students in the capstone way. Administrators value the way in which capstone shifts the focus in their schools away from traditional learning and toward the values and attributes that they are in charge of making a reality—like the fabled 21st-century learning skills enshrined in their mission statements. Parents are amazed by what their children can accomplish when they are properly supported and encouraged to explore what they are truly interested in, and grateful to all who make it possible. All of these positive impressions are on display during presentation day, when a program wraps up a year with impressive stand-and-deliver moments. The resounding applause, looks of amazement on faces, and exclamations fill the school with positive reinforcement for the remarkable capstone program.

The capstone community needs to come together to share ideas and experiences for the benefit of all. The commonalities among all of our programs mean that there is great benefit to be had by learning from each other. The way a capstone program begins each year is surprisingly similar across all the different kinds of schools that offer it. The same is true of navigating the middle of the year and presentations at the end. There is much to be gained for new school programs through collaborating with experienced ones to avoid reinventing plans that already exist, and instead focus on the special parts of the program that are unique to their school. This is the primary purpose of this book: to give teachers what they need to go from zero to high speed in a reasonable amount of time, avoiding many potholes along the way, by considering the advice of seasoned capstone teachers. As we noted at the outset, this is a book by teachers, for teachers, to effectively create and run a capstone program at a school. This is also the purpose of the National Capstone Consortium, whose mission statement is "Connecting vision with experience by supporting peer-to-peer collaboration between capstone educators at all K–12 schools." We are looking forward to connecting with you all, to talk capstone and collaborate on our programs, because we have so much inspirational work to do with each other and our students.

Notes to Conclusion

Note 1, page 267: **natural selection creates adaptations**—Richard Dawkins explains the astounding power of natural selection, an inherently simple process, in his excellent and accessible book, *The Blind Watchmaker: Why The Evidence of Evolution Reveals a Universe Without Design* (New York: W. W. Norton & Company, 1986). Here is a snapshot of the idea from the start of Chapter 2 (page 21): "Natural selection is the blind watchmaker, blind because it does not see ahead, does not plan consequences, has no purpose in view. Yet the living results of natural selection overwhelmingly impress us with the appearance of design as if by a master watchmaker, impress us with the illusion of design and planning."

BIBLIOGRAPHY

"A Robot Wrote This Entire Article. Are You Scared Yet, Human? | GPT-3." *The Guardian* (Guardian News and Media), September 8, 2020.

Aguilar, Elena. *The Art of Coaching Teams*. San Francisco: John Wiley, 2016.

Badke, William. *Research Strategies: Finding Your Way Through the Information Fog*. Bloomington: iUniverse, 2011.

Beilock, Sian. "How Diverse Teams Produce Better Outcomes." *Forbes*, April 4, 2019.

Blythe, Tina, David Allen, and Barbara Schieffelin Powell. *Looking Together At Student Work*. New York: Teachers' College, 2015.

Bond, Sarah. "Dear Scholars, Delete Your Account At Academia.Edu." *Forbes*, January 23, 2017.

Bringle, Robert G. and Julie A. Hatcher. "Reflection in Service Learning: Making Meaning of Experience." *Evaluation/Reflection* 23 (1999): 179–185.

Brown, Tim and Jocelyn Wyatt. "Design Thinking for Social Innovation." *Stanford Social Innovation Review* (Winter 2010): 30–35.

Bryk, et al. *Learning to Improve: How America's Schools Can Get Better At Getting Better*. Cambridge, MA: Harvard Education Press, 2017.

Campbell, Joseph. "Ep. 6: Joseph Campbell and the Power of Myth -- 'Masks of Eternity'." BillMoyers.com, June 26, 1988.

Capstone Consortium. "Summer Summit 2013 Report." www.bit.ly/35xR11d

Coates, Ta-Nehisi. "The Case For Reparations." *The Atlantic*, June 2014.

Crawford, Matthew B. "Shop Class as Soulcraft." *New Atlantis* (Summer 2006): 7–24.

Crawford, Matthew B. *Shop Class as Soulcraft.* New York, Penguin, 2009.

Csikszentmihalyi, Mihaly. *Flow: The Psychology of Optimal Experience.* New York: Harper Perennial, 2008.

Dawkins, Richard. *The Blind Watchmaker: Why the Evidence of Evolution Reveals a Universe Without Design.* New York: W.W. Norton & Company, 1986.

Dewey, John. *Experience and Education.* New York: Free Press, 1938.

Douglas, Bruce, et al. "The Impact of White Teachers on the Academic Achievement of Black Students: An Exploratory Qualitative Analysis." *Educational Foundations* 22, no. 1–2 (Winter-Spring 2008): 47–62.

Du Bois, W.E.B. *The Souls of Black Folk.* Dover Thrift, 2016.

Duarte, Nancy. *Slide:ology: The Art and Science of Creating Great Presentations.* Sebastopol, CA: O'Reilly Media, 2008.

Dweck, Carol. *Mindset: A New Psychology of Success.* New York: Ballantine, 2006.

Dyment, Janet E. and Timothy S. O'Connell. "The Quality of Reflection in Student Journals: A Review of Limiting and Enabling Factors." *Innovative Higher Education* 35, no. 4 (August 2010): 233–244.

Emerson, Ralph Waldo. *Five Essays on Man and Nature.* Arlington Heights, IL: Crofts Classics, 1954.

Evans, Robert. *The Human Side of School Change: Reform, Resistance, and the Real-Life Problems of Innovation.* San Francisco: Jossey-Bass, 1996.

Gabrielle, Bruce R. *Speaking PowerPoint: The New Language of Business.* Insight Publishing, 2010.

Gates, Henry Louis. *Loose Cannons: Notes on the Culture Wars.* New York: Oxford University Press, 1992.

Graff, Gerald and Cathy Birkenstein. *They Say, I Say: The Moves That Matter in Academic Writing.* New York: Norton, 2010.

Guha, R., T. Wagner, L. Darling-Hammond, T. Taylor, and D. Curtis. *The promise of performance assessments: Innovations in high school learning and college admission.* Palo Alto, CA: Learning Policy Institute, 2018.

Hanover Research. "Best Practices in Capstone: Prepared for Northwest Independent School District." Washington: Hanover Research, 2013.

Harford, Tim. *Adapt: Why Success Always Starts With Failure.* New York: Farrar, Strauss, and Giroux, 2011.

Heffernan, James M. "The Credibility of the Credit Hour: The History, Use, and Shortcomings of the Credit System." *The Journal of Higher Education* 44, no. 1 (January 1973): 61–72.

Heidegger, Martin. *The Question Concerning Technology and Other Essays.* Harper Torchbooks, 1977.

Hidayat, D., S. Pratsch, and R. Stoecker. "Principles for success in service learning–the three Cs." In *The unheard voices: Community organizations and service learning,* edited by R. Stoecker, E.S. Tryon, and A. Hilgendorf, 146–161. Philadelphia, PA: Temple University Press, 2009.

Higgins, Lesley. "Jowett and Pater: Trafficking in Platonic Wares." *Victorian Studies* 39, no. 1 (Autumn 1993): 43–72.

Hutt, Ethan. "A Brief History of the Student Record." Ithaka S + R. September 6, 2016.

Jabr, Ferris. "The Social Lives of Forests." *The New York Times,* December 2, 2020.

Kannapel, Patricia J. "High School Capstone Courses: A Review of the Literature." Nashville: Appalachia Regional Comprehensive Center, 2012.

Kohn, Alfie. "The Case Against Grades." *Counterpoints* 451 (2013): 143–153.

Kolb, David. *Experiential Learning. Experience as the Source of Learning and Development.* First Edition. Englewood Cliffs, NJ: Prentice Hall, 1984.

Kolb, David. *Experiential Learning. Experience as the Source of Learning and Development.* Second Edition. Upper Saddle River, NJ: Pearson, 2015.

Kolb, Alice Y. and David A. Kolb, *The Experiential Educator: Principles and Practices of Experiential Learning.* Kaunakakai, HI: Experience Based Learning Systems Inc, 2017.

Kuhn, Thomas. *The Structure of Scientific Revolutions.* Chicago: University of Chicago Press, 2012.

Levy, Frank and Richard Murnane. *Dancing with Robots: Human Skills for Computerized Work.* Third Way. July 17, 2013.

Liebow, Elliot. "Preface: A Soft Beginning." In *Tell Them Who I Am: The Lives of Homeless Women*, vii–xxi. New York: Penguin, 1993.

MacKenzie, Trevor. *Dive Into Inquiry: Amplify Learning and Empower Student Voice.* Irvine, EdTechTeam, 2016.

Maher, Frances A. and Mary Kay Tetreault. "Constructing Meaningful Dialogue on Difference: Feminism and Postmodernism in Anthropology and the Academy." *Anthropological Quarterly* 66, no. 3 (1993): 118–126.

Maietta, Andrea and Paolo Aliverti. *The Maker's Manual: A Practical Guide to the New Industrial Revolution.* San Francisco: Maker Media, 2015.

Malley, Susan Blum and Ames Hawkins. "Chapter 2: Framing Ethical Research." In *Engaging Communities: Writing Ethnographic Research.* Open-access book, December 31, 2015. www. engagingcommunities.org

McLaren, Peter. *Schooling as a Ritual Performance: Toward a Political Economy of Symbols and Gestures.* Lanham, Maryland: Rowman & Littlefield, 1999.

Mehta, Jal and Sarah Fine. *In Search of Deeper Learning: The Quest to Remake the American High School.* Cambridge: Harvard University Press, 2019.

Meyers, Peter and Shann Nix. *As We Speak: How To Make Your Point and Have It Stick.* New York: Atria, 2012.

Milner IV, H. Richard. "Race, Culture, and Researcher Positionality: Working Through Dangers Seen, Unseen, and Unforeseen." *Educational Researcher* 36, no. 7 (2007): 388–400. DOI: 10.3102/0013189X07309471

Bibliography

Mitchell, Tania D. "Moments to Inspire Movement: Three Seminal Moments in Community Engagement." *International Journal of Research on Service-Learning and Community Engagement* 4, no. 1 (2016): 345–349.

Mitchell, Tania D. "Service Learning as a Pedagogy of Whiteness." *Equity and Excellence in Education* 45, no. 4 (2012): 612–629.

Mitchell, Tania D. "Traditional vs. Critical Service-Learning: Engaging the Literature to Differentiate Two Models." *Michigan Journal of Community Service Learning* 14 (Spring 2008): 50–65.

Morris, Aldon D. "Preface." In *The Scholar Denied: W.E.B. Du Bois and the Birth of Modern Sociology*, ix - xxiii. Oakland: University of California Press, 2015.

Nakamura, J., and M. Csikszentmihalyi. "The concept of flow." In *Handbook of positive psychology*, edited by C. R. Snyder and S. J. Lopez, 89–105. Oxford: Oxford University Press, 2002.

National Capstone Consortium. "Summer Summit 2013 Report." www.bit.ly/35xR11d

Page, Scott E. *The Diversity Bonus*. Princeton University Press, 2019.

Pang, Alex Soojung-Kim, *The Distraction Addiction*. New York: Little, Brown, 2013.

Partnership for 21st-Century Learning (P21). "Framework for 21st-Century Learning." www.bit.ly/3w8rGWu

Phillips, Adam. "On Interest." *London Review of Books* 18, no. 12 (20 June 1996).

Pope, Denise. *Overloaded and Underprepared: Strategies for Stronger Schools and Healthy, Successful Kids*. San Francisco: Jossey-Bass, 2015.

Popper, Karl. *The Logic of Scientific Discovery*. New York: Routledge Classics, 2002.

Reich, Justin and Peter Senge. "Launching Innovation in Schools." Online Edx course, archived open-access. MIT Open Learning Library. www.bit.ly/3w7BkIY

273

Resnick, Brian and Julia Belluz. "The war to free science: How librarians, pirates, and funders are liberating the world's academic research from paywalls." *Vox*, July 10, 2019.

Reynolds, Garr. *Presentation Zen: Simple Ideas on Presentation Design and Delivery*. Berkeley, CA: New Riders, 2012.

Rilke, Rainer Maria. *Letters to a Young Poet*. Trans. M. D. Herter Norton. New York: Norton, 1993.

Ritchhart, Ron, Mark Church, and Karin Morrison. *Making Thinking Visible: How to Promote Engagement, Understanding, and Independence for All Learners*. San Francisco: Jossey-Bass, 2011.

Rose, Todd. *The End of Average: How We Succeed in a World That Values Sameness*. New York: HarperOne, 2015.

Rothstein, Dan and Luz Santana. *Make Just One Change: Teach Students to Ask Their Own Questions*. Cambridge, MA: Harvard Education Press, 2011.

Rothstein, Richard. *The Color of Law*. New York: Liverwright, 1917.

Sarris, Greg. "Peeling Potatoes." In *Keeping Slug Woman Alive: A Holistic Approach to American Indian Texts*, 1–14. Berkeley, CA: University of California Press, 2015.

Schneider, Jack and Ethan Hutt. "Making the grade: a history of the A–F marking scheme." *Journal of Curriculum Studies* (2013). DOI: 10.1080/00220272.2013.790480

Senge, Peter. *The Fifth Discipline: The Art and Practice of the Learning Organization*. New York: Doubleday, 2006.

Senge, Peter, et al. *Schools That Learn (Updated and Revised): A Fifth Discipline Fieldbook for Educators, Parents, and Everyone Who Cares About Education*. Revised Edition. New York: Crown, 2012.

Suzuki, Shunryu. *Zen Mind, Beginner's Mind*. New York: Weatherhill, 1970.

Sweeney, Camille and Josh Gosfieldjan. "Secret Ingredient for Success." *The New York Times*, January 19, 2013.

Toulmin, Stephen. *The Uses of Argument*. Cambridge: Cambridge University Press, 1964.

Tufte, Edward. "The Cognitive Style of Powerpoint: Pitching Out Corrupts Within." In *Beautiful Evidence*, 156–185. Cheshire, CT: Graphics Press LLC, 2006.

Westheimer, Joel and Joseph Kahne. "What Kind of Citizen? The Politics of Educating for Democracy." *American Educational Research Journal* 41, no. 2 (Summer 2004): 237–269.

Wigfield, Allan, Jacquelynne S. Eccles, and Daniel Rodriguez. "The Development of Children's Motivation in School Contexts." *Review of Research in Education* 23 (1998): 73–118.

Wiggins, Grant and Jay McTighe. *Understanding By Design*. Alexandria, VA: ASCD, 2005.

Wiggins, Grant and Jay McTighe. *Essential Questions: Opening Doors to Student Understanding*. Alexandria, VA: ASCD, 2013.

Zemliansky, Paul. "Chapter 10; Ethnographic Research." In *Methods of Discovery: A Guide to Research Writing*. Open-access book. www.bit.ly/36Cndks.

CPSIA information can be obtained
at www.ICGtesting.com
Printed in the USA
JSHW031711100921
18534JS00001B/1